REFFING HELL

STUCK IN THE MIDDLE OF
A GAME GONE WRONG

by Ian Plenderleith

Illustrations by Tim Bradford

Published by Halcyon Publishing

First published 2022

Edited by Adam Bushby & Rob MacDonald

ISBN: 978-1-9196240-2-0

Cover design: Peter Rowson

Illustrations: Tim Bradford

Layout: Rob MacDonald

Back cover photograph: Natascha Lotze

Printed & bound by:
CMP (UK) Limited
G3 The Fulcrum
Vantage Way
Poole
Dorset
BH12 4NU

For Mrs. Ref, with love and gratitude

CONTENTS

SEASON 2016-17

INSULTS, THREATS, WEED AND WANKERS   15

- Danny (Part 1) • Friendly kick to the shins • Respectable praise
- 'The spirit of the game' • Advantage! • Vinyl mystery
- The child in the man • He's lost control • Authority
- 'I'll break your neck' • Fairground • Eyesight query
- A touch of the Collinas • Invite to re-patriate • The insult (Part 1)
- Mellow smells • Deafness query (The insult, Part 2) • Laughter
- Football, I love you • Lips on the whistle • November (Part 1)
- Danny (Part 2) • Lambchop • Warnings • Semi-final • Nationality
- Needy ref • Dying • Fistfight • Gods • Bankers

SEASON 2017-18

HATRED, DISSENT AND IMAGINARY LINESMEN   81

- Inane optimism • Refugees • Coward! • Putting out fires
- Intimidation at work • Maradona moment • Imaginary linesmen
- 'Let them know you're pissed off' • Mourning has broken
- Danny (Part 3) • No respect • Pinball • Traffic wardens
- Dad's the wanker • November (Part 2) • Hatred on the touchline
- Snowballs • The odd bunch • No cards on Valentine's Day
- Reason vs emotion • Teenage kickers • Strike!
- Come on you reds • Model behaviour

SEASON 2018-19

ANGER, ARSEHOLES, BRAWLING PARENTS AND A LONG AFTERNOON IN HELL   137

- Let the old shit begin • Quiet comeback • I'm not Dr. Felix Brych
- My least favourite things • Model parents in mass brawl
- Just a skirmish • 'Körper!' • The monologue of thwarted justice
- Flood of youthful contrition • Oh, beautiful! • Danny (Part 4)
- The Jules Rimet trophy • Fun and games with Archie of the Arseholes
- Take me to Nagoya • Glorious rain • The goalkeeper's tears, and a penalty
- How I knocked Ajax out the Champions League • Hidden key
- The game from Hell (Danny, Part 5)

SEASON 2019-20

SEASON 2020-21

SEASON 2021-22

ADDENDUM

About the author

Ian Plenderleith is a freelance journalist and writer who grew up in Lincolnshire and now lives in Frankfurt am Main. He's been a regular contributor to *When Saturday Comes* magazine for 30 years, and writes a weekly opinion column for *Soccer America*.

His previous books include *For Whom the Ball Rolls* (fiction), *Rock n Roll Soccer: The Short Life and Fast Times of the North American Soccer League* (self-explanatory), and *The Quiet Fan* (kind of a memoir). His blog, *Referee Tales*, has morphed into the book you are about to read. Thank you for that.

You can follow him on twitter @PlenderleithIan and @RefereeTales.

Acknowledgments

A massive thank you to Rob MacDonald and Adam Bushby at Halcyon for being among the most understanding, communicative and enthusiastic collaborators, advisors and editors I've yet to encounter in the weird world of books and book people.

Thank you to lifelong friend Tim Bradford for illustrating this book and adding a wonderfully expressive extra dimension.

Thank you to my youngest daughter, Natascha Lotze, for her extra-fine filming and photography out on the field, and for always being there to listen.

Thank you to my football club in Frankfurt, VfR Bockenheim, for supporting me as a referee and coach.

Thank you to all my refereeing colleagues in Frankfurt for their solidarity and counselling, in particular Kan-Wa Tang and David Sanchez.

Thank you to Goran Culjak at the *Schiedsrichtervereinigung Frankfurt* for being so receptive to our Manifesto.

Thank you to all the players and coaches who apologised. Thank you even more to those who behaved in a sane and sportsmanlike manner in the first place.

Thank you (I think) to Drew Whitelegg, for suggesting that I become a referee to start with.

And thank you above all to the late Richard Antony Bradford, my cricket coach in 1970s Lincolnshire, who taught me the values of true sportsmanship to start with. RIP, Tony, with love from 'Mr. Politics'.

And also love and gratitude to my dad, Robert Plenderleith, a lifelong Rangers fan who who taught me to deplore sectarianism, and that it's fine to applaud the opposition and judge games in a fair and detached manner.

Introduction

It's a cold Thursday night in February, in the 89th minute of a friendly game between two men's teams. Grown-up, adult men, of voting age. The game has kicked off for the second time tonight. Everyone's shouting, many are shoving, all are absolutely indignant. "Ref, did you hear what he said to me? Did you see what he did to me?" Sometimes, the quietest game can skid off the rails for no good reason. Just bad reasons, such as perceived insults, unseen fouls or a marginal offside. Even a contested throw-in.

"Why in the name of all that's holy would anyone spend their free time refereeing amateur football?" is the question posed to me time and again by family and friends who've just heard my latest tale from the sporting fields of Frankfurt am Main. What reason could any even halfway sane person give for volunteering to stand among 22 athletic and highly motivated players, with the added bonus of coaches, parents and fans to hem us all in, in order to be the sole person subject to disrespect, cursing, abuse and the threat of violence on a weekend afternoon or a weekday night?

It's a fair question. Of course, not all games are fraught and stressful, and my stories focus on the extreme examples. No one wants to hear the yarn about the two well-behaved teams who contested a 1-1 draw and then everyone went home with a smile on their face. The extreme games, though, really affect you, and not just as a referee. Sometimes I cycle away from a football pitch and succumb to the facile temptation of bracketing the entire human race in with the players who just lost their rag at me about a late penalty kick. I try to keep such negative thoughts in check, though, and to remember that a well-managed and sometimes even light-hearted game can put a spring in my step (or a ping to my pedals).

Starting my weekly blog *Referee Tales* was my way of exploring an answer to the question, 'Why?' It was also a means to offload my frustration after a hard weekend, to vent my bile in a way I couldn't in my role as the neutral man with a whistle, charged with keeping order. I really didn't expect the blog to be going strong into its sixth season, and that its strapline 'Every game tells a story' would turn out to be as accurate as all my decisions. That is, not always correct, but pretty close most of the time. I think. But the stubby left-back has another point of view. "He was two yards offside, ref! TWO YARDS!"

And so here we are in print, with a volume of long-forgotten games on rutted grass fields, over-bouncy plastic surfaces, and bumpy, flooded cinder pitches, seen purely from the eyes of a referee. Each of these matches unveiled their own narratives, also throwing up issues and incidents that are relevant to the wider game. Added to that were moments of humour, insight and conflict. And as anyone who watches a soap opera knows, it's conflict that keeps us watching.

Starting with a readership of nought and a Twitter account with zero followers, I wondered if anyone would really be interested in my perspective of an 8-0 hiding at Germany's 10th level. I searched, but couldn't find a referee anywhere else in the world regularly documenting their experiences at this or any other level. With nothing to lose, and an audience that could only increase, I decided to try and reveal what's going on inside a referee's head — before, during and after the game. And I promised myself I'd be honest. If the away team's striker was screaming into my face and I really was thinking that I'd love to just slap him and see what happens, then that's what I was going to write. I'm sure the players' thoughts about what they'd like to do to me follow the same deviant arc that stretches far, far away from Fifa's hallowed Laws.

Soccer America, the longest-running football magazine in the US, once asked me a version of the 'Why?' question. The obvious answer is that I love football, and always will. In this case, I came up with a less sentimental response. "Despite the abuse, I keep doing it because I love being out on the soccer field — most days, it's where I feel like I belong, where I'm happiest." When you can't quite cope with the fact that your playing days are over, refereeing is the closest you'll come to the action, even if it means taking a misplaced shot right in the nuts.

During that Thursday night mass confrontation that started just before we were all about to head for the changing rooms, I remained quite calm. I'd seen it all before. I knew that everyone would pipe down eventually, once their bellicose posturing was over and done with. I blew three times on my whistle and began to walk off the pitch.

"Wait, where are you going?" a couple of players asked. "I'm off home because you're all acting like idiots," I replied. Does that mean the game's over, they wanted to know. It certainly does. Though there'll be another one next Sunday afternoon, and no doubt we'll all be back out there again, ready to hotly contest another highly controversial throw-in decision...

SEASON 2016–17

INSULTS, THREATS, WEED AND WANKERS

Danny (Part 1)

The away team's striker is called Danny. That's not his real name. I find it hard to write his real name without a picture of myself walking slowly into a stagnant pond where I submerge myself until I disappear and drown. I last saw him three months ago in front of the city's football disciplinary panel. A few weeks before that, I'd sent him off while he was coaching a youth team because he wouldn't shut his mouth.

I'd given Danny four warnings about his conduct before dismissing him, which was two more than he deserved. Two more than it states you have to give in the Laws of the Game, a leniency born of a genuine dislike of sending anyone off — player or coach. Danny treated the four warnings like dandelion fluff in the breeze. That is, he saw them as a distraction, at best, and continued objecting to every call against his team as though he was on a rolling contract to harass the referee, paid on a cash-per-yell basis. In front of the disciplinary panel he denied everything, right after I'd given my detailed account of his tantrums and refusal to cooperate.

What did I make of Danny's wholesale denial, the panel asked me. I answered their question with one of my own. Did they think I'd cycle halfway across town on a weeknight to tell lies about a youth team coach just for the hell of it? They nodded and sent us both outside to wait. Danny then chatted away like this was some sort of party game, like he hadn't just accused me of being a vindictive liar who was out to get him. Summoned back inside, the panel fined him €150. "You're not a blank sheet of paper, are you?" they pointed out, before recalling the day he was ordered to the stands during a tournament the previous summer. If they saw him here again, he'd face a lengthy ban.

Before today's pre-season friendly, Danny greets me like we're old friends. We shake hands. "How's it going, how was your summer?" We chat about football like blokes at the bar, all smiles and small talk.

Danny plays for a reserve outfit in one of the city's lowest divisions. Once the game begins, there's no more small talk. Danny and his striking partner, both in their mid-20s, work well together — at gobbing off to me, the referee. As football players, they are less talented. The pair's main complaint is that they are being fouled every time they don't win the ball (that is, almost every time), while I mostly see things from a different point of view. They're simply being outmuscled by the defenders. Ten minutes before half-time I show his partner a yellow card for dissent, hoping that will shut them both up. But it doesn't.

So Danny's partner is still mouthing off at me, moaning with diligence at every last decision. In a league game I'd have shown him a second yellow and bid a tearful adieu. But it's just a friendly, and they only have 11 players, so I give him a last chance in the form of a firm but friendly warning: "Hey, how about you just play football and shut your trap?"

The two players are thoroughly indignant at this. How dare I speak to them in this fashion? I laugh and tell them that I can say whatever the hell I want (which is not strictly true, but 'shut your trap' falls well within the realm of acceptability in a rough, dog-end of a game like this). Danny then has a brilliant idea and calms his partner down. "Don't worry," he tells his fellow forward, "we'll *report* him." Clearly he's imagining an hour of revenge in front of the disciplinary panel, bearing witness, and this time it's me in the dock. It's this future call to justice that causes his striking partner to indeed shut his trap for the rest of the game. Or maybe he's still in shock that the nasty referee was so rude.

At half-time, I talk about Danny with an official from the home team, who's also a referee. "I've come across him at youth games," he says. "If his team's ahead, he tries to sub in every 30 seconds to waste time, and then gets mad if you wave him away." That sounds like Danny the coach I came to know, love and dismiss on a miserable, wet afternoon last winter.

Danny the player continues to moan in the second half, but I've moved ahead. "What did you see this time, Danny?" I ask him when he whines about me giving a goal kick rather than the corner he wants. "A deliberate handball? Did he trip you? Did he grab your balls?" He says it was a corner, and I just laugh, and then every time he whinges I sing a little song to myself, "Shut up Danny, you twat/Oh shut up Danny, you twat." At the final whistle, with the score at 3-3, he doesn't come over to shake hands.

It's July. There are still several weeks to go until the start of the new season. It's going to be a long and frustrating year for Danny, thanks all to those unconscionable referees. Will he report me for telling his team-mate to shut his trap? The return match in front of the disciplinary hearing has yet to be scheduled.

Final score: 3-3 (2 x yellow)

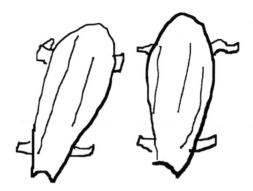

Friendly kick to the shins

We're just about to kick off when I notice that at least half of the home team are not wearing shin-guards. I turn around and look at the away team. Same thing. No, it's not an under-7s game. These are all adult men. Though sometimes it's hard to tell the difference.

Everyone's ready to go, it's very hot, and it's only a friendly. I hadn't bothered checking the players' equipment because, for adult games, everyone usually knows the rules. So I point out the all-round lack of leg protection. "Ah, come on," says one player. "We all know each other. It's going to be very laid back." With an uneasy feeling, I start the game.

Ten minutes later I stop it again, and order all the players who don't have shin-guards to put them on. The tackles are going in thick and hard. This is about as laid back as Jürgen Klopp barefoot on a hot tin roof. One player has already limped off with an ankle injury. I picture a health insurance company suing me on behalf of its client and his triple shin fracture, while my refereeing association will wonder why on earth I overlooked such a basic law. I will be banished for five years to the pre-adolescent leagues, kicking off on Sundays at 8am.

Most of the players without shin-guards just stand and stare at me. A few are annoyed that I'm delaying the game and urge me just to play on. One player yells at me. I ignore him and instead send the manager of the home side off to the changing room to grab as many shin-guards as he can find. He's a nice bloke, but very chaotic.

He returns with a sack of extra equipment. The away team's been standing around like the directive doesn't affect them, so I send them one by one to the bench to grab any spare shin-guards going among the substitutes. Every single player on the pitch thinks I'm a wanker for enforcing this.

As though I'd expressly told them before the game not to wear shin-guards, and now I'd changed my mind just for the hell of it.

Finally, we start again. Someone asks about injury time, which would probably be around seven minutes, but no one complains when I blow for half-time on the dot at 45 minutes — they're all too knackered and out of shape from doing fuck all over the summer.

In the second half, they get cranky. Teams can turn extra dirty after the break. Either they've been bollocked at half-time for not being aggressive enough, or they're pissed off at missing their afternoon naps. There's some pushing, threats and half-hearted squaring up, so I get the captains to substitute the worst perpetrators because I can't be arsed to card anyone in a meaningless game. Besides, they're all friends, right? The away goalkeeper then has a bust-up with an opposing forward, and again I step in. "He insulted my mother!" the keeper shouts at me in self-mitigation. The accusation of lost virtue among players' mums is a recurring theme in football games at all levels in this city.

Despite all this, I'm in a serene mood, unfazed by fights, fouls or fractiousness. After the game, the nice team manager thanks me some more. We talk about the shin-guard thing. "Well, they have to learn some time," he says cheerfully, as though they were all playing their first game ever, and he bears no responsibility for the situation at all. Nothing stops this bloke from smiling, not even his team getting soundly beaten. If only everyone at a friendly was this friendly.

Final score: 1-4 (2 x yellow)

Respectable praise

A very local derby on a hot August day between two small towns just outside of Frankfurt, separated by three kilometres of road and several fields of corn. Here's how I picture my day in the countryside: after a lively game played in great spirit, the hearty locals will toast each other while quaffing copious beers and chewing on browned meat from an open grill. They won't care about the result. I stand among them, spinning great yarns from my refereeing travels, enjoying a couple of ales and some roasted pig before they bid me a cheery farewell, telling me I'm welcome at their club any time.

Well, that's how a whimsical film director might have scripted it. The reality is as grim as the away team's assistant coach, who comes over to brief me while I'm warming up. "There's a fierce rivalry and a lot of bad blood between our two teams," he tells me with a certain macabre sense of anticipation. "Last season we lost here 2-1 because the referee fucked us over." He proceeds to describe in great detail what happened — something to do with a red card and a free-kick. "Sounds like the ref had an off day," I reply brightly. "It can happen to all of us. Maybe it'll happen to me today." Then I run off to check the corner flags.

It's the last time I speak to the away team's assistant coach, though I hear him screaming at me a couple of times during the game. It's hard to make him out, though, because the derby has attracted a crowd of around 150, most of them crammed into the shady protection of a small stand, while others sit beneath trees and bushes. They make a lot of noise. If I blow for offside (I have no linesmen), around half of them howl at me in despair. It's a micro-version of the big time, and I love every minute, despite the heat and the dead-eyed intensity of the players.

The away team's striker puts his side 2-1 up just before half-time after dribbling around the keeper. He does a little celebratory dance right in front of the still-prostrate goalie, and I think about a yellow card for unsporting behaviour. But he breaks it off after less than a second in order to get mobbed by his team-mates. Overall, they just about behave themselves — there are five yellow cards, and a few niggly square-ups. Once or twice there is even a freak outbreak of sportsmanship.

At the end it's 3-3, a pretty fair result, though neither side is happy. Clearly both teams were coveting the opportunity to gloat and ululate in front of their neighbours. A spectator yells at me as I leave the pitch — something about not showing a yellow card. The nicest thing about being yelled at by spectators is that you can walk right past them and act like you haven't heard a thing. And the best thing about being neutral is not having to give a fuck about the result. I'm just happy when I'm not surrounded by a crowd of angry players.

In towns like these there are always a lot of older spectators who've been involved with the team for decades. They are the memory and conscience of the club. One revered elder stops me in the bar when I'm picking up my expenses and asks me where I'm from. He wants to put some background to an unfamiliar face. At the end of our exchange, he says, "Your performance today was respectable. Enjoy the rest of your weekend." There's no beer, no barbecue, no village festival, but I feel like I've been awarded the freedom of a small town in Hessen.

Final score: 3-3 (5 x yellow)

'The spirit of the game'

Fifa directives this season advise referees to control play not just according to the Laws of the Game, but in "the spirit of the game" too. They could hardly have phrased it more vaguely if they'd written, "Yeah, just go out there and blow your whistle whenever you feel the urge. Actually, we don't care any more what you do. Most of our laws are open to interpretation anyway. Do whatever the hell you want."

I'm not complaining about this directive. We can interpret "the spirit of the game" to suit ourselves. Can I kick the niggly midfielder bleating about every decision hard in the bollocks? That would seem, under the circumstances, to be in the spirit of the game. Can I accept a bundle of hard currency in a brown envelope to favour the team that discreetly placed the cash inside my sports bag as I walked into the changing room? Sure. What could be more in the spirit of the game nowadays than the richest team buying victory?

Anyway, to this first-round Cup game. The away team has as its honorary president a prominent ex-parliamentarian and anarcho-communist revolutionary of the '68 generation. His son founded the club with friends a few years back to create a playing field without allegiance to any specific city area, ethnicity or religion. In other words, all are welcome. They have a good reputation for sporting behaviour and progressive campaigning, though when I checked their disciplinary record before the game it wasn't anything special.

Yet it's clear from the kick-off that this team is different. They don't foul. They don't complain. It seems to have an effect on the home team, who follow suit. For the first 15 minutes I blow my whistle only once, for an offside. I feel like stopping the match, hugging them all, and then walking off to leave them to their own devices. Clearly, they don't need me.

During that first half, I rule out two goals for the away team for offside. The calm is almost uncanny. Usually any offside decision, even when it doesn't involve a goal, provokes collective uproar, and it's more effort than I'm prepared to make to point out yet again that I don't have linesmen, and the reason that we don't have linesmen is because the clubs themselves voted against having them. Too expensive, apparently.

Lest I start to idealise this group of players, things warm up a bit in the second half. There's an aggressive one-on-one confrontation following a foul, and a yellow card for dissent. An away forward slams the ball into the ground after an offside call, and his team-mate points out that he too thinks I've made the wrong call — one of those where the player comes back to get the ball from an offside position, so no one can comprehend how he's offside when receiving the ball with two defenders now between him and the goal. A few minutes later, though, he apologises for speaking out of turn, and again at the final whistle.

The team with the former anarcho-communist revolutionary as its honorary president wins 4-1. Mainly they prove that it's easily possible to play hard without fouling an opponent, and that you can win a game without remonstrating constantly with the referee. They play "in the spirit of the game", and for the most part their opponents (two yellows for foul play) manage to do the same. Thank you. It was an absolute pleasure.

Final score: 1-4 (3 x yellow)

Advantage!

Occasionally, referees may experience a moment of glory. It's not like scoring a goal, but it's similar. And no, it's not when you — straight-armed and righteous — raise the red card to that purple-faced midfield goblin who just called you a blind, clueless twat. It's when you cry the word "Advantage!" and just a few seconds later the attacking team sticks the ball in the net.

It happens just over an hour into a closely fought and very well played game between the first team of a small town and the reserve team of a neighbouring, much bigger town. The score is 1-1. The home team's number 7 — a hot-headed but extremely nimble central midfielder — has been sandwiched by two opponents just inside the away team's half. As he falls and howls for the foul, the ball squirts forward to one of his team-mates, who with a first-time pass puts their number 11 through on goal. The whole time I have my arms stretched out and am exhorting them to play on. The number 11 needs only two touches to score from just inside the penalty area.

In such moments, you remember what it was like to score a goal. In the interests of neutrality, it's best not to scream out "Yes!" and punch the air. Or to run over and join in the goal celebrations. But that's exactly what you feel like doing. And for the next few minutes I have that pleasant 'after-goal' sensation I used to feel after a successful strike, at the same time as having to keep myself in check and return to fully concentrating on the game.

Still, fucking excellent call, ref! Says precisely no one. Not during the game, and not after. Three minutes before time, with the score now at 4-1, I miss a handball by the away team thanks to the glare of the floodlights.

It's a very obvious handball judging by the incredulous cries of the 40-odd spectators and the querulous yells of the home team. When the home manager shakes my hand after the game he says, "That was a clear handball, you know."

Yeah, I know. Didn't matter much by then, though, did it? Main thing was my application of that critical advantage call, right? Forget it, you idiot, that was half an hour ago. They'll only remember you here as the ref who needs night-vision glasses. If it's gratitude you want, go found a charity.

Final score: 4-1 (1 x yellow)

Vinyl mystery

There should be an online database of referees' changing rooms so that we can warn our colleagues of the potential hazards. At one club where I'm a regular ref, the changing room seems to be right over a severely defective sewage outlet. Sometimes you do without a shower because you know you'll come out dirtier than when you went in. The groundsman might have left his overalls and a long history of their sweat out to hang on a peg. If the floor's been swept of last week's pebbles, mud, scuzz and dead skin then you're generally happy.

Occasionally, though, you're in for a pleasant surprise. There are three different kinds of drink and a snack laid out on a clean table. The team sheets have been printed out and signed with over half an hour until kick-off, just like they're supposed to be. There's a working radio so you can keep up with the action in games around the country. Or there's a box of used LPs.

I doubt that there are many refs who get as excited as I do by the latter, but there's nothing I'd rather see when I walk into any room, let alone a referee's changing room, than a box of used vinyl. Like a child heading towards a flashing red button with a sign saying 'Press Me', I can't resist dropping anything in my hands at that moment and heading for the box to see what might be inside. It's not so much curiosity as compulsion.

Why would there be a box of used records in a referee's changing room? Presumably someone in the club has dumped them there ahead of a future fund-raiser. It's not mine to reason why, it's mine to get down on my knees and start frantically thumbing through them for an unexpected rarity.

The records are very old but in beautiful condition. I suspect their original owner is no longer alive. Does that thought ever prompt vinyl raiders to pause from fervently rifling through the discs and take a moment to reflect upon mortality, and how life is as cyclical as a 12-inch piece of plastic rotating on a turntable? No, not for one second. Even in the confines of this small room where I have the key to the door, I'm wary that someone might take advantage of any hesitancy to elbow in and claim the precious object that might be just a few flips away from my probing fingertips.

They are mostly classical, but there are some old jazz and blues records too. I would love to take the whole box and sit alone with them in a cool room on a soft chair for hours, with a record player and a bottle of single malt whisky. But kick-off is approaching. I need to get changed, warm up, check the nets, the corner flags and the player passes. It's the same feeling I used to get when heading off to work evening shifts on the weekends while everyone else was gathering in the pub. The possible pleasure's being dangled in front of my nose just as duty directs me towards a dusty cinder pitch on a hot, close afternoon.

The home team lost their first game last week by 15 goals. The coach says a lot of his players are still on holiday. They wheel out their youth team coach to play at centre-back, a bloke so old that he was born two years before me. It's an afternoon of desperate defending as the more mature XI belts the ball as far up the field as possible to kill time. They gallantly lose 9-1, with the game played in a decent spirit. There are no yellow or red cards, which in this league happens about as often as finding a box of used LPs in your changing room.

I think about asking them to waive my expenses in exchange for the mint copy of the Verve-released 'Night Train' LP by the Oscar Peterson Trio. But it seems too weird a thing to ask in a football club. In the end, I prefer the thought of leaving the records as they are, their presence in the referee's changing room a pleasant minor mystery.

Final score: 1-9 (no cards)

The child in the man

I used to run a football team for mature men. Like every team, it had its minor share of hotheads. If they didn't fall out with referees and opponents, then they fell out with each other, and I'd find myself in the strange position of reconciling an economist, who had screamed for the ball out on the right wing, with a management consultant who had refused to pass to him because he didn't like being screamed at. Instead of giving the economist the ball, the management consultant had kicked it into touch and squared up to him.

At half-time or after the match I'd take these professional men to one side and tell them off. The day after one such incident, the management consultant wrote me an email saying he would no longer be playing on the team because he didn't appreciate being treated like a child. I didn't respond to the email because the retort was too obvious — if you don't want to be treated like a child, then don't act like one to start with.

I'm reminded of him during this game — two men's reserve teams on a crappy old plastic pitch out on the edge of town. I have to book a fellow referee who is playing on the home team. He's a lovely, mild bloke off the field. I've reffed with him at tournaments and chatted to him at meetings. But just before half-time he receives a light blow to the nose from the raised foot of the striker he's marking, and completely loses it.

Rather than apologise, the striker loses it too, and the pair of them square up and scream at each other. Threats and insults override my whistle and the attempts of team-mates to pull the two apart. Eventually I stand back until their anger peters out, call them over, and show them both the yellow card, with the unequivocal warning that repeat theatricals will mean an end to their afternoon's sport and leisure.

It works. Peace is re-established, and the only other yellow was for a mouthy git who excitedly disagrees with an offside call. At full-time, my refereeing colleague comes over with a rueful smile and apologises, but points out that he's a little over-protective of his nose because it's been broken three times. "I understand," I say. "But you're the team's coach, and you're also a qualified referee — if I'd sent you off, you'd have been banned from reffing for several months. You're supposed to be setting an example."

So, a big moral speech from me there, who just 24 hours earlier had almost provoked a fight in the car park at the DIY store by showing the finger to an aggressively honking driver. The young driver and his mate got out of their car and made it clear that they wanted to sort things out the old-fashioned way. I walked away — I'm a whistler, not a fighter. They followed us into the hardware store, where perhaps the presence of several dozen witnesses and some security cameras prompted them to turn around again and leave.

It only takes a second to start a fire, to start a fight. Even though referees are supposed to extinguish fires rather than set them, we are just as susceptible to the laws of ill temper as anyone else. I will aim to heed Mrs Ref's firm advice: don't do that ever again, you idiot. She might even have said: stop acting like a child.

Final score: 1-3 (3 x yellow)

He's lost control

Four minutes to go, the score's 2-3 in a furious and foul-ridden boys' under-17 game, and I blow for a penalty to the home team. It's an unnecessary foul from the defender, who keeps his feet on the ground as he backs into a forward jumping for the ball. The forward goes arse over tit and lands in a heap. I'm five yards away — a clear foul, a clear penalty.

The away team sees it differently. Five players surround me and yell. Their bench is up on its feet, expressing solidarity through raised arms and rubicund outrage. It's been like this the whole second half, from both teams. I don't change my mind, but I show a yellow to the loudest dissenter and they back off. The home team converts the penalty.

So often with penalties the foul doesn't fit the punishment. A few years back, I was reffing in a men's league in Washington DC and a defender committed a soft foul at the top corner of the penalty area, seven minutes after kick-off. I blew for the spot kick, and the captain pleaded, "You can't give that, we've only just kicked off!" In a way, I sympathised. I'm sure he and his defender would have liked to go back 10 seconds to make it not happen. His team didn't deserve to go 1-0 down for such a pointless infringement.

Referees often don't make these calls, reasoning exactly that — a 'soft' foul isn't worth a penalty kick. But a foul's a foul. If you'd call it in any other part of the pitch, you should call it in the penalty area too, provided you're 100% sure it was a foul. The problem for referees is that, like last night, we then have to take the blame for the foul. As though I had used my mental powers to control the defender and back him into the forward. God forbid that his trainer talk to him about why he committed an anodyne offence in such a dangerous area of the field.

"You lost control of the game in the second half," the away team coach tells me afterward. I walk away without telling him what's on my mind in that second, tempted to show him what 'lost control' really looks like. Another way of looking at it would be to say that he lost control of his team, as did the home bench. Fired on by the bellicose reaction of the coaches to every foul, the behaviour of the players deteriorated, leading to more fouls, more dissent, and a deeply unpleasant atmosphere. In the first half there were no cards, because I was a touch too lenient. In the second half, I handed out eight yellows and issued multiple appeals for the players and the coaches to calm down. Aside from abandoning the match, there wasn't a lot else I could do.

I can remember hearing this old cliché in the stands as a kid. The ref would book a couple of players, there might be a flare-up, and an old bloke would turn around to another old bloke behind him and say knowingly, "The ref's lost control." The other old fellow, usually smoking a pipe, would concur with a nod born of wisdom and experience. It's not the wankers kicking opponents and squaring up to each other who are losing control. It's the referee.

After a long inquisition at the final whistle — the away players laugh with open contempt when I explain the penalty decision — I walk back to the changing room feeling that, for €14, I could have better stayed at home laughing at my own reflection in a mirror. "Well reffed," says one kind spectator as I leave the pitch. "Don't let the bastards get to you."

Before the game, I'd met a young referee who'd just done a boys' U13 game. He's still at school, and has only been reffing since the start of the year. He thought it would be a good way for him to stay involved in the game when he stops playing. "Are you enjoying it?" I asked him. "Not really," he replied. "I'm thinking of packing it in." Why? "The coaches," he said, without hesitation. "They never stop complaining." Soon they'll be able to complain that there's no one around to ref their sorry games.

Final score: 3-3 (8 x yellow)

Authority

The two teenage players are in buoyant mood, sitting on a moped, ready to leave the ground. They're honking at some fellow players about to set off in a car. They're young, they've won, and Saturday night's about to start. They see me come out of the changing room and heading for my bike. "Referee! Referee!" they start chanting in sync with the moped's horn. I give them a wave and they scoot off to whatever awaits them — most likely girls, weed and alcohol. Lucky bastards.

Not that it's necessarily a good thing to be honked and waved at by the winning team. A senior referee at one of our recent training seminars claimed that he doesn't like to be told "Well reffed!" by the victors. Ideally, both teams should shake your hand, but without any compliments. Critical comments can be a truer sign that your performance was up to scratch. (However, if the losing team says "Well reffed!" that's presumably a different matter. And it does actually happen.)

Ultimately, you know yourself if you had a good or a bad game. When things get out of hand, you can spend the next two days wondering if you could have kept a lid on it. Today's U19 boys' game is tight, fast, rough, and full of fouls. I talk from the start, justifying my decisions loud and clear. I book a player for dissent in the first half. There's a flare-up in the second — I show yellow to both players and give them the statutory lecture.

Despite that, the atmosphere's not too bad. The coaches focus on their teams, and I don't hear a single comment from the benches. Is that the difference compared with games that have apparently got out of hand? Or am I the difference, because I'm acting with greater authority? Either way, I enjoy the match, despite its niggly, nasty nature, and despite the intense summer heat that's persisting through September.

And I like the fact that the two lads were cheeky enough to chant at me from their moped. The game's over, we're all human again, now we can do the more important things in life — smile and go drink a beer.

Final score: 4-2 (7 x yellow)

'I'll break your neck'

Before this game I'd only once been threatened with violence while refereeing. I sent off the coach of a boys' U11 team who had gone nuclear over an apparent handball and didn't want to let it go. For several minutes he refused to leave the field. When he finally went, he asked me if he should wait by my car. I should have called the game off right there and called the police, but two teams of 10-year-old boys were staring at me and I didn't want any further drama, or to ruin their Saturday morning.

On this occasion the threat is less nuanced. The usual Sunday afternoon scenario: two men's teams with little ability, a very elastic plastic pitch, temperatures in the low 30s, lots of fouls, lots of moaning (mostly at each other, some at me), the odd piece of football. A bullet-headed player on the away team becomes conspicuous by his general anger. After one foul against his team, he screams and whacks the ball against one of the subs' benches out of frustration (fortunately, there's no one sitting on it). I show him a yellow card and he looks at me and asks with genuine bewilderment, "What's that for?"

A few minutes later, the same thing — a free kick against his team, he yells in frustration and kicks the ball again, though this time not as hard. It narrowly misses my head. I go to talk to him, and he claims he was just playing it back to the opponents so they could continue play as quickly as possible (his team were 4-1 down). I give him the very slim benefit of the doubt.

Three minutes before time he starts a stramash after facing down an opponent who's just fouled one of his team-mates. The team-mate is writhing dramatically on the ground — this happens a lot, and almost every time the player is back up on his feet and playing again within two minutes. There's a brief mass confrontation, which I break up with the usual loud whistling and appeals for calm. At this point, I should have shown the player a second yellow. But I'd sent off one of his team-mates a minute earlier, and the entire team are growling at me that I should now be sending off the player who just fouled the man on the ground (I gave him a yellow — it was a bad foul, but not bad enough for red). The game's nearly over, and in the interests of peace and harmony I once again let him off.

My angry friend is standing right next to me at the final whistle a few minutes later. Rather than offer me his hand, he speculates that I was bribed by the home team. Now I finally show him that second yellow and then the red, just as he's walking away. He's incredulous. "Did you just show me a red card? I'm going to break your neck!" he breathes, low and threatening. His team-mates pull him back. I walk away and back to the dressing room, protected by the home team. He continues to scream at me all the way back across the adjacent field to the clubhouse.

I'm outwardly unperturbed, but my hand is shaking as I put the key in the changing room door. I lock myself in and try to remain calm. There's a huge commotion outside, lots of yelling. I gather my things and wait to leave. I'm escorted to my bicycle, a scene with comic potential. There's no sign of my would-be assailant.

"One game soon," says Mrs Ref when I tell her all about it, "you're going to call me from the ER."

Final score: 4-2 (6 x yellow, 2 x yellow-red)

Fairground

A game where nothing remotely controversial happens, and exactly the game I need just over 24 hours after being threatened with a broken neck.

I'm refereeing a boys' U15 Cup tie, first round. These lads are fit and fast, but they're also playing a compressed game, trying to spring the offside trap. I not only have to keep up with a game that flows in both directions, but I'm trying to straddle the final line of defence to get the offside calls right.

I run my ass off, and even though the game's only 70 minutes long, it's another humid evening where the hard running makes it feel like I'm in a gratifying race to get back into the whistling groove. The longer the game goes on without protests from either on or off the field, the more I can feel my brain and body becoming re-infused with self-assurance. "Maybe I'm not a shit ref after all," goes through my head.

There's just one squeak of dissent, from a pubescent home defender after the away striker has yet again slipped past their broken offside trap and finished. "Clearly offside," he mutters. "Clearly a good goal," I mutter back as I note down the scorer's number and the time of the goal, resisting the temptation to add, "And clearly crap defending." That's the end of the discussion.

The away team plays in a higher division and tears the home side apart with some nice passing football, even using an out-and-out left winger who teases and terrifies the home right-back. The night ends with smiles and handshakes, and not a single question about a single decision. The waxing moon is a beautiful pallid pink, and on the other side of the park the kinetic, poly-hued lights of the fairground's revolving rides showcase a field of alternative pleasures. It only took me a day to become besotted with football again.

Final score: 2-6 (no cards)

Eyesight query

"Are you blind?" the player wants to know. A goal has just been scored by the opposition, and from his position 50 yards away in the waning daylight, the home forward maintains that the goal was offside. And yet, I'm allowing the goal to stand. Is there perhaps a problem with my vision?

It's a reasonable question, right? If you're playing a game of football with a match official, then one of their core competencies (a concept I learned while working at John Birt's BBC in the 1990s) should be the ability to use their eyes as a decision-making aid. I consider my answer, and then summon my personal secretary from the touchline. I dictate the following letter, which is soon enough delivered by my butler on a silver tray to the home number 10:

"Dear Home Team Forward,

Thank you so much for your query concerning my eyesight. Your compassion does you great credit as a human being. Without such touching fraternal concern, the football community would doubtless fall apart at the seams.

Fortunately, I am able to allay your fears that I am optically damaged. Let us recall that incident in the first half, for example, when you received the ball in your opponent's half. I clearly remember seeing you at least five yards offside. And I can, with total clarity, recall the vision of you running towards me in a state of uncontrolled rage at my decision to blow for an indirect free-kick. I then pulled a yellow card from my pocket, held it up directly to your face, and recorded the time of the incident and the nature of the offence on the back of a piece of cardboard. Using my absolutely fine eyes the entire time.

Let us now jump forward in time to the second half of tonight's game, and the fourth goal scored by the away team. You will recall that their number 5 followed up on a shot your keeper could only parry, and put the ball into the net. I saw that. Then I saw you run from your position inside the opposition half, still fuming about another (sadly correct) call against you, push through your protesting team-mates and, just a few centimetres from my face, pose the question that has prompted this response. "Are you blind?"

You were maybe worried too about my hearing, because you screamed the question at a high volume. Once I'd explained my decision to your more rational team-mates (the number 5 had not been offside when the original shot was taken), they backed off and left you to it. You were still very passionate about the perceived injustice. Therefore, using my fully functional ocular capacities, I located my top left pocket, withdrew my yellow card from said pocket for a second time, and again held it up to your face. According to the Laws of the Game, this meant it was followed by a red card, which in turn sadly meant the end of your (un)sporting activity for the night.

You left the field still cursing at me, and using your own eyes to stare at me in a manner you perhaps thought would intimidate me. I saw that, because I stared back at you. But you don't scare me, and I don't give a fuck about you or your anger issues.

Yours sincerely, The Referee."

Final score: 2-6 (2 x yellow, 1 x yellow-red)

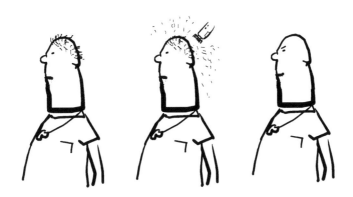

A touch of the Collinas

I went for a haircut before last night's game. I like my hair cut very short, and it's been hard to find a barber's shop in this city willing to meet my wishes. They always try and talk me out of it, and when I insist, they just ignore me and present my greying strands to me the way they think is best. I thank them, pay, and look for another barber next time. When you've got a bald patch, less is more — the barren circle is less conspicuous when the rest of your hair is cut right down.

Yesterday I found my perfect salon — they listened, and cut my hair as I asked them to. "We've had this business for 48 years. Do you think we're not going to pay attention to the customer?" the barber asked me after I'd explained my dilemma. "I'll be back," I promised. And looking in the mirror, I felt ready to referee. It's not that my short haircut makes me look psycho, it's just that... well, maybe there's a hint of psycho. A suggestion that, under certain circumstances, I might get pushed over the edge. Beware the unhinged arbitrator — he's got a touch of the Collinas.

It's a men's third-round Cup tie. I talk to the coaches before the game, because the away team plays higher up the pyramid in a league where they actually have assistant referees. "Remember, I have no linesmen," I say. "Please tell your players not to bother shouting about my offside decisions. Last night I showed three cards, all to players moaning about offside. I'm not going to change my mind because they moan or yell at me, but I promise you that I will show them cards."

They nod — coaches are always very understanding people before the match. It's a pacey, hectic encounter on a cinder pitch under floodlights and a full moon, tabbed as the last balmy night of a long, sweaty summer. It's not dirty, and the players play, though there are a lot of high balls.

I'm right in line to cancel out an offside goal for the away team — when they see where I'm standing, they don't complain.

The away team scores just after half-time, and the defence calls for offside — again, I'm right in line. Then there's just a mild protest over a penalty call which the home team claims was outside the box — they point to the scratch lines in the cinder, which stretch from just outside the penalty area to three yards in. That is, from where their overstretched defender started fouling the fleet-toed away winger, all the way to where he finally brought him down.

"That was an easy game for you," says the club treasurer as he counts out my wages. Well, it depends which way you look at it. A few years ago, an assessor said the game he'd just watched me ref wouldn't count because it was "too easy". Maybe, I suggested, it was me that made it easy. A few days later he sent me an email saying that he agreed, I had kept the game well under control, and so it should count after all.

So I feel like saying to the club treasurer that it's difficult to say what comes first. Was the game "easy" to ref because the players were focused on the sport and played in a sporting manner? Or was it because the absolutely fucking impeccable referee made the right decisions and the players had nothing to moan about?

Or was it because they saw my new haircut and decided that I looked just a little bit psycho?

Final score: 0-3 (no cards)

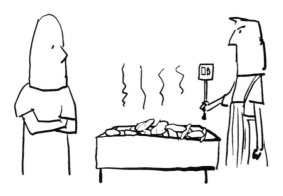

Invite to re-patriate

"No, he's a shit ref!" the coach screams. He's not actually yelling at me this time, he's screaming at one of his own players, who's just offered me his hand after the game and said, "Well reffed." I'd sent the trainer off half an hour earlier for his seemingly addictive hysteria. Even after I'd sent him off, he kept on screaming, "You should fuck off back to England! Go anywhere, as long as it's far away!" (Oh, my friend, you can't imagine how far away from here I'd like to be right now.) Now, after the game, he curses at me non-stop until I've disappeared into my changing room and shut the door.

His team lost 1-5. It's my fault, obviously. He isn't the only member of the host side unhappy with my performance. One of his players has a predilection for using his hand to control the ball, which — as many of you will know — is contrary to the Laws of the Game. The first time's right outside his own penalty area, and when I whistle, he yells, "Why don't you just give a penalty and be done with it?" A highly curious suggestion, but I stick with the free-kick, which his opponents score from anyway.

Ten minutes later he does it again, this time to the left side of the penalty area. He loudly protests the decision once more, so I give him a yellow card. "I don't give a shit!" he shouts.

One minute later I'm standing next to him, after having actually awarded his team a free-kick. But he must be in a hurry to get somewhere, because he informs me, "Your refereeing's a pile of shit today." I show him a second yellow, then the red, and he walks off giving me the old hard stare and calling me a bum.

Meanwhile, up front there's a 44-year-old striker who, like many of us, has seen better days but doesn't want to admit that the only rectangular-shaped box he should be in is a wooden one with handles and a lid.

Every time the young centre-back beats him to the ball, he moans that he was fouled. Eventually he moans so much that I card him too. When he misses an easy chance I consider asking him if that was my fucking fault too, but I cling on to the moral high ground and hold my tongue. I do, however, get to enjoy his sarcastic applause as he serenades me off the ground. He's not stupid — he knows I can't red-card him once we've left the pitch. It all has to go in my disciplinary report.

Because, after refereeing three games in less than 24 hours, there's nothing I'd rather do than sit down at the computer to write up all these misdemeanours. Not just all of the above, but the fact that the club officials wouldn't confirm the name of the coach to me, and one even lied that it hadn't been the coach at all, just "some guy" who happened to be spontaneously coaching the team, and whose name he didn't know. Is that right? I tell a whole crowd of people standing by the grill (I don't get offered any food, even though that's generally the custom) that the reason I've had to ref three games in 24 hours is because so many referees just can't be arsed with the hassle any more. We're quitting, and I can completely understand why. I get half shouted down, half laughed off the premises.

"You all have a nice evening now," I say as I cycle away. The previous afternoon, I'd refereed a boys' U19 match. There was only one yellow card, and at the end both coaches said "Thank you." That's pretty much all I ask for. Even if you really think I've been a shit ref who should fuck off back to England.

Final score: 1-5 (4 x yellow, 1 x yellow-red, 1 x coach dismissal)

The Insult (Part 1)

Uproar in the 70th minute. We're waiting for the home team to take a corner kick when all of a sudden the defending lads — a boys' U17 team who are seven goals down in a last-16 cup tie — erupt in outrage at "an insult" from one of their opponents. The only problem is — I didn't hear it, and even if I had heard it, I wouldn't have been sure which of the players had said it. Play on.

This leaves the away team with a sense of injustice for the rest of the night, enough to sway focus away from the fact they took a hammering. At the final whistle, a player makes a comment about my reffing, but I ignore him. Can't be arsed with another red card and writing up a disciplinary report. Their coach comes over and says that though I had a good game, surely I'd heard The Insult. Everyone heard it, even over on the touchline.

I tell him that what I didn't see or hear, I can't whistle. I make my favourite point about having no linesmen. I also tell him that I'm hard of hearing and wear hearing aids. He's understanding about all of this and, for once, I part on good terms with a losing coach. I mention the incident to the home coach and he says, "They always find something to moan about. Sometimes it's best not to have heard something."

There could be something in this. I've been thinking a lot about the 'fuck off back to England' game and how I could have calmed things down. When the player in that game told me that my refereeing was shit, I could have laughed and said, "Well, mate, when you're a shit player in a shit league, you're gonna get a shit ref." But I only thought of that later (though I'm still going to use it at some point). Alternatively, I could just have stared into space and ignored him. Officially, the red card was absolutely the correct course of action. Unofficially, I'm no longer so sure.

A recent article in the German magazine *Der Spiegel* highlighted the abuse that amateur refs have to put up with. In the city of Hamburg, more than half of new referees give up during their first two years because they can't handle it, and they don't get enough support and protection from the football authorities. "Who wants to get sworn at for a couple of Euros while doing their hobby?" asks Wilfried Diekert, chairman of the Hamburg Referees' Committee, adding: "The old refs are hardened, they don't hear it any more."

In recent years, in both Hamburg and in Frankfurt, referee associations drew up Codes of Conduct that all clubs were asked to sign. In reality, that's about as effective as a dozen stoned peaceniks in an empty field holding hands, closing their eyes and praying for an end to war. Clubs all agree on the record that, of course, all their players should respect the referee. Then once the game kicks off, all those beautifully crafted, well-intentioned words about sportsmanship are as relevant to football as a declaration of intent from the Fifa Ethics Committee. In short, without the feeling that abusive players are going to be properly disciplined, referees are faced with three choices: 1. Pack it in. 2. Take the time and trouble to prosecute violent players via the legal system, given that football's internal disciplinary system ranges from lenient to impotent. 3. Develop an even thicker skin.

Option 1 is tempting, and often considered. Its time will surely come. Option 2 requires time, a tough constitution and a support network that's rarely available. Option 3 is an ongoing process and tends to work with practice, while hardly enhancing any pleasure taken from the job. The longer I ref, the more often I'm forced to behave like the mean bastard ref of stereotypical repute. Still, some teams get the ref they deserve.

Final score: 10-2 (1 x yellow, 1 x time penalty)

Mellow smells

It's a gorgeous, warm weekend, despite the first yellow notes of autumn. My game's south of Frankfurt, across the Main and then five miles through the forest. The whole world's out doing normal Sunday afternoon things. Couples cross the footbridge holding hands, on their way to an art gallery or a museum. Others lie by the water, reading books, unpacking picnics, drinking a beer. In the woods, people are dog-walking, bird-watching, horse-riding.

Every time I head off to ref on an afternoon like this, I feel bad that I'm not doing the same with my family, who have all got used to doing their own thing. When my daughters were small, Sunday afternoons were lazy affairs usually involving walks, ice cream, and then meeting up with friends for some cheap and greasy food. I miss those days now. Back then, by contrast, I missed being out on the football pitch.

The strong smell of weed hits me before I see two young men finishing off a joint and flipping the tab end away. That's something else I wouldn't mind doing on a day like this. But hang on a minute, I'm already at the ground, and these lads are walking in there too, just ahead of me. One of them stretches out his arms and runs onto the field like an aeroplane. His friend laughs and then they make their way towards the away team's changing room. Well, maybe today's game will be all relaxed and mellow fruitfulness.

Yeah, right. It only takes 13 minutes before the first histrionics. Two away forwards are behind the home team's defensive line, but it's a third forward — the only one of the three to run through the back line as the ball is played — who receives his team-mate's pass. He scores. The home team screams that three men were offside, how could I not see them? The club linesman is unhelpfully standing with his flag raised, shouting, "Referee, that was offside!" 0-1.

A few minutes later, a different away forward receives the ball, level with the second to last man. He also scores. The club linesman again stands with his flag raised shouting the same thing, "Referee, offside!" Again, I ignore him. 0-2, though this time at least the defenders don't complain. But then the home team's winger is played free out on the left, a yard offside and I call it. His fellow forward runs up to me and screams in my face — how come I'm only calling offside against them? Dude, because life's a bitch, and here's a yellow card to prove it.

By half-time they've pulled it back to 2-2. The little linesman comes over to me, all upset. What's the point of him being there if I'm going to ignore him? I explain why neither goal was offside, and that his role is only to flag when the ball goes out of play. It would hardly be credible if I kept ruling out goals for the away team based on the decisions of the home team's voluntary linesman, would it? He nods curtly and walks away, looking like he's about to burst into tears. He must be almost 70 years old. I wonder why no one's explained this to him before.

As usual it gets rougher and louder in the second half. Stacks of fouls, copious whining, and then just as it seems we've made it through, there's a stupid flare-up between two players over a throw-in near the corner flag in the 88th minute. Now, finally, it's Kindergarten Time — within seconds everybody's there, pushing, cursing, sweating, threatening, letting it all out. There's at least one insult about somebody's mother. I'm about to blow early for full-time, but then I think, "Fuck it, we've made it this far, let's see it out." I show the two instigators yellow cards, and everyone settles down. There's still time for one more yellow for a nasty foul in midfield, but to my amazement it doesn't set everyone off again.

Even without their linesman's help (he never showed up for the second half), the home side takes the three points. For once, no one seems to blame me for the result. Maybe they're all chilling in the clubhouse together with a post-match bong.

Final score: 4-2 (8 x yellow)

Deafness query
(The Insult, Part 2)

"Hear less, see more." That's the advice of 77-year-old Artur Alt, who's been refereeing for 56 years. According to a feature in the German football monthly *11 Freunde*, Mr. Alt recently refereed his 8,000th game. In the last 1,000 games he says that he's only shown two red cards. "He's very relaxed at dealing with agitated players," says a fellow member of the club he represents, TSV Steppach, near Augsburg.

I think of Artur Alt at the end of this boys' U15 game. The two losing coaches are looking for someone to blame. I can see them marching towards me as the home team shake my hands, and the dejected away team troop off the field. I know they aren't coming over to wish me well and thank me for turning out on a wet, windy afternoon. They've already spent the entire 70 minutes of the game screaming, "Referee!" at every single hint of contact. They only shut up when I threaten to send them off.

So, here we go. Hey ref, why did you give a free-kick for that foul on the edge of the area when it had clearly been a penalty? Also, had I not heard The Insult? They were both babbling so fast that it was impossible to determine who had been insulted and when. I should have pointed out that they had spent so much of the game screaming (and, to be balanced, so had the home coach) that it would have been impossible to hear any insult on top of their ranting.

"No, I didn't hear any insult," I say. One of their players comes over to join in. "Are you deaf?" he wants to know. I point to my hearing aids and say, "Yes, hearing can be problematic for me." I move away from the circle and part with a courteous (if possibly sardonic), "I wish you all a very nice evening." They continue raving at me, but I'm gone. In my head, I'm already at home with a beer on the sofa watching the Bundesliga highlights.

The perceived insult seems to be a distraction from defeat in youth football right now. It leads to the comical indignation and inflated outrage from grown men who've just spent the afternoon demonstrating to their players how to behave in an unsporting fashion. Better to get all exercised about bad refereeing calls than face up to the truth — we got hammered because we weren't good enough. Neither the players, nor the coaches, despite all the yelling.

These encounters at the game's end are pointless. If you give a reasoned explanation, the coaches mostly keep on shouting at you anyway. They've got themselves into a state, and the last person who's going to get them out of it is the referee. If you raise your voice and tell them to back off, they'll get madder too — you're just upping the temperature. If you walk away and ignore them, they act affronted that you are refusing them the explanation they so richly deserve. This ref's so arrogant!

Artur Alt is an old and wise man. He wants to referee for four more years so that he can complete six decades in the game. If he's perfected the art of calming down or pretending not to hear hot-headed wankers then he's a better referee than I am. He's given me a great idea, though. From now on, I might just leave my hearing aids in the dressing room.

Final score: 5-2 (3 x yellow, 1 x time penalty)

Laughter

"And so ends this instalment of The Game of Moans," I announce as I blow the final whistle. The player standing near me starts to laugh. "Heh, sorry about that," he says. "I know it was pretty bad today." It's always pretty bad, I reply. But really I'm just delighted that he laughed — it doesn't happen often enough on the football pitch.

Next I walk up to the home team's left-back. A few minutes earlier he'd made a fairly sour comment about me needing glasses. "Thanks for your touching concern about my eyesight," I say, "but in fact I already wear contact lenses." For the first time that afternoon, he cracks a smile too, then shakes my hand.

It was a bit of a knockabout afternoon. While inspecting the pitch before the game, I found the abandoned packaging of an eight-inch rubber dildo. I picked it up to take it to the rubbish bin, and passed a group of players waiting outside the changing room, not yet in their kit. "Can anyone tell me which team this belongs to?" I asked, holding it up. Ho ho ho, much laddish chuckling.

Otherwise, though, amateur football is a deeply serious affair. The occasional moments of lightness usually come when some gawky hacker tries the spectacular, like an overhead kick from 30 yards out, and misses the ball completely. Only goals result in smiles. Even at this level, goalkeepers do that thing of pulling off a spectacular save and then chewing out their defences for letting the shot happen at all. You'd think they'd be happy to get the chance to show off their skills.

Then again, I was once linesman on a game with a referee who told me before the game, "If you can't referee with a smile, then you shouldn't be in the game." He was one of the worst referees I ever worked with —

neither he nor the two teams we reffed were smiling by the end of the afternoon. As the old joke goes, What do you call a referee with a sense of humour? A. "Don't call me anything, son, or you'll be off."

Final score: 2-2 (4 x yellow)

Football, I love you

I'm cycling to the game and already there's a fight going on, but only between summer and winter. A chill breeze cuts across a silent Sunday afternoon, while a brittle sun struggles to find cracks in the clouds. The result: the comfort of festering autumn and the dying of the leaves. It's back to long-sleeved shirts for the next five months at least.

I'm also thinking about all the things that could go wrong today. You try not to expect anything bad ahead of your games, but I last refereed today's home team 18 months ago. On that day, I red-carded three of their players in the last 12 minutes of a fractious and filthy match that ended with them losing 1-0 to an injury-time penalty. After the game, I had to lock myself in my changing room while a drunk representative of the club banged on the door, demanding a face-to-face audience.

When I saw today's match-up in my inbox last month, I thought about asking for another game. Then I thought, What for? What are you scared of? Nothing really, is the answer. Today, I check the team line-ups, and two of the players I'd red-carded are not in the squad — one had been dismissed for violent conduct, the other for twice screaming in my face about decisions he'd somewhat disagreed with. The third player, whose sin had been a mere brace of reckless fouls, is on the bench.

When I arrive at the pitch I recognise many of the faces, though the drunken club rep's absent — maybe because there's no bar this afternoon. Everyone's friendly, courteous and welcoming, which is not always a given. My guess is that while the game has possibly gone down in club folklore, they have forgotten who the hell I am. Maybe they kicked out their psycho players. Or they've long since come to terms with that particular defeat and have decided to forgive me.

The first half is as placid as Sunday itself. No cards, and the home side deservedly leads 1-0. At half-time, the groundsman comments on what a sporting game it's been. "I've had quiet first halves before," I reply. "The main lesson I've learnt from that is not to automatically expect a quiet second half." Sure enough, after the restart things get tasty — many more bad fouls, players niggling each other, and a sequence of loud and ludicrous penalty appeals.

There's a confrontation between the away team's number 9 and one of the home team's central defenders. I give the defender a yellow card for pushing the striker in an off-the-ball incident. After being 2-0 down, the away team comes back and eventually equalises in the 92nd minute. At the final whistle there's a lot of barging and boisterous debate. I guide them all off the field, after which anything that happens is beyond my realm of giving a fuck.

Laughably, we referees are supposed to encourage teams to shake hands in a line at the end of the game in the same way they are also obliged to do before kick-off. I've never enforced this. There's always someone who's pissed off at the final whistle, no matter what the result. Most days, it'd be like asking Donald Trump and Hillary Clinton to end one of their piss-and-vinegar hate-ins by jumping in a hot tub together for a joint and a glass of Pinot Noir.

Today, thankfully, no one at all is narked at the ref. The home coach mentions the "obnoxious" away team number nine. "Yeah, but you need to be a bit obnoxious if you're a striker," I say. He was just very competitive, and put himself about a bit. The coach agrees, and bemoans three injuries to his own team. He knows they should have put the game away at 2-0. As a neutral, I'm cool with the egalitarian outcome.

Two weekends ago I'd just come out of hospital with a lung embolism after being attached to a heart monitor for 36 hours. Last weekend I was in another hospital, listening to my dad — recovering from a bowel cancer operation — telling me that he no longer wants to live. No matter what happened on the field today, nothing was going to beat the joy of being back in the fresh air, running up and down a pitch and blowing a plastic whistle. Football, autumn — I love you.

Final score: 2-2 (5 x yellow)

Lips on the whistle

City Cup, quarter-final. I'm standing on the end line in my usual position for a corner kick, about 35 minutes in. It's 0-0. The corner comes to the home team's defender directly in front of me, just ahead of the near post. He tries to clear first time but, because it's a wet evening, the ball slices off his right foot and hits his arm. It bounces back down favourably for him and he clears.

"Penalty!" scream several players on the away team. Instinctively, I'd raised the whistle to my lips as the ball hit his hand, but in that split second I decide against blowing. "No intent!" I yell and start to follow the game upfield. There's an immediate foul committed against the home team as they try to quickly break, and in the ensuing pause the away team further protests about the non-call.

Their main lobbying point is not that it was a clear penalty, but that I'd raised my whistle to my lips. To them, that meant I was already on the way to making the decision in their favour. To me, it was just a preparatory move in case I made the handball call. I do it a handful of times every game, largely unnoticed — it's the sound of the whistle players react to, not your body language.

In my pre-reffing years I used to sometimes see officials do the same, and it irked me too. To an observer, it's hard to understand that a referee can see a possible foul one second but then change their mind the next. That's not the mental process, though — as described above, we're still thinking it through. At the same time, I can fully understand why the away team was aggrieved.

The non-decision has repercussions for the next few minutes. I blow for a blatant foul throw (one foot high in the air) against an away team player and he remonstrates, "You're blowing for that and you didn't give us the penalty?" Logically, he might know that the two incidents are not related, but at this moment it's all about the perceived injustice of my overall decision-making. At half-time, I explain the penalty call to their captain. By this time they're fairly good-natured about it, even if they disagree with the call and are still banging on about the fact that I'd had the whistle on my tongue.

Just after half-time, they go 1-0 down. The away team is from a superior league, and they pound the home team's goal for the rest of the match. The home team, egged on by around 50 partisan fans in the increasingly heavy rain, defend like bastards and almost snatch a second on a couple of counter-attacks. Their goalkeeper makes one astonishing save from a deflected shot, leaping high to his right to turn the effort over the bar — involuntarily, I jump with him and under my breath emit a low "Whoo!" of admiration.

There's the obligatory flashpoint and shoving match after 75 minutes, with spectators involved too. I send them all back to stand behind the fence (where they should have been anyway) and book the two miscreants. Aside from that and the non-penalty call, it's one long, glorious evening of thrilling, floodlit, end-to-end cup football in the almost freezing rain on a slippery grass pitch. My watch tells me I ran 5.2 miles, the longest distance I've ever measured over 90 minutes. The home team hangs on and makes it to the semi-final, and there is general delight in front of the clubhouse.

As I claim to learn something new from every game, here's the obvious lesson: in that brief second when you're analysing a possible penalty, try not to raise your whistle to your lips. Even though the players should be watching the ball and not you, it's not going to do you any favours if you decide to play on. Although if you decide it is a penalty, but you wait too long to blow, then the other side might think you were influenced by the loud appeals of the attacking team...

Final score: 1-0 (4 x yellow)

November (Part 1)

"November seems odd," Tom Waits once sang, and the gravel-voiced troubadour would have had his suspicion confirmed if he'd shown up to watch this cinder-pitch game on a still, grey, dying day.

The first thing I notice is how crooked the freshly painted touchlines are. I'm about to ask the groundsman, Horst, if he can quickly re-do the goal-line at least. Then I smell his breath. It's 1pm on a Sunday afternoon and he's already shit-faced — very slow to move and barely present in thought. I stick with what we have for fear he'll paint something worse. Jackson Pollock in the penalty box.

The two teams are second and third bottom, but both are near the top of the Fair Play table. Only one red card between them all season. Should be a quiet game, I think. Right.

The two defences are just as wobbly as the touchlines, and both teams hare out of the paddock with four goals in the first 13 minutes. 2-2. There's another burst of scoring just before half-time, and we go in with the away team leading 4-3. They've only won a single game all season, and seem touchingly surprised and delighted every time they score a goal.

In the second half the goals dry up, and the spectators (two young boys — the sons of one of the home team's players) are now subject to watching something more akin to 22 blind bush-pigs digging their own graves in a mud pit using only their snouts and their hooves, with the ball a mere inconvenience that's constantly getting in the way. The longer the game goes on at 3-4, the more the away team scents three unlikely points. They start to waste time.

After several verbal warnings, in the 83rd minute I finally yellow-card the away team's number 2 for kicking the ball away at a free-kick. He'd already seen yellow for an earlier tantrum when I'd given a free kick against him for upending an opponent. So off he goes. Four minutes later, his team-mate, the number 7, throws the ball over a fence and down the hill rather than leaving it for the home side to take a throw-in. Unfortunately, he too had already seen yellow for a pre-meditated foul. So off he goes as well, prompting a mass ruckus.

How dare I send off two players just for time-wasting? That's what several away team players now want to know as they surround me and stage a colossal drama. Another good way to waste time. The number 6 is particularly vocal, and eventually I show him a yellow for dissent. But he won't shut up, and as I walk away and signal the restart he keeps telling me what he thinks of my officiating. Should I now show a third yellow-red card in five minutes?

Instead I look at him and say, "Yeah, the fucking shit referee's a fucking arsehole, but what can you do about it, eh?" This stuns him into silence, and the last three minutes, plus five minutes of added time, pass without further incident. The time-wasters win, getting their precious three points to take their season's total to seven. And bollocks to the Fair Play table.

When I leave my dressing room after the game, the away team's number 6 is sitting on a bench waiting for a lift. He smiles sheepishly and says, "I'm sorry for yelling at you. Sometimes during the game I just lose all control." I tell him that I'm used to it, and explain why I'd no choice but to send off his team-mates with the game so tight, and so much time being blatantly wasted. More players come out and we all shake hands and wish each other a pleasant Sunday evening.

Finally, just the two young spectators are left, waiting for their dad as I wait for my cash. There's no sign of Horst, who's either passed out in his office or long since been carried home. "What did you think of the game?" I ask the boys. "Exciting," says the older one. The younger one looks at me shyly. "Where do you get your red and yellow cards?" he wants to know. I give him a spare set out of my kit bag and he rushes into the dressing room to tell his Dad.

Well, there's another first — I've made someone really happy by giving him a red card. Like I said, a very odd day.

Final score: 3-4 (4 x yellow, 2 x yellow-red)

Danny (Part 2)

It's just before noon with 45 minutes until kick-off, and I'm waiting outside the locked changing rooms with players from both teams. Nobody seems to know who's got the key. "We had our Christmas party last night," a bleary-eyed player from the home team tells me. "It went on until 5.30." A couple of his team-mates manage a tired, knowing smile. They're almost bottom of the table, with 14 points. The visitors are top, with 46. No one's expecting any shocks today.

The home team represents Sunday football in all its glory. Late arrivals dribble in looking pale and fragile, then once out on the pitch chug around like dysfunctional steam trains clanking between randomly programmed lower gears. The ball seems to be permanently just out of their control, as though it's being manipulated remotely by a snickering deity with nothing better to do on a Sunday afternoon than taunt hangover-prone amateur sportsmen. Somehow they hold out for 20 minutes until the league leaders finally go one-nil up.

The hosts do have one good player, though — a grey-haired but slim number 10 who controls their game, distributes the ball, turns up wherever the play is, and pretty much does the running for all 10 outfield players. Improbably, he scores the equaliser just before the half-hour mark, but that's it. He can't carry his rapidly fading team for the whole afternoon and eventually they bring him down to their level.

The number 10 is a talker too, but he doesn't know the local language — he chivvies his team-mates in English. He complains to me in English too, but I act like I don't understand a word he's saying. I wonder if he'll break out into profanity, at which point I'll have some choice rejoinders, but despite his numerous optimistic appeals for offside when the visitors are carving his side's defence to shreds, he keeps his cool. There's a small part of me I'm not especially proud of that's a little disappointed.

With 25 minutes to go, the away team bring on a sub I know well — Danny, the youth team coach I ended up testifying against at a disciplinary hearing earlier this year. He manages to behave until the 87th minute, then complains at great length about me not blowing for a foul against an opponent — dangerous play, he claims, as the defender had his foot way too high as he cleared the ball. Except that Danny was nowhere near the ball at the time.

As we're walking off at the final whistle, one of Danny's coaches starts laughing and asks me if I hadn't been tempted to show the choleric striker a red card again. "You held out until three minutes to go," I say to Danny, "but you couldn't help yourself, could you? You had to have a moan about something." Danny makes the case for dangerous play once more, but his coach says, "It only seems like dangerous play to you because you're such a short-arse." Which is not only funny but, in the case of this particular non-foul, true. Even Danny manages to laugh, to give him some credit, though I'm sure we'll meet again in less convivial circumstances.

The next several weeks are off until play re-starts in February. I should be happy at the thought of a break from people like Danny, but I'm not really — I'm into a confident rhythm now stretching back several weeks. Plus, it's difficult to keep fit over the festive season without the incentive of games at weekends. Once the hangovers have subsided and the smoke has cleared from the New Year's fireworks, we'll all be more than ready to start again.

Final score: 1-7 (one yellow card)

Lambchop

Three friendlies in four days to warm us all up for the second half of the season. The first two games pass as you would hope — with very little bother, and just one card in 180 minutes. I'm grateful for this, as it helps me get back into the rhythm of refereeing. For the opening 20 minutes of my first game for two months, my mind was wandering until I could wrestle hold of my concentration.

On Saturday evening, I was mentally composing a column along the following lines: friendly games are the ideal in terms of player behaviour, but only the incentive of an arbitrary number of points for winning injects the game with enough needle to make it worth playing and watching over the long term. Not a massively profound theory, it's true, but I was hoping to raise a sporting-philosophical conundrum. Is it better to play in harmony and safety for the joy of the game and the exercise? Or is it better to play for points in a perpetually competitive atmosphere with the ever-present possibility that things will turn sour and maybe violent?

On Sunday, this poser was blown out of the water by the third 'friendly'. Two young, fit teams from levels 7 and 8 of the national tier, both of them doing well in their respective divisions. Ironically, one of the team's names translates as 'Friends of Sport'. Previous visits to this club have not been relaxed. Their vocal crowd is, to put it generously, opinionated.

Neither the 'Friends of Sport' nor their opponents are in the mood for brotherhood. In short, it's an ugly game marked by multiple fouls that are initially niggly, mutate to pre-meditated, and eventually become borderline dangerous. Because it's a friendly, I'm lenient on showing cards at the start, and by the end even a total of seven yellows is still way too generous. I regret not having clamped down sooner — my mistake; poor game management.

The game's other main marker is the moaning, which at this level seems to be institutionalised. The worst, but by no means only, offender is the short-legged number 4 on the away team. He's much older than all the other players, and makes up for his diminishing speed and skills by whining all game long. When the Friends of Sport score a perfectly good goal, he is the only player from his side to scream that it was offside, and he demands to know why I didn't blow the whistle.

What to do? Yet another yellow card? There comes a point where it's as effective as ordering sugar-crazed toddlers at a wild kids' party to go and stand in the corner for five minutes. I say to him, "I didn't blow my whistle, because it wasn't offside. The reason it wasn't offside is because I didn't blow my whistle." While he tries to wrap his angry little brain around my circular logic, I blow for the restart.

There's a space in the match report for 'Notable incidents'. You're supposed to write about missing or irregular player passes, serious injuries, or game interruptions for bad weather. Usually I leave it blank, though occasionally I'll comment on a particularly unsporting coach or team. After this game, I really wanted to write the following:

"Today we experienced 90 minutes of sporting joy. Both teams positively radiated universal goodwill and a generous spirit throughout the match. Each decision of the referee was greeted with a hearty, 'Well judged, sir, that was a jolly difficult decision to get right' and, 'Mr. Referee, while I may not agree with your last call against my team, I respect your right to express yourself using a whistle.' Not that there were many fouls to call aside from the odd unfortunate collision that immediately prompted an avalanche of gentlemanly apologies and warm handshakes. The seven yellow cards I showed were merely to break up the monotony of the unstinting fellowship. These two teams are shining beacons of excellent conduct, and I salute their impeccable human qualities in these times of political uncertainty."

I didn't have the time, though, as we had tickets to see Lambchop and had to run for the train. Two hours of beautiful, mellow music to counter an afternoon of witless snivelling and vindictive ankle-tapping. I wish that I could have taken all these Friends of Sport along to wind down too.

Final score: 3-2 (7 x yellow)

Warnings

First clash for points after the winter break, and it's Third v First in a boys' U17 league. As always, I check the disciplinary records of both teams. The first-placed team have only accrued eight cautions all season. The home team have been far less shy about disturbing the referee.

In the refs' changing room, I talk to the lad who's just finished whistling the U13 game before me. By coincidence, he plays for the second-placed team in the U17 league. When they played today's hosts, he tells me, "they tried to kick us off the park".

Does that mean I go into the game expecting trouble from the home team? Not at all — just as the game starts at 0-0, so does the punishment card. It does no harm, though, to be aware of a team's reputation. If shithousery's a habit, it's unlikely to be taking a day off.

In fact the opening yellow card goes to a visiting player's midfielder, for a tactical foul. Then the home team's robust approach begins to kick in. I book their number 6, a central midfield enforcer, for three successive hefty fouls. And I notice how their striker, number 11, keeps following through on challenges long after the ball has been played by his defending opponent. Our exchanges for the rest of the half are as follows:

Minute 20, warning 1 — verbal: "Quit playing like that."

Minute 30, warning 2 — yellow card: for a late challenge, crashing into a defender full body and knocking him to the ground.

Minute 32, warning 3 — stern lecture for a trailing elbow to the side of a defender's head. "You're on a yellow, final warning." He nods.

Minute 35 — straight red card for violent conduct. Just three minutes after his final warning, number 11 deliberately kicks an opponent in the ankle after the ball has already gone out for a throw-in.

His team's already 3-1 down by this point, and after that they fold. At half-time I hear their captain, who's also got a yellow card for gesturing at the opposition bench, absorb a bollocking from one of his coaches for his lack of control. A club official apologises for the striker's conduct and says they have no quibbles with the straight red. They all saw me repeatedly talk to him.

All the same, there's little joy in a game like this. The red card kills it as a competitive encounter, and I dislike sending players off, especially in youth matches. The away team's coaches are grateful that I clamped down on the violent play, but to have reacted any other way would have been negligent.

Still, it took 35 games this season before I had to show a straight red card. On the other hand, it could easily have been avoided. Even allowing for the fact that the player was too dim to take on board my clear signals, his coach should have taken him out after the third warning, at the very latest, and had a proper word. Or have taught him not to play like that in the first place.

Final score: 1-9 (5 x yellow, 1 x red)

Semi-final

City Cup, semi-final — what's at stake? The City Cup winner goes into next season's State Cup, and the winner of the State Cup goes into the first round of this country's FA Cup. Win that, and you're in the Europa League. Win the Europa League and... well, let's say that tonight I'm reffing two potential Champions League participants. Though probably not.

What I'm really reffing tonight are two quick but very physical teams. My left arm begins to ache from raising the yellow card. At the end of 90 minutes, the central defender of the losing team shakes my hand and kindly adds, "I haven't seen such a bad referee in a long time."

It's understandable that he's disappointed after narrowly missing out on making it to the final. So in response I'd just like to say — though I didn't at the time, because I can be courteous if I clamp my tongue between my teeth until it bleeds all over my gums — I haven't seen such bad defending against a team almost at the bottom of the league below you for such a long time, Mr Bitter-Grape-Sucking, Sneaky-Foul-Addicted, Like-A-Child-Losing, Twatty Number 5. Mr. Beaten-In-The-Air-By-A-Winger-A-Foot-Shorter-Than-You-For-The-Winning-Goal, Mardy-Faced Wanker.

If I seem a bit sensitive to criticism, it's because there was really just one mildly contentious incident all night, although Number 5 and his central defending partner were the biggest moaners about it — mainly because they got burned. To spare you too much detail, an attacker in an offside position stood passively and allowed a team-mate to run on to a through ball from an onside position, from where he scored a cracking goal to make the score 2-2. The defending team claimed that the passive attacker had been active.

The terrible referee, though, allowed the goal to stand. It was a lovely finish, and a football world where goals like that are cancelled out — because another forward looked for half a second as though he was going to run after the ball but then changed his mind — is not one in which I want to watch, play, coach or officiate. Suck it up and stop making the ref a scapegoat for your shite positioning.

In a game this intense, though, there will always be a few players who'll find something to moan about. "Handball!" screams one player in my ear after an opponent briefly handles, but with no intent. "Calm down," I tell him, so he looks at me and screams "Handball!" even louder. Like the sole instruction the coach gave him when he came off the bench a few minutes earlier had been, "Never mind winning the game, make sure you get a yellow card by yelling at the fucking ref!"

The decisive goal from a glancing header comes 10 minutes from time, and the 80 or so home fans celebrate their unlikely progress into the final. On the way they've beaten four teams from higher leagues. They're less critical of my performance than the opposition's number 5, needless to say, and cheerful at the prospect of Europa League football a few years down the line. An online match report mentions the flurry of second half yellows, but neither the journalist nor the two coaches cite any refereeing influence on the outcome. For me, that's the best possible result.

Final score: 3-2 (9 x yellow)

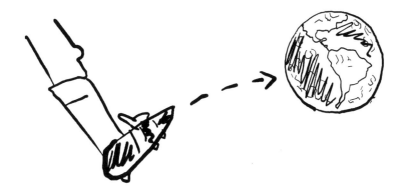

Nationality

I've been assigned another game out of town and when I look at the laughably christened Fair Play Table, my heart sinks a little. I'm being sent to officiate between teams who, in the disciplinary rankings, are third bottom (the home team) and bottom (away). This is in a league of very few angels, where you have to be almost conscientiously deviant to hit last place.

I presume that the idea is to ship an unknown ref in for a potentially explosive game, then let him flee the scene never to be heard of again in that neck of the woods. It's true there are some players you encounter on a weekend afternoon you'd not want to meet on a quiet street late at night. I've retained a clear image in my head of the player who threatened to break my neck last autumn. You know, just in case.

I talk with the referee who's just officiated the game before me, between the reserve teams of the same two clubs. How was it? He shrugs. "Well," he says of the away team. "They're ... " And he names their nationality, like it's understood. I say that in my experience, there are no national boundaries to foul play, mean tempers and crass stupidity. Well yes, he replies a little guiltily, I suppose that's true.

Before kick-off I wish both teams a fair and sporting encounter, but I might as well have been standing on a beach spitting at a tsunami. Right from the start they set about fouling each other. Almost every challenge ends in a free-kick, and almost every free-kick is subject to dispute, particularly from the away team. I give out a couple of verbal warnings about the level of dissent, but it's like telling a flock of starving vultures to please leave that cow's rotting carcass alone on the grounds that it should be granted a dignified burial.

After half an hour I've had enough of the away team's central midfielder wittering on, and I book him for dissent. "Are you refereeing against us because we're … " And he names their nationality. "What are you accusing me of?" I ask back loudly, expressing the necessary outrage at having had both my partiality and my world view called into question. He walks away. Can you call a game off and then call a lawyer to instigate a case for slander?

By half-time it's 1-0 to the home team, with two yellow cards on each side. It would take a colossal entry to document all the ways that the away team in particular infringe the values of sporting conduct, fair play and respect, but suffice to say that by the final whistle, they are three men down. Two go for yellow-red offences involving varying degrees of dissent and dirty play, and one player gets a straight red for deliberately following through on a tackle some weeks after the ball was played. When down to nine men they equalise in injury time through a gratuitous own goal and celebrate like they've earned more than just a point.

One of those yellow-red cards provokes a scene I've not yet dealt with as a referee. I send off the away team's captain — already booked for screaming at me for the second time about an offside non-call — after he scythes through a home team forward. The away players surround the forward, who is black, and accuse him of making a meal out of it. The fouled player remains calm, and I intervene and send them away. One of the away team's defenders mutters a racial epithet that I'm almost sure that I hear correctly, although he is too far away from the scene for anyone else to have heard.

If I'd shown him the straight red, it would have not only meant yet another angry scene right there on the field, but also a long disciplinary process over the coming weeks. It would have been my word against his, and because he only muttered it, I could not with full conviction say that I definitely heard the words I think that I heard. Instead I follow him, with the red card in my hand, and ask him if he's prepared to repeat what he just said. Of course, he pretends not to know what I'm talking about. I look him in the eye and warn him not to utter one more word for the rest of the game — an unsatisfactory solution perhaps, but the best I can come up with in the already fraught circumstances.

After the game, which finishes 1-1 after seven minutes of added time (because many bad fouls lead to many injuries), the player who was red-carded comes to apologise, claiming that the foul was "unintentional". I thank him, but say that wasn't how it looked from where I was standing five yards away. He's brought his small son along to project the image of an easy-going family man. Which he probably is. The football field can do wicked things to one's mind.

I give the player passes back to a representative of the away team standing outside their dressing room. How long will the red-carded player be banned, he asks? I tell him I don't know, it's not up to me. "He's one of the club chairmen," he says, and both of us and several by-standers burst out laughing. As the sun goes down behind the trees, casting lanky shadows over the now peaceful pitch, at least we all share that common outlet.

Final score: 1-1 (6 x yellow, 2 x yellow-red, 1 x red)

Needy Ref

How important is refereeing to me? I found out this weekend, when it looked like I wouldn't have a game. I had no idea what to do with myself.

It's alright when I travel out of town for the weekend. I don't even think about it. But if I'm at home and available on both Saturday and Sunday, then I'm almost always assigned at least two games. This weekend I was only assigned one, on Sunday morning as a mentor to a newly-qualified referee on a boys' U13 game. Standing on the touchline taking notes — I don't mind doing it, but it's not the real thing.

On Friday, I sent an email to the game assignors. Just to let them know I was around, like, and available if anyone called off at short notice. I got a sniffy email back saying there were plenty of refs this weekend, thanks, and that I shouldn't bother them by lobbying for games. Blimey, I was just trying to help. Or do they get a dozen emails like that from needy refs every Friday afternoon?

On Saturday, I got up late, had a leisurely breakfast with the family, and then Mrs Ref wanted to know what we should do with our afternoon. I admit that I was half waiting for a call to tell me to pack my things, get on my bike, and heroically step in to whistle a game abandoned by some unreliable and impetuous colleague who'd decided to fly to Vegas for the weekend instead. In the absence of this call, we cycled to the market, walked around, bought some fruit and veg, then had an ice cream.

"I feel like there's something not right about today," I said. "That I should be somewhere else." Mrs Ref gave me that look generally reserved for the incurably afflicted. I assured her that I really was enjoying my afternoon with her at the market, only that it felt a little odd. Almost like I was being punished for wanting to ref so badly.

Later, we went to watch the city's pros fail to win again and after that we met some friends in a restaurant. I'd just picked up the menu, it was 9pm, and my phone vibrated. Caller ID showed it was one of my game assignors. Ha! I rushed outside to answer. Where and when do you want me? Tomorrow afternoon, one o, clock, Reserve League. I resisted the temptation to triumphantly yell down the phone, "So you needed me after all, eh? EH? FUCKIN' EH?"

"Happy now?" asked Mrs Ref. Not as happy as I am 16 hours later, stamping my damned authority on the game with three cards in the game's first half hour — two for reckless fouls, one for dissent. They set the tone nicely and both teams settle down. I possibly screw up a late offside call, but by then the outcome is far beyond doubt and the protests are mild.

There are handshakes from both teams, despite the lopsided score-line. I did my job and the weekend feels complete. It may be only for 90 minutes, but sometimes it feels like I need theose amateur teams as much as I suppose that they need me.

Final score: 6-0 (3 x yellow)

Dying

Ten minutes to go, the home team is 1-2 down but pressing for the equaliser. They have a corner, and there's lots of movement and bustling about in the penalty area. I watch the away team's number 14 holding one of the home team's players, who is fighting back a little. I'm about to blow my whistle to stop the corner and tell them to quit when the home player lightly shoves the number 14 away from him. Number 14 falls to the ground, clearly dying.

Well, not dying, obviously. But it seems really serious. The emphasis here is on 'seems'. In fact the home player hardly touched him, but it's sparked a huge kerfuffle. I blow loudly and go over to intervene in what is becoming a massed swinging of purses and airing of playground-like whines. "Referee, red card! Violent conduct!"

I lose sight of the home team's player, who's merged into the melee. Very crafty. But I hadn't planned to send him off, or even book him. I just wanted a chat with him and the number 14 to tell them to stop acting like twats and get on with the game. We're nearly done, and there haven't been any cards so far. But I no longer have any idea who he is, so it's a non-issue. Especially as number 14 is still down receiving treatment for the cracked ribs, punctured lung and shot knee-caps that must surely have resulted from the push, judging by the heroic cry of agony we all heard as he fell.

"What are you going to do?" demands the away team's captain. "Nothing," I say. "I didn't see which player it was, and as I've no linesmen to help me, that's it. Get your number 14 off and we'll play on." Number 14 limps off, supported by his coach. A pathetic, stooped figure, who will surely never kick a ball again. After the corner is taken, he sprints back on, quick-heeled and quickly healed. What a recovery!

I suppose you could argue that the push was a sending-off offence, if you're the kind of referee who thinks that David Beckham deserved to be red-carded for flicking his heel at Diego Simeone during the England-Argentina game at the 1998 World Cup. But I'm the sort of referee who, even though he's anything but an England fan, thinks that Diego Simeone acted like a complete wanker. When I see players composing a Wagnerian opera on a kid's xylophone, I tend to have no sympathy at all.

There's another reason I didn't want to show any cards yesterday. Three hours before kick-off we got news of a death in the family. It wasn't unexpected, but it was close to home. It may seem like a strange tribute to show no yellow or red cards in a completely unrelated game of football, but it was the best I could do. Only four weeks earlier, we'd been sitting in a restaurant and talking about the game I'd reffed that day. Two games later — gone.

So that's why I'm lenient on a couple of fouls that are borderline cautions, but no one protests. There are two penalties — one for each team, and neither call raises even a snort of dissent. The two teams know nothing of the death, of course, but until the 80th minute it seems like they are somehow tuned in to the temporary hippy floating around the field as their referee.

At the final whistle I tell the away team's captain that I wouldn't have sent off their opponent, even if I'd been able to identify him, mainly because his number 14 did the Kindergarten Flop. By this time his side's scored another goal and won the game, so he's very magnanimous. A few players are exchanging unkind words as they leave the pitch, but aside from the little drama in the penalty area, it was about as sporting as it gets in this particular league.

Another game. Just another game among mortals.

Final score: 1-3 (no cards)

Fistfight

The coach of the away team is on the pitch and yelling at me, even though his team are 3-1 up. I've just shown one of his players a red card. He's so outraged that he wants to take his team off the field and concede the game. Even his own players are telling him that's a bad idea. They would rather play another 10 minutes and take the three points than forfeit on a matter of principle.

What's going on? It's a boys' U17 game, and up until the 68th minute it has been relatively peaceful. Only half an hour in, when the home team substitutes in a burly latecomer, do things heat up a little. He slots into the back four and immediately starts a little something with the opposing number 7 after a clash of adolescent bodies and egos. "It was pretty peaceful until you turned up two minutes ago," I say. "Cut it out." And he does.

The away team are league leaders and on the verge of winning the title. The home side are in mid-table, playing out the season without too much enthusiasm. One of their players, the number 16, takes exception to being fouled near the halfway line. He pushes the player who fouled him, the away team's number 15, who then pushes him back. So the number 16 thumps the number 15, and the number 15 thumps him back, and in the course of a two seconds it has escalated to a full-blooded fistfight. Think Billy Bremner and Kevin Keegan at the 1974 Charity Shield.

I run over, blowing away on my whistle, but by the time I arrive at the scene of the scrap the coaches on the touchline have intervened to break it up. I show both players the red card. The home team's miscreant is already running off to the changing room, but the away team's player cannot believe he has to go too. Neither can his team-mates. Neither can his coach, which is why he starts yelling at me.

"Our player was only defending himself!" they all proclaim, and they are quite serious. It takes two to have a fist-fight, though, and after the first shove all he needed to do was raise his arms in the air and walk away. I'd have shown the number 16 a red and that would have been it.

"If we play on, anything that happens from now until the end of the game is your responsibility!" the coach raves at me. I'm confident that things will be fine, though. I talk to the 20 remaining players and ask them to play a calm and sensible final 10 minutes. There's one more goal and no more incidents. The home coach apologises and tells me he's already thrown the number 16 out of the club. The away coach is no longer speaking to me, but that's fine because he's a twat.

Next morning I'm back out for another U17 encounter. I look at the match report from when the two teams met earlier in the season. Seven yellows, three reds. Fuck, here we go again. As we line up to walk out on the field, I let them know that I know — that there were more cards than goals the last time they played. They all look sheepish, with the exception of a couple of smirks — these are teenage boys, after all.

The away team behaves impeccably, the home team accumulates a quartet of yellows for foul play, mainly because they're one step slower than their opponents. There are no full-on fist-fights, however, and I just about hang on to my faith that football is a worthwhile and wonderful game.

Saturday: 1-4 (2 x yellow, 2 x red)

Sunday: 1-7 (4 x yellow)

Gods

"Once apparently the chief concern and masterpiece of the gods," HL Mencken wrote, "the human race now begins to bear the aspect of an accidental by-product of their vast, inscrutable and probably nonsensical operations." And that was without him ever having watched an amateur football match.

A visitor from another planet might have wandered past yesterday's game at the butt-end of a league so low that there's no way out but upwards, and rightfully asked, "What on your increasingly dysfunctional planet Earth is all the fuss about?"

Well, you might patiently explain to the alien, this is what we call a game. Games are played for leisure, fitness and entertainment purposes as an escape from daily toil. It's the final day of the season, and the team in orange, who are mid-table, are hosting the team in green that is third from bottom.

"So the game in itself has no importance," muses the alien. Correct — it has none, you reply. "Then why," the baffled visitor continues, "are the men in green surrounding some of the men in orange and shoving them, and why is everyone shouting, and why is that funny bloke in the red shirt trying to get in between them while ferociously blowing his whistle?"

I think, you reply, because it's so hot. Our planet's warming up, and humans can't cope with it. Psychologically, most of us are in denial and continue to drive our cars, fly in planes, eat mass-produced meat and generally act like it isn't happening. Physically, it causes us to melt down like two-year-olds denied an ice cream and being told instead that it's time for our afternoon nap.

"I still don't really get it," shrugs the alien, looking at its watch and thinking it's about time to get back to the spaceship. "And I'm not even going to ask why the bloke in the red shirt is now waving a little piece of yellow cardboard in the faces of some of the angry players."

Later, the referee helpfully sends the alien his match report, which goes like this: "The intense heat had a strange effect on the players of Wankers FC. In the absence of any substitutes, scoring chances or creative attacking ideas, many of the team's players began to moan, complain and dissent, and were unable to stop. The fact that they went on to lose 8-0 had absolutely nothing to do with the superiority of their opponents, and was solely down to the poor decisions of the idiotic referee. The idiotic referee would nonetheless like to wish the whole delightful squad a wonderful and peaceful summer break, and hopes that they make a full recovery."

The gods, as Mencken assumed, have in the meantime long since given up.

Final score: 8-0 (3 x yellow)

Bankers

Should referees ever lose their calm and take the low road? Absolutely not. Not ever. Though that isn't to say that it doesn't happen. Today, for the first time in over eight years of refereeing, I feel that I don't need to take the shit being thrown at me any more.

It doesn't help. In fact, it almost leads to me being physically assaulted.

It's the time of year for corporate six-a-side tournaments, and I am one of several refs at an all-day jamboree spread out over eight mini-fields. It's also a good chance to exchange views and experiences with colleagues in the referees' tent, and the pay's generally a lot better than at our officially sanctioned games. The downside is that the tournaments follow a pattern as predictable as an unregulated teenage party when the parents are out of town for the weekend.

Things start peacefully at 9am. The sun's out and everyone's in a good mood, apart from the team in green, already marked out in the first 13-minute game of the day as serial moaners. For the first two hours, though, the consensus in the refs' tent is that it's all "very relaxed". But the weather's turning quite sticky, and there are storms forecast. As though in a badly-scripted soap opera, dusky clouds start forming on the horizon. And beer is now being served in the main tent.

As the group stage comes to a close and teams are on the verge of elimination, a handful of games get tense. In one match, I separate two feuding teams who then have to be prevented by several stewards from belting each other after the final whistle. It's not yet noon. Then I finally get to referee the stroppy green team. They are hanging on to a 2-1 lead with two minutes to go when one of their players wellies the ball as far out of play as possible, way beyond the other fields. I give him a three-minute time penalty for unsporting behaviour, and in the minute of time I add for time-wasting, their opponents make it 2-2 with the very last kick of the game.

Three of the green team's players surround me and yell about the injustice of the time penalty. They say they've had enough of the shit refereeing and they're going home. "Have a good journey," I say. They stay on anyway, to nobody's joy.

The green team's just a warm-up for the main act, though. The rain's now coming down steadily and there's thunder in the air, but we play on. In a round of 16 game, I meet one of the teams that earlier had to be calmed down by the stewards. They're from a bank, and it's not a bank I'll ever do business with if they're as dirty in finance as they are on the football field.

At 1-1, they're furious when I send one of their players out for three minutes for his second bad foul. Their Angry Number 3 then slides into a tackle with a straight leg and takes out an opponent. He then yells at me for giving the free kick, but as he's remonstrating an opponent takes the free-kick quickly to a forward in space, and he makes it 2-1.

My new friend, the Angry Number 3, squares right up to me and yells right in my face, "The ball was moving!" I tell him there was nothing wrong with the goal and that he needs to move away from me right now. A minute later I blow the final whistle and, now that his team is out, he runs back up to me and does the same thing, with the same complaint, but more aggressively still. For the second time, I order him to move away. Now he turns and sprints to the referees' tent and starts yelling at my colleagues, demanding... I don't know what. Video evidence? A replay of the game? A steward's enquiry? A hearing before the European Court of Justice?

When he gets no sympathy there (hard to believe, but refs don't like being yelled at by furious little twats), he confronts me again, grabs my hand in a macho way, shakes it hard and says, "*Very* well reffed. *Very* well reffed." He lets go of my hand, and this is the second when I lose control. Even as I do it, I know it's a mistake. I show him the finger.

At this, the Angry Number 3 crosses a line into the arena of the unhinged, but another ref is just passing as his rage goes off the dial and stands in his way as he runs back towards me. I walk off casually to the changing room, because I'm leaving early to ref a boys' U17 game across town. As I go, I can still hear Angry Number 3 screaming at me, and turn to see him being restrained now by several people.

As I'm in the changing room gathering up my things, one of my senior colleagues comes in. "A player out there says you showed him the finger," he says. "Is that true?" I explain the circumstances, and then confess that it is indeed true. I did it, and I'm not going to lie about it. And the funny thing is, I don't actually regret it. After the senior ref has gone (he's not happy),

I say to another colleague, "If that means they suspend me for six months, then so be it."

I cycle five miles across town in the thunderstorm and arrive absolutely soaked. I change into dry gear, and by the time we're ready to kick off at 4pm the rain's subsided. "The season's nearly over — stay calm, stay decent, be good sportsmen," I say to the two teams, somewhat hypocritically. The game, though, goes well, apart from an inflammatory clash of two strapping lads just before the end. "Hey, just three more minutes," I tell them. "We can get through this, right?"

And we do.

Final score: 8-1 (2 x yellow)

SEASON 2017–18

HATRED, DISSENT AND IMAGINARY LINESMEN

Inane optimism

The German football press is pregnant with pre-season flam. It can't wait to give birth to the new football year, but for now is hampered by interviews in which every coach, player and manager is obliged to say that this time around they have a really strong squad, and that everyone's worked very hard during training camp. 110% has been given all round, and there's a great team spirit among the lads or lasses. The clubs are all in such amazing shape that clearly no one will be getting relegated next spring.

Cycling towards my first game of the season, I wish that we referees could be afforded a platform for such inane optimism. "This year," I would tell the reporter from The Referee's Recorder, "I think that all players will be so focused on improving their game that they will allow the referees free rein to call the game as they see fit. We will see unprecedented levels of sportsmanship, and I doubt that I will have to whistle a single foul all season, let alone show a yellow card.

In fact, what dulls my mood on a warm, breezy day is the prospect of all the inevitable cards and complaints over the coming months. This opener is a friendly game, but we've all learnt by now that classifying a football match as 'friendly' is like calling the civil war in Yemen a temperate discussion ground for some minor variants in interpreting the word of the Koran.

Indeed, with 20 minutes of the match to go I have to take both captains to one side and offer them a choice. Either I call off the game and write up a disciplinary report, or they can tell their players to stop acting like idiots and play out the remainder without a single further incident. It's a bit of a gamble, because I have no intention of blowing up early and spending hours writing up this playground spat (I have other plans). On the other hand, neither side wants to have to explain how they went off the mental rails two weeks before the season even started.

Both captains roar at their players to calm down, for Christ's sake. One day later, and I can't even remember why they got so upset. Someone pushed someone else at a corner-kick, and then a few more people pushed a few more people and everyone started shouting. The kind of really important stuff that leads to an ululating swarm of restless stupidity just inside the 18-yard box.

In the first half, the away team's number 9 had complained at length about me blowing for a foul when he went into a tackle with his foot raised. "Ah, Mr Referee, what happened to the idea of Scottish hardness?" he says after the game. "Your refereeing was too fussy today."

I mutter something about it not having been me who committed any of the endless fouls. Later, a far better answer occurs to me: "I may have been too fussy, but at least I wasn't so shit that I got subbed out at half-time." Oh, and what the hell is "Scottish hardness"? The sound of a Glasgow Kiss cracking up against the Stone of Scone, or the physically-oriented approach to football that means Scotland haven't qualified for a major tournament for almost 20 years?

The valves have been reopened for the legitimised ventilation of excess testosterone on a field measuring approximately 60 x 100 yards. We've got a good bunch of lads and they've been training hard. All ready for another 10 months of kicking opponents, and crying out loud at the injustice of an erroneous whistle. Here we go again.

Final score: 1-4 (1 x yellow)

Refugees

Some of the grounds I referee at are located near accommodation for refugees. A couple of seasons back, I walked into a dressing room looking for the home team's captain, and found a man from the container houses next door on his knees praying to Mecca. It must be both strange and challenging when you've been forced to swap your normal house of worship for the grubby tiles of a seventh-level football team. Five times a day.

I'm refereeing a peaceful and mainly uneventful friendly game. Over the 90 minutes, a few short, sharp words are enough to keep things calm when trouble twice vaguely threatens. No cards, no controversy.

So, nothing much to say about this match. Except that at one point, when standing on the end line for a corner kick, I notice three men from the nearby refugees' home watching the game from behind the railing. They are all holding plastic bags with a small amount of groceries. They watch the action intently.

Sport, I've long contended, attracts us not just because we want to see which team or individual wins, but also because it represents a benchmark of normality. Where games are being played, wars are not usually being fought. In London recently, I was standing before a room of people where I had five minutes to explain why they should crowd-fund my next book, *The Quiet Fan* (published in 2018 by Unbound). I held up my battered copy of Purnell's 1972 *Encyclopaedia of Association Football* — my first ever football book, and which became my bible at the age of seven — and nervously babbled something like this:

"When I first got this book I ravenously scanned its pages of stats and began to memorise the results of historic cup finals. I couldn't understand, though, why there were no results for the years 1916-19, or for the period

1940-45. What could possibly have been happening during those times that stopped football being played?"

Because as long as there are games going on, life feels stable enough. Organised sport is only suspended when it's overwhelmed by matters of life and death (or, temporarily and more prosaically, by bad weather, but you know what I mean). I love the scene at the end of *Traffic* when Mexican police officer Javier Rodriguez is contentedly watching kids in his town play baseball, thanks to the floodlights he requested from the council to keep young people out of the drugs trade. It's the kind of facility we take for granted in countries that are at peace.

So I imagine the three young men who stop to watch the game remembering with melancholy a space in the town or village they grew up in, where they'd played themselves. Maybe they want to play again in their new country, but lack the language, the knowledge or the courage to ask how. From their expressions, I sense a sullen, silent longing.

Then the corner's taken and my attention is diverted back to the game. The next time the ball goes down that end of the field, the three men have left. Back to unpack their meagre groceries in a shared kitchen, thousands of miles from home and family, in a country where the means of feeling like they belong — membership of a football club, say — are not necessarily denied them. But there's probably a giant leap to be made (trials, paperwork, misunderstandings) before they're allowed on board.

The rest of us involved in the game must remember that sport is both a leveller and an immense human right that should be available to all.

Final score: 2-7 (no cards)

Coward!

Anyone who's ever had a job has fantasised about just walking out and sticking a finger up to their boss or manager as they leave. It's how I feel at half-time of this fractious men's game on a warm Sunday afternoon. Of course, just abandoning a game at half-time would mean giving up refereeing for good, but still I'm tempted. Just to see their faces when you say, "You can referee your own fucking game, you wankers. And you're all crap at football too."

That day may come, though I'm not quite ready for it yet. Still, if I'd known how the second half was going to play out, it might well have happened.

Sometimes you referee a team that commits lots of niggly, deliberate fouls, then complains every time you blow the whistle. It's not a loud enough complaint to draw a yellow card, rather it's a deliberate campaign to intimidate you and make you feel insecure. In this game, it's the policy of both teams. After 25 minutes, as the ball's being fetched for a corner kick, I announce loudly:

"*Hey ref! Hey ref! Hey ref!* It's all I'm hearing. Shut up and play the game."

They duly ignore me, so in the next 10 minutes I yellow card the next two complaints (away team) and the next two fouls (both home team). I also twice warn the home coach for yelling at me from the touchline. This works much better than my appeal for sanity. Half-time: 0-3. The only major decision is a penalty for the away team, but the foul was hard and clear, despite the home team captain's claim that it "might have been a penalty, but look where the ball is". The ball is at the corner flag. I don't get his point.

After resisting my own half-time urge to leave, the game's as good as killed in the 47th minute when a home team defender, who'd already been booked in the first half, pulls the shirt of the away team's number 12 in the penalty area just as he's about to shoot. He doesn't even wait for the second yellow — he walks off, and after the game he apologises. "I forgot I'd already had a yellow," he says, and we both laugh.

So at 0-4 and one man short, the home team calms down because they're now too knackered to protest. The away team have shut up moaning too, happy with their lead. There are lots of requests to know how long we still have to play — summer's returned after three days of cool rain. Everyone, including me, is already thinking about their evening plans.

Until, in the very last minute, two players — the home team's number 13 and the away team's number 8 — become entangled while fighting for the ball. The ball squirts away and they end up pushing and shoving each other in a wee playground struggle. All of a sudden a dozen players are weighing in, but most of them are actually trying to separate the two miscreants and shouting, "Calm down!"

Except for the away team's number 9, who attacks the home side's number 13, yelling at him and shoving him until he's also pulled back. The home team claims he hit the player, but I don't see that — by this time there are two arguing groups of grown men, and if an actual punch was thrown then I missed it in the hullabaloo. Still, I decide that once things have calmed down, I'll show the number 9 the red card for violent conduct, and then I'll blow the final whistle.

As I'm waiting to do this, out of nowhere the huge number 14 from the home team's defence — who's not misbehaved much bar a couple of fouls — walks aggressively up to me and says, "Can I just say something? Your refereeing's shit." Well, that may be so, you great hulking lump of dumb humanity, but you're going to get a red card anyway. He then completely freaks out. "Why don't you have my shirt as well?" he screams mysteriously. Then he takes it off and throws it right in my face. It doesn't smell of French perfume and freshly-mown summer meadows. He walks off, turns back around and marches towards me again, then two team-mates intervene and point him towards the changing room.

Meanwhile, the home trainer has marched on to the pitch to have his say. "You are a coward! You are a coward!" he screams. "Why aren't you sending off their player?" He means the number 9. I ask him if he could please calm down and take a short walk with me away from all his still remonstrating players. He actually does, and I tell him that I'm just waiting for the situation to calm down before I hand out the punishment (absolutely standard practice — you don't barge into a scrum of yelling, pushing players waving a red card).

So, the number 9 finally gets his red. Then I blow the final whistle and wish everyone a beautiful day. Some players thank me, some apologise. The number 14 sits outside the changing room making conspicuously loud comments about the shit ref. The number 9 comes to my changing room and wants to know what the consequences will be for his red card (this happens a lot). I don't know, I tell him, I just write a report and send it off. Good chance this one will be going to a disciplinary hearing, though. He sighs and walks out.

A boys' U19 game the day before was very quiet. Not a single complaint throughout the entire match. "They're good lads," said one of the coaches. And they were. Because it's really not difficult to keep your mouth shut and play football at the same time.

Saturday: 2-2 (1 x yellow)

Sunday: 0-4 (5 x yellow, 1 x yellow-red, 2 x red)

Putting out fires

Three days after being assaulted for the first time as a referee, you'd hope for a gentle game. Maybe a friendly in an U9 league where both teams have kittens for mascots. Instead, I've been assigned to a City Cup first round game between two teams of distinct ethnic origins. They hail from a part of the world far from my city, and have been in conflict for well over a century. It's the luck of the draw.

It's due to get dark around half-time, so the home team asks if it's okay if we play the first half on their smooth and kempt grass field (no floodlights), then move to the neglected cinder pitch, weeds and all (but with floodlights), at half-time. The answer: no. So they haul the wheelie out of the shed, paint the lines, and clear away the debris from a storm the night before. What follows on this decrepit surface is the most intense and challenging game I've ever refereed.

There are so many fouls that it's hard to recall more than a handful of clean challenges throughout the entire match. I play advantage multiple times just to keep the game flowing. This irritates the away team in particular when they don't make good on the advantage. Yet in between the dirty play there are some cracking goals. We go in at half-time with the score at 3-2 and a count of three yellow cards.

I fear, though, that they are just getting started, and I'm right. In the second half the game remains closely fought, and highly fractious. I run around putting out fires like a lone United Nations envoy with a water bucket in the middle of a city under siege. My appeals for calm and a steady stream of yellow cards for foul play and dissent are about as effective as a UN resolution drafted and passed in faraway New York. There is something going on here far beyond my remit, on the brink of an explosion —

five times I have to separate players or groups of players yelling and squaring up to each other. A chat with both captains makes no difference at all.

I don't help matters by making a significant mistake. I let play continue after an aerial challenge between the home team's robust centre-back and the away side's already fuming centre-forward. The striker goes down with a dramatic yell (not for the first time — every foul in this game is a short and outraged three-act play), clutching his back. When I go over to look, I realise that he was genuinely hurt in the challenge — a knee or an elbow into his back that I hadn't seen under the poor floodlights. The away team now feels that I'm 'against' them, and start to foul with even more deliberate intent, while letting me loudly know that I'm the carrier of injustice.

Of the 10 cautions I issue, at least half a dozen could easily have become reds for second offences. Gauging the already blazing temperature, though, I refrain from sending anyone off — it feels like that would be the final spark needed to propel the random skirmishes into an ugly, full-on mass confrontation. Instead, I continue to talk, to try and mollify the aggrieved, even the ones accusing me of bias and incompetence. The away team's number 21, already booked for dissent, rants on and on until I tell him, "I'm not even listening any more. Save your breath."

I run like a fledgling hare throughout the 90, petrified of missing the foul that might push us over the edge, though this at least helps me to stand on the back line for several offside calls. That's the one area tonight where no one actually moans. I'm so relieved when I blow the final whistle that I don't give a fuck when the away team's number 7, already booked, tells me what a useless waste of space I am. "Have a nice evening," I reply. Although I should have said, "You're right — if I was any good, I'd have sent you off hours ago, you moaning, fouling twat."

To my surprise, that's the last of the abuse. Players from both teams thank me and shake my hand and say, "Well reffed." Some even come into my changing room to drop a kind word. I've a suspicion they might have been told to do so by their club officials for fear of a searing disciplinary report, but it could also just have been an acknowledgment that I'd done my best during a grimy, belligerent encounter.

I'd give myself six out of 10 — I feel the game got out of control in the second half after I missed the foul. Still, we all came out the other side alive and mainly unscathed, which is more than you can say for the real-world conflict between these two ethnic groups. I come home mentally and physically shattered, unable to eat and feeling nauseous. But I also belong to a nation state, enjoy freedom of movement, and live in a wealthy democracy. I got a lucky draw. I think I'll survive.

Final score: 5-3 (10 x yellow)

Intimidation at work

Two more excitable teams who are poor at football, but extremely talented at fouling and shouting. You get the picture by now. Things start out calm at 3pm with the score at 0-0, defenders peacefully passing the ball among themselves to the sound of bird-song. We end the afternoon with shins bruised, tempers AWOL, faces as hot and purple as a mad radish, and so many unhappy players that a better man than I would have summoned them all to the centre circle for group therapy.

And today I wonder if the problem really does, in a way, lie with the referees. The sporting culture in this city is so messed up that many now seem too scared to hand out the necessary punishments. Players increasingly think they can get away with anything. Here's what I witness before my game:

When I arrive at the sports ground, there are two games still going on. While warming up behind one of the goals, I watch as a defender trips an opponent just inside the box. The referee correctly awards the penalty, but a huge number 13 on the defending side begins to remonstrate. He is a foot taller than the ref, and towers over him, pointing at the spot where the foul occurred and yelling at him that it was outside the box.

I think, "Yellow card for dissent." But the referee just tries to appease him. The big number 13 continues to yell. By now I would have sent him off. The referee then blows his whistle and points to the edge of the penalty area. He's changed his mind and given a free-kick instead. I know why he does it — he's simply scared of this huge bastard, and has no other protection. He has no authority.

In the refs' changing room after his game's over, I tell him that his original call was correct, and that I was surprised he didn't send off the number 13. He just shrugs. He was doing his best to keep the peace, he explains.

I also watch a few minutes of the other game. Both teams are very loud, and at one point several players surround the young, 16-year-old referee, waving their arms, vocally invoking the Gods of justice. Afterwards, I ask him how many cards he'd shown during the game. "Oh, none at all," he says.

I then go out to referee the First XI of the team with the big number 13. Clearly there's a philosophy at this club that intimidating the referee can work. Two of the goals they concede are vociferously appealed as having been offside — this is what happens when lumbering defenders turn around and see a quicker opponent through on goal. When I let the goals stand, they gesture and moan and claim that I'm biased against them, and they continue to claim this all afternoon. Yes, lads, you only lost because the ref was biased. No need to look any further.

In the online match report section Other Remarks, I write: "An awful, ugly game — bad fouls from both teams; endless moaning in particular from the away team; a mass confrontation among hotheads that almost led to the game being abandoned because the home team understandably had had enough. It was the kind of day when you think — why do people bother playing football at all? And why am I so stupid to sacrifice spending a Sunday afternoon with my family, for the sake of €22, refereeing 22 men who take absolutely no pleasure at all in their sport? At some point you've had enough, and at some point there will be no more referees for the xxx League. And then this beautiful league will cease to exist because they won't find anyone willing to be sworn at and reviled for chump change. In conclusion: the human condition is all fucked up."

I, on the other hand, press 'send', then immediately feel that my condition's much, much better.

Final score: 5-3 (9 x yellow)

Maradona moment

This boys' U19 first round cup tie is not untypical. I reckon there are about a dozen appeals for handball throughout the evening. Most of them I ignore. The only good thing you can say about the handball rule is this: it's so open to interpretation that even the players appealing for it rarely do so with complete conviction. It's often more of a hopeful question, as opposed to the raging demand you get with fouls and offside calls.

Like snowflakes, no two cases of handball are ever the same. It's one of the most difficult calls to make, but one of the easiest to turn down. After most appeals, the game moves quickly on, and even if a player follows up at the next stop in play, all you have to say is, "Ball to hand" or "There was no handball." Or touch your shoulder or upper chest to indicate that the ball was not, as one side is claiming, controlled by the upper arm.

I don't really blame the players for all the appeals. Shouting "Handball!" is instinctive, and if it prompts the referee to blow for a free-kick, then why not try? It's not particularly sporting behaviour, but then what kind of idiot expects that any more?

The appeal is particularly impassioned when a shot is fired towards goal and hits a defender in the penalty area. It can hit the defender's head, thigh, stomach, back or arse, and there will still almost always be an attacker who raises his arm and screams, "Handball!" Sometimes it really has hit a defender's arm or hand, but the ball was travelling at such speed, and from such a short distance away, that the contact was unavoidable. Any kind of actual upper limb contact does, however, tend to ramp up the thermometer of outrage when you don't blow.

My approach to handball is the same one I have to penalties: I only blow if I'm 100% sure that it was an offence. Borderline decisions I wave away.

Given the impossibility of translating the game's theoretical law of 'intent' into actual practice*, it's the only fair way that I can think of to proceed.

In this particular game, I experience a first in my decade of refereeing. The home side are 0-1 down and there are two minutes to play. They loft a long ball into the box from a free-kick, the defending team steps up too late, and three attackers are left alone in front of goal. As the ball bounces, it looks like the goalkeeper will catch it, no problem. But then the attacking team's number 17 deftly flips his hand up and knocks the ball over the keeper's head and into the net.

The home fans — numbering around a dozen or so very expressive friends and relatives — cheer wildly. Bizarrely, the away team don't appeal for handball. The sun is almost down, the groundsman hasn't turned on the floodlights, and that end of the ground is covered by trees — the light is beyond poor. For a second, I wonder if I've seen correctly. Then I blow the whistle and make the gesture to indicate handball. The number 17 looks at me sheepishly. There's no protest, and he doesn't object to the yellow card, even as the home supporters are demanding to know why I cancelled out the 'goal'.

The game ends that way after three minutes of stoppage time. There was just one flare-up and a shoving match between two players, quickly snuffed out by two yellows and The Lecture, then followed by good coaching. That is, the coaches tell their players to calm down and play football, and don't yell at me for punishing their stupidity.

A fast, well-contested game on a tricky cinder pitch that flew by, and one that I really enjoy. I shouldn't start relaxing and fooling myself that it's a sign for the better, though. On my way out, I pass a men's game in the dusk on the adjacent grass field. It's the team whose coach told me last year to fuck off back to England. They've just had a player sent off, who's now mouthing off on the touchline and arguing with some spectators.

That's not my problem tonight. I cycle off through the park and enjoy the sunset instead.

Final score: 0-1 (5 x yellow)

*Prior to 2019's even less helpful law change, eliminating the concept of intent and replacing it with some bollocks about players making themselves 'unnaturally bigger'.

Imaginary linesmen

"We were very impressed with your pre-match speech," says the steward. "We've never heard anything like that before." Look, I don't want to show off here, but it's extremely rare as a referee to have someone tell you they are impressed by anything you've done. So forgive me for cherishing the moment and going into some more detail.

I've tried lots of different pre-match speeches down the years. In the US there was a particularly difficult boys' 'elite' league where all the players had supposedly signed a Code of Conduct. During the games, though, there was little sign that they'd taken it on board. I ended up taking a printout of the Code to games, holding it up to the players, and telling them I was sure that over the coming 90 minutes they would all be taking very seriously the document that they'd read, signed and promised to honour. It was surprisingly effective.

In Germany, I've tried being nice and I've tried to be stern. Any nods or even short applause following these speeches were frequently rendered laughable by the ensuing game (see previous chapters). I've also tried keeping it very short: "So, let's play. Good luck and enjoy the game." That particular speech will appear in the satirical version of *My Life as a Referee*.

So this is my latest attempt to set the tone (the one that apparently impressed the home officials), which I've used twice this week as I stood in front of both teams at the halfway line ready to take the field: "I'd like to introduce my assistants today, Mr X [I point to my left] and Ms Y [I point to my right]. Also [pointing vaguely towards the club-house], my video assistant, Mr Z. On the off-chance that these people are not visible to you, then please show some understanding for the fact that I only possess two eyes. Don't moan about every single foul and every single offside decision. For dissent there's always the possibility of a yellow card. So, good luck and enjoy the game."

As I'm pointing at my imaginary linesmen, some players laugh, some look baffled, but in both games it's seemed to work — just one card for dissent. In this game, when an away team forward instinctively howls about an offside call early on, I snap, "Hey, what did I say before the game?" and his team-mates shush him. He apologises. The yellow card stays in my pocket. The three first-half cautions — all for persistent fouling — remain the sole yellows of the day.

I'm not naive enough to expect a revolution of good behaviour, because I've already experienced too many false dawns of apparent enlightenment. Still, I really enjoyed both games this weekend. On the other hand, the past few weekends are still weighing on me. I just had an email assigning me to a game at the club who last season invited me to fuck off back to England. I replied that I would never referee this team again.

That was just the first paragraph. I felt compelled to write more, and to copy in all my refereeing overlords. The situation in the city's lower amateur leagues is catastrophic and out of control, I went on. There's an almost constant threat of violence, while fairness and sporting values have been usurped by endless tantrums, foul play and intimidation. I was sick of spending my Sunday evenings writing long disciplinary reports and never hearing anything back, apart from seeing that certain players, like the one who threatened to break my neck, were still playing several weeks later. Referees were receiving neither the protection nor the support they needed from the state FA and the refereeing body.

Maybe someone will be "impressed" enough to take me seriously. So far all I've had back is a formal notice that I've been withdrawn from that particular game. In the medium term, however, the frank discussion that everyone's avoiding needs to take place, but that will probably only happen once there's been a serious assault.

Saturday: 3-1 (2 x yellow)

Sunday: 5-2 (3 x yellow)

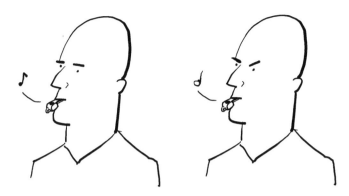

'Let them know you're pissed off'

I'm faced with anger almost every game, and the general idea is that I, as the referee, must remain a steady rock of calm amid a thunderous sea of foaming fury. Yet there are times when it pays to show that you are, at the very least, mildly irritated. Here's my guide to the referee's anger management:

1. Before the game. Both teams should have signed off on their final line-ups half an hour before kick-off, and the home side must produce a print-out of the teams for me to check against their player passes. This happens maybe once or twice a season. Upon arrival, I always introduce myself to both coaches with a smile and a handshake, but I become less genial the closer we are to kick-off and the coaches are still faffing around with passes and mobile phones. If it's still going on less than 15 minutes before kick-off, I become exasperated. And if it turns out I can't check the passes until half-time, then I pass into 'stern lecture' mode to let the wayward coach know I've already marked his card as incompetent.

2. Just before kick-off. You know the scene. Hands shaken, coins tossed, we're ready to start, but one of the teams has hunched into a huddle for a doubtless inspiring last-minute speech from the captain. That's okay, if they keep it short, but often they don't. I give a double-blast of the whistle to let them know that I don't like waiting around. Then sometimes there's one of those stupid, ritualistic team chants which, to my knowledge, has never yet helped anyone to win a game. Congratulations, wannabe Maori warriors, you've already shown your disrespect for me and the opposition before we've even kicked a ball.

3. Bad fouls. During my first year of refereeing in the US, an experienced ref who was my assistant that day took me to one side at half-time and taught me about using my whistle to communicate. "All your whistles sound the same," he said. "For minor infringements, give a short whistle. For bad fouls, blast it long and hard, let them know you're pissed off!" No such useful information had been given on my training course, but it was the best 30-second seminar I've had in 10 years of refereeing.

4. Dissent. If a player is genuinely outraged at a call (or non-call), I'm as likely to be worried that I screwed up the call as I am to be angry, depending on the circumstances. I might even say, "Sorry if I missed that, I was at the wrong angle." Last night (boys' U19 Cup game, second round) I got angry at the other kind of dissent. A perfectly legitimate away goal is claimed as offside by a home defender who stands before me, points to his peepers, and says, "Open your eyes, ref." Doesn't sound so bad on paper, but that doesn't convey the insolence and disrespect. I show him a yellow and vociferously explain why he'll be off the field if he opens his mouth again.

5. Not knowing the rules. When a player tries to tell you that you don't know the Laws of the Game. This really tweaks my ire. Again, an example from last night's game: I wait for an offside player to get to the ball before I call it. One of his team-mates very stroppily asks me why I've waited so long to blow the whistle. "Have you even read the Laws of the Game?" I ask him sharply. "Until you have, keep your mouth shut." I concede this last order was too harsh, and probably would be frowned upon by referees' assessors, but there are never any assessors at my games so occasionally I'm a law unto myself.

6. Flare-ups. Controlled anger is the key here, because obviously you don't want to wade in drunkenly scattering absinthe on to an already open flame. Again, use the whistle, and preferably blow so loud that it hurts the players' ears and they get distracted from pushing, shoving and insulting each others' mothers. Continue to look like you're mightily pissed off right through the ensuing lectures and disciplinary measures, even if you're thinking, "This whole situation is so absurd that I just want to laugh in their faces and tell them to grow up, for Christ's sake."

7. Post-game. It's been a horror show from both teams, both coaches. The home coach hands you your match fee and tries to apologise with a weak smile, saying something like, "Relegation fight, you know how it is." I say nothing, but think, 'Too late, mate. You helped make this a shit afternoon for everyone, and I won't forget you or your rancid club the next time we meet.' And home I go without a civil parting shot.

Final score: 2-5 (6 x yellow)

Mourning has broken

The away team, like many in this city, has a reputation. The stats tell me that they've already picked up three red cards in their opening four games. The home team, meanwhile, is top of the table with maximum points (no reds). There are rarely any surprise results in amateur football, so I'm expecting an easy home win, but with the potential for their opponents to turn defeat into drama.

The guests are wearing black armbands and ask for a minute's silence because the father of one of their players had died during the previous week. Everyone's fine with that, and we duly observe a solemn 60 seconds. Although the mourning side take an undisputed yellow card three minutes in for a tactical foul, the rest of the half is as peaceful as they come — very few infringements, and not a murmur of complaint.

In my mind, I'm already thinking, "If they continue like this, I'll note in the match report what a pleasure it was to referee two such sporting sides." I've only ever done this twice. You'd think I'd know better. Because it turns out that the cut-off point for honouring the dead is exactly 45 minutes.

The away side are deservedly 4-1 down at half-time, but as soon as the second half is under way they lift their embargo on behaving like twats and start to complain. I immediately tell them that the first half was great, so we don't need to start dissenting now. The number 8 with the suspect 'populist' hair-cut, who is standing right next to me, cups his ear and says sarcastically, "Sorry, I can't hear you." Number 8 is now very much in my sight-lines, even though it's one of his team-mates I book a few minutes later for going nuts about a throw-in decision.

Number 8 suddenly looks like he has a red-card mission to fulfil. Two nasty, deliberate fouls later and he's off, no protests. One of his team-mates tries to remonstrate, but there's no conceivable way to argue the decision. They ship more goals and we reach the point where everyone just wants the match to be over.

Incidents often seem to occur in the last minute of games like this, just as you're mentally preparing to round things off. The burly away team goalkeeper goes right through the home team's striker as he's shielding the ball with his back to goal in the six-yard box. Almost reluctantly, I blow the whistle for a penalty. I say reluctantly because it's the final minute and the score's already 8-1, but I have no choice.

It's a cue for the guests to surround me and start yelling. The captain is particularly inventive: "That wasn't in the penalty area, it was the six-yard box, and the goalkeeper can do what he wants there!" Is that right? Another player demands, "What else was he supposed to do?" Well, he could have refrained from going through the back of his opponent, or tried to play the ball.

The captain tries a new tack. "It's already 8-1," he yells, "what difference does another bloody goal make?" Exactly, I respond. So why are you getting so worked up? He gives up now and we line up for the penalty, which the goalkeeper saves with a decent dive to his left.

After the game I catch the goalie having a tab outside the clubhouse. "I knew you'd save it," I say. "I just wanted to give you the chance to be a hero." This attempt at humour, it's fair to say, bombs like a 70s sitcom. He just tries to claim again that it wasn't a foul. And Kim Jong-un is a peacenik from Mendocino.

"Maybe it wasn't," I say in an attempt to be conciliatory (although it was). "Maybe I got that one wrong." I shrug and leave. I suppose I should just be grateful that today at least I got to referee half of a peaceful, civilised game.

Final score: 8-1 (4 x yellow, 1 x yellow-red)

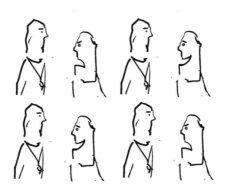

Danny (Part 3)

Another day in the familiar proving grounds of the city's reserves leagues. The men who only play for fun, but never seem to be having any. The average, the bad and the hopeless. The unsightly, the unfit and the sporadically unhinged. Speaking of whom, there on the bench as substitute and assistant coach of the home team is my old friend Danny.

"New club, Danny?" I ask as he hands me the player passes. "What happened — did your old team finally kick you out?"

"Ha ha, no," he replies. "I'm still coach of the U19s there." As we're so chummy these days, I don't ask him if he's had any trouble with referees lately.

Danny's team captain remembers me too from previous games, and it seems to be a fond memory, for once. "You're from England, right? Or is it Holland?" We're still all smiles at kick-off after I give my 'imaginary linesmen' speech and one player even shakes hands with my non-existent assistants. It's 10 minutes before I even have to call a foul, but I know in this league the peace won't hold.

At 1-2 down, my pre-match friend, the home captain, trips an opponent in the box and I point to the penalty spot. It's such a clear call that no one protests, except the player himself. How could it have been a penalty when he had his hands held up high? "Yeah, but you didn't commit your foul with the hands, did you," I point out. He argues all the way to a yellow card. The goalkeeper punches the penalty away to his left. The captain encroaches, but the saved ball is nowhere close to him. I've been reffing in these leagues long enough now to know when to ignore an infringement like that.

A few minutes later, right outside his own penalty area, he makes a challenge, plays the ball, but also leaves a man lying on the grass in the wake of his 'robust' tackle. When I blow for the free-kick, he can't believe it. "I played the ball!" I hear this claim week after week — the rule change from several years ago forbidding such tackles has still not trickled down into the consciousness of at least half the players at amateur level. Especially defenders.

The captain now walks towards me, grabs me by the shoulder and begins to argue the toss. I take a step back and order him to keep his hands off me. At this point I'd have been quite justified in sending him off — for the foul, for the physical contact, and for the dissent. Take your pick. But from the touchline I hear a voice. It's telling his captain to calm down, to back off, to accept the call. The voice belongs to Danny, the new darling of discipline! His captain walks away, and at half-time, with the score now at 2-2, I see Danny taking him to one side for a quiet talk.

He may be giving him a gentle lecture on the importance of fair play and sporting behaviour. Or he may, just possibly, be saying something along the lines of, "I know this ref, he's a fucking arsehole, he'll write up a blow-by-blow two-page disciplinary report and take you all the way to the hearing. Then the bastard will cycle halfway across town to show up and repeat it all with added details, and you'll get a €150 fine and the threat of a long-term suspension. So just leave it, Captain, he ain't worth it."

Whatever he says, it works. In the second half, the captain utters not a word and commits not a single foul until, in the act of tripping an opponent, he somehow knackers his ribs and has to be helped off. Danny, though, subs himself in with 10 minutes to go. How does the reformed assistant coach act when out on the field? I'm hardly surprised when he starts moaning about every call. At one point, while one of his players is receiving treatment for an ankle tap, he stares at me like a psychopath for a full 30 seconds. I try to ignore him.

"What do you want me to do, Danny?" I say eventually. "I'm not a doctor."

"He was fouled!" Danny pouts. Yes he was, I agree, which is why I blew for a free-kick.

There should be at least five minutes of injury time, but the temperature's too high and there are too many niggly little battles going on by now. One unhappy couple gets away with The Lecture instead of the yellow cards they deserve for a mutual shoving match. After another midfield square-up just two minutes into stoppage time, I blow for full-time. The away team's coach moans like hell. I tell him that the players didn't deserve injury time the way they were behaving. Plus, they got a point each, so everyone should go home happy. Which he clearly isn't, but just like I'm not a doctor, I'm not a fucking therapist either.

Danny continues to argue about something or other all the way to the changing room, until I say, "You'll never learn, will you?" And then he cuts short his moanologue, breaks into a smile, tells me that I had a good game, shakes my hand, and wishes me a nice Sunday. It's that same slightly unnerving dual personality I saw when he shook my hand and wished me all the best right after he got his fine and severe ear-bashing from the four-man panel at the disciplinary hearing.

All the way home I have The Fall's 'C'n'c s-Mithering' in my head where Mark E Smith sings a chirpy, "They say, *See you, mate!*" Then he replies in his own tired, lowered voice, "Yeah, see you, *mate.*"

Final score: 3-3 (3 x yellow — none for Danny!)

No respect

I'm reading the walls in the referee's changing room before a men's game some way out of town. There are four framed certificates honouring one man's dedication to football — a referee who's a member of the home club, and who has put in 50 years of service to the amateur game. I mentally salute his steadfast devotion. I'm only in my 10th season, but I feel like I've been reffing much, much longer.

A few minutes later, having inspected the pitch, I'm warming up close to the touchline when an elderly gentleman ambles by and begins to chat about refereeing. I soon work out that he's the ref whose certificates are on my changing room wall. He tells me how he skipped the country when he was young to avoid doing military service and travelled the world. He ended up playing for a Scottish ex-pat club in Adelaide. "Boy, could they drink," he says. "Every last one of them."

We also talk about the problems facing referees now compared with when he started out. "What I notice now throughout the game is a lack of respect," he says thoughtfully, and with some sadness. Then he elaborates: "A complete lack of respect." I agree, although I don't mention that I've a blog full of stories to back us up.

The game starts well for me in the fourth minute when I play advantage after a dirty tackle, and the home team races up field to take the lead. I have to really focus on not smiling as I note down the goal-scorer and the time of the goal. There's a crowd of 40-50 people and they all shout out, "Well played, ref!" (I just made that last bit up — in fact they spend the entire game contesting every last call against the home side.)

A quiet first half ends 1-1, but there are a number of notable incidents after the break:

1. A penalty for the home team after their captain heads a through ball over the keeper, who stands his ground and intentionally blocks the attacker's path, knocking him down. "What else was I supposed to do?" the goalkeeper yells at me. This seems to be the now recurring question from an updated edition of *The Goalkeeper's Book of Alibis and Excuses*. The penalty is scored: 2-1.

2. A home attacker beats a defender for pace just beyond the halfway line, and the defender upends him. He wasn't in on goal and another defender could have caught up with him, so I only yellow-card the defender — the first card of the game, in fact, after 74 minutes. Several players on the home team tell me hotly that it should have been a straight red.

3. Two opposing players get in a shouting and shoving match. I caution them both and tell them we've only got 10 minutes to play, so can they just keep a lid on it, otherwise they'll be off. The away team player, the number 19, leaves it a whole two minutes before he starts shouting at and shoving a different opponent. So he's off, and his captain goes in the book for running up to me and yelling in my face about the terrible injustice of it all.

It's still 2-1, and the away team twice tries to buy a penalty when forwards go down in the box and yell dramatically, but I see no fouls. Their bench and followers bellow along in anger and disbelief. Then they get caught at the back in the last minute and the home side seals the game with a breakaway goal.

After the final whistle, the away team coach comes to shake my hand, but then proceeds to outline all the ways I was biased against his team. That wasn't a penalty, that should have been a penalty, the sending-off was unfair blah blah. "It's funny," I say, "but almost every week the losing team says the same thing."

I think I've had an okay game, but immediately start to retrospectively doubt my decisions. Did I miss something in the box? Was the red card too harsh? At least there are handshakes from both teams, and no further comments. And then, by the clubhouse door, I see the elderly gentleman with 50 years of refereeing experience waiting for me.

Fellow referees in this country are never usually shy to tell you where you went wrong. I steel myself, expecting to hear once and for all that I messed up the penalty call. He steps forward and shakes my hand. "Congratulations," he says warmly. "Man of the match. You were the best man on the field today. I won't let it go unmentioned."

Instead of shaking his hand I want to give him a man-hug. I'm genuinely moved and can barely stammer out a thank you. During the 14-mile cycle ride home on a mild, cloudy evening, I'm humming all the way and thinking things like, "Foul. Play on. Goal. Get fucking in there!"

Final score: 3-1 (4 x yellow, 1 x yellow-red)

Pinball

Just how bad is it possible for a game of football to be? Today, all the ideal conditions are in place. The home team is bottom of the table with zero points after nine games. The likewise winless away team is one place above them with two points, and we're playing on one of those bald, hard, 1980s-style astro-turf surfaces you occasionally get out in one of the city's satellite towns, where time does indeed feel locked inside that plastic, Day-Glo decade.

The visitors bag a fortuitous early goal when a scuffed shot finds its way into the corner of the net, more thanks to the intrinsically malevolent bounce of the pitch than any skill on the shooter's part. It turns out to be the most accurate attempt on goal all afternoon. The remaining 83 minutes are for connoisseurs of random pinball — though Roger Daltrey's deaf, dumb and blind kid would have played more accurate passes than all these lads put together.

In their favour, they're a sporting bunch. Decisions are once or twice politely questioned rather than loudly scorned, other than by a female follower of the away team, who sees my throw-in calls as reason to squawk so vehemently about my crass incompetence that I'm tempted to turn around and parrot her complaints right back at her. That would be satisfying, but unprofessional, and as she's the only irritant during the quiet first half I let her get on with whatever therapeutic process she's been prescribed. I hope it's helping.

Meanwhile, the ball continues to run off the pitch like a marble off a glacier. As the game continues, mutual desperation sets in. The away team sense their first victory of the season, two months in. The home team realises that if they can't at least get a point off this hopeless bunch, then the season's already over in the first week of October. The game morphs into a combination of flailing aerial challenges, blatant shoves, desperate tackles and theatrical flops. Fouls multiply like midsummer maggots on a rat's corpse.

With about 20 minutes to go, I can sense the game's taking a darker turn. The temperature rises to hot and irascible — the previous polite enquiries have transformed into loud appeals and bawls of protest. It's only a matter of time before something flares up.

Instead of booking the away team players for time-wasting (which just takes up more time), I add six minutes to the end of the game. And it's in the sixth minute of injury time that it happens. A last desperate free-kick from the home team passes over everybody's heads, and as I'm checking the ball's trajectory to see if it's gone out of play for a goal-kick, an away defender goes down, clutching his face. Everyone on his team surrounds the apparent perpetrator — a striker built like a rogue walrus who's been in the thick of the afternoon's multiple low points.

It's quite possible he elbowed the defender (who recovered without the need for an ambulance, or even the magic sponge), but I didn't see it. I blow my whistle and separate the madding mob, and ask them to see out the final 30 seconds without any more unpleasantness. At the end, both teams are pissed off — the home team because they lost, the away team because I didn't show the red card to the naughty striker. Though one player says, "Thanks, ref. That wasn't an easy game."

That was a game? I thought you boys were just trying to set some kind of record for the number of times a ball can be ejected out of play from a given rectangular area over the course of an hour and a half. Anyway, you're welcome. Good luck with your forthcoming six-month battle against relegation. And if it gets any uglier than this, please don't bother letting me know.

Final score: 0-1 (4 x yellow)

Traffic wardens

Fifteen minutes to go, and I'm surrounded by four people, all of them screaming at me. One of them is the home number 9 I've just sent off for stamping on an opponent, a crime he vigorously denies. The other three belong to his team's touchline entourage — they may be coaches, spectators or even the stewards. I'm not looking at them, I'm staying calm and ordering them to move away.

There's nothing like a straight red card to ignite the tinder of outrage at the referee's very existence. Only when there's been a fist thrown does the miscreant usually accept their fate and walk away. For filthy fouls and acts of minor, stupid and unnecessary violence like this one, the punishment administered is apparently beyond the realms of human belief. How, how, how could I possibly send this player off? "I was only going for the ball!"

Here's another club where I'm making few friends for applying the Laws of the Game. This must be how traffic wardens feel every day. The red card has been hanging over an intense, angry, foul-plagued game all afternoon. I've been appeasing conflicts throughout the second half, exhorting disputatious players to please just calm the hell down. Even when you call the foul and show the yellow card, they still rage at each other, and order me to come down harder on the other team. Both sides do this.

For all that, I have two good moments. The first comes when the home team, 3-1 down, takes a corner kick and, after a huge scramble where they twice appeal for a goal (both times the ball's blocked on the line), a third attempt does indeed cross the line, albeit for a brief quarter second before the keeper claws it back. I'm standing in my usual place for corner kicks, on the end line next to the goal, and see it all perfectly. This of course doesn't stop three players from the away team encircling me and loudly maintaining that the ball never went in. I point to where I was standing. "That's why I stand there." End of dissent. 2-3.

The second comes a few minutes after the red card. The away team's left winger is running alongside the opposing full-back, who fouls him twice, or at least he tries, but the winger keeps running, and twice I call advantage. The winger crosses and the number 10 converts. I mention in passing to the away team's number 4, a perpetually aggrieved mountain of a moaner, that, "Hey, did you see that? The fucking shit ref played advantage twice there. You're welcome."

He stares at me for a moment, probably wondering why the fucking shit ref is talking about a fucking shit ref. And then he gets it and smiles. Yes, one of the players actually smiles. The clouds open and a chorus of scarf-waving angels sing, "Hallefuckinglujah." The football Gods chant, wave their rattles, and crack open a crate of heavenly beer. The home team simmers. Still, they can always blame the ref for sending off their number 9.

That number 9, by the way, was built like a Belarussian shot-putter. He'd come in to the game less than a minute before, with his coach presumably having given him the following instructions:

"It's a nice autumnal day. Show off some of your tricks. I'd like to see a feint or a pirouette. Maybe some step-overs, a wee shimmy, or a back-heel. Hell, you can even sing while you play, if you like. The main thing is, enjoy yourself!"

Or maybe he said, "We're one goal down with 15 minutes to go. Don't hold back, get fucking out there and mix this fucker up."

What could possibly go wrong? In his first challenge, he charges into an opponent and takes him out, which on its own is worth at least a yellow. They fall to the ground and their bodies become entangled, like two writhing, polyester-clad, sado-masochistic lovers in a muddy field full of curious voyeurs (and a referee). The fouled player lets out a cry, and in the ensuing struggle to get up (or is it for dominance?) the number 9 stamps on his left thigh. Not brutally, but enough to warrant the punishment.

I share the changing room with a ref who's just whistled the reserves on the next pitch over. He looks like a broken man. "An absolute nightmare," he says. Outside we hear shouts and cursing. He nods to the window and says, "They're still at it." All in all, a tense and shouty afternoon's sport. I cycle home in a mood, glad to eventually reach the river and see normal people out for a walk.

The previous day's game offers up a different kind of misery — a boys' U15 match where the home coach of a team boasting a 100% record moans incessantly about every decision that doesn't go his way. This in spite of a 2-0 win and no controversial decisions whatsoever. I ignore him all afternoon. At the end of the game, not a single player shakes my hand or says thanks. Thanks for being a role model, Mr. Adult.

Saturday: 2-0 (2 x yellow)

Sunday: 2-5 (6 x yellow, 1 x red)

Dad's the wanker

One of the teams I coach is at the boys' U7 level, and on Saturday morning we have a home game in the Fair Play League. I am very hands-off and let them scurry around after the ball, backed by lots of encouragement and very little guidance. I stick closely to the League's instructions to keep my team's parents well away from the field of play.

The away team, however, allows a father to stand behind one goal coaching his son. The kid has the ball in his hands and kicks it straight to one of my players. The father screams at his son for the mistake. My player shoots, the goalie saves (very well), but then another one of my players nets the rebound. Making the score ... it doesn't matter. We're not supposed to count the score. The father is now gesturing emphatically and screaming at a whole bunch of wee lads: "Where was the defence?"

His two coaches are doing nothing, so I walk up and ask him what on earth he's doing yelling at five- and six-year-old kids. He suddenly looks ashamed, apologises, and then moves away from the goal. Afterwards, he comes to shake my hand and makes an excuse about it having been "in the heat of the game". I'm so irritated by this remark that I just ignore him. Though in hindsight I wish I'd said, "Look, you porridge-brained tosser, just like you don't go down the street randomly insulting, assaulting or groping people, you don't ever yell at six-year-old kids, in the heat of the game or not."

The incident's a fair indication of the football culture in this city. So far, I've only encountered one other team that sticks to the Fair Play League's stated philosophy of treating kids like kids and just letting them play. Most are (at best) constantly chivvied, or (at worst) bellowed at by over-motivated coaches commentating every last kick and stumble.

The bad sportsmen of tomorrow are already being moulded by mouthy, ambitious trainers and clueless, over-involved parents.

And we haven't even got to my refereeing in the League of Crisis. It's Sunday lunchtime, and it's raining hard. The away team is running late and wants the kick-off delayed by 10 minutes. The home team can't get hold of its player passes and asks if I can wait until half-time before I check them. I accede to both requests, because at the start of the afternoon I always try to be a nice bloke, but later I wonder if this was a mistake. If you're accommodating, they take you for a sucker.

There follows the by now almost expected 90 minutes of fouling, moaning, shouting and theatricals, mostly from the away team. In the 10th minute, I book their striker for a dive as he tries to catch a penalty. Just before half-time, it's a yellow card for their archetypal hatchet-man centre-half for his third foul, and his sour-gobbed team-mate for complaining loudly about it. By the interval, I'm wet through and properly pissed off. A home player complains that the hatchet man should already be off, and he's probably right.

Just after the hour mark, the hatchet-man's indeed off for another bit of attempted butchery — almost as though he expected to be. (I also notice he seems to be wearing a shirt number different to the one he has on the official line-up — a quick Google search when I'm home confirms his real identity. Caught you, you cheating bastards!) Despite being down to 10 men, the away team scores from a free-kick with nine minutes to go. 0-1. Now it's all about defending their lead by illegal means.

In the 86th minute, I send off another away team defender for his second reckless foul (swung by him 'having a word' with the player he's just kicked in the shin). Several of his team-mates go nuts, surrounding me and screaming at me. In the last minute, the home team equalise, and the away team hail the end of the world as we know it — "Offside!" they cry and weep and howl (it's not). The sour-gob yells at me again and should be off too, but at this point I'm just keen to reach the end of the game.

I play only one minute of stoppage time and then wave away all the away team's players who are still very keen to continue expressing their low opinion of my refereeing. Much of the yelling has turned to sarcastic congratulations on what a great game I've had. And congratulations to you gentlemen too on a hard-earned away point. I sincerely hope you've enjoyed your afternoon of sport.

The home team coach (quite politely) asks me, "Only one minute of stoppage time?" At this point, regrettably, I lose it and tell them all to fuck off and wish them good luck in finding someone else to referee their shitty league. The coach later apologises. He realises that I'd "had enough". But still, only one minute of injury time ...

Quite right, I'd had enough. It was another one of those cycle rides home where you can feel the urge to quit almost as much as you feel the urge to chain your bike up outside the next bar and drown the whole sorry Sunday in a barrel of extra-strength Pilsener. And wish that everyone could just stop yelling. At kids. At referees. At anyone and anything. What the fuck is the matter with you?

Final score: 1-1 (6 x yellow, 2 x yellow-red)

November (Part 2)

There's a short history of family members coming to watch me referee over the past decade. The pioneer was my father-in-law, who watched me in action all day at a US youth tournament a few years ago. On the drive home, he was resolutely silent. Two days later, while we were watching a game on television, he remarked drily: "This referee's a lot like you. Very frugal with the whistle."

Last year, Mrs Ref came along to a men's game, bringing a book in the expectation that she would be bored. She never even opened the book, being in equal parts horrified, fascinated and entertained by all that unfolded before her, with her husband the centre of attention for 90 minutes. For the next two weeks, she followed me around the flat shouting, "Hey ref, what the fuck is that dirty fork doing on the draining board? And where the fuck's my dinner? Come *on*, referee!"

This weekend it was my youngest daughter's turn. She had an assignment at college to take a photograph to illustrate an article for the headline: "Compassion is an unlimited resource." Come along to my game tomorrow, I said, you're sure to see plenty of examples. She took that as a challenge and decided this would be a fun way to spend an afternoon.

So here we are. It's raining steadily, for the third Sunday running. November has been allocated the colour grey and is refusing to relinquish it to any shade of cheer. With the face of a flinty Scottish pallbearer, it ushers in the dark, frigid months to come. Want something to cheer you up? Here — go referee third-placed v second, with both teams near the foot of the Fair Play table.

The home team takes an early lead, misses several easy chances, then allows the visitors to equalise with a goal half-heartedly claimed as offside.

Just before half-time, one of their players comes away from a challenge in midfield with the ball, but then stumbles and loses control. The away team counter-attack and score their second. The home team moans that their player was fouled. Now they decide that I'm 1. incompetent and 2. against them.

"Did you get any pictures of compassionate behaviour?" I ask my daughter at the break. The home steward has kindly given her coffee to warm her up (teenagers never dress for winter — don't ask me why. I was the same.). "Oh yes, loads," she replies, to my surprise. She proceeds to show me several snaps of players helping each other to their feet, almost all of them smiling. I've barely any recollection of this happening. "Maybe," she says, "you just don't notice because it happens so often."

Well, there's also maybe an element of players doing their best to avoid a yellow card, so they apologise for the foul, and help the opponent up. Nothing wrong with that. It also makes me wonder if I'm programmed only to see the unsporting conduct, and never see much good in the players around me. Still, I caution, this game's just warming up. The second half is always worse.

The home team equalises soon after half-time, but then two minutes later one of their players decides to go on a hare-brained sideways dribble and runs straight into me. The ball runs loose to an opponent, he passes it out wide, and the number 10 heads the ball in from the cross. 2-3. Of course it was an accident, a collision, and they all know I'm part of the field of play. All I can do is hold up my arm and apologise. But it accentuates the feeling that I'm 'against' them (I'm now unofficially against both sides), and they start to complain about every call, while making a number of loud and dramatic penalty claims.

The game gets progressively louder and muckier, and there's a stream of yellow cards, mainly for the away side. Plus one for dissent for the home captain, the number 10, just one of several players on his team to loudly express their feelings about my calls. They lose, and obviously it's my fault, not the fault of the players who missed all those first-half chances, or the fluffed indirect free-kick right in front of goal I gave for a dangerous play deep into stoppage time.

"Well, there's another club that hates me," I say to my daughter as we walk away from the ground. She says that I did miss one foul down at her corner — she has a picture of it. "And yes, that number 10 really did hate you," she adds. "He was cursing you the entire time." I wonder how much more I missed, and if I should have given him more protection, and if I should have booked more away players earlier on. Had that maybe been a foul after all in the lead-up to the second goal just before half-time? I don't feel like I had a particularly good game.

"Oh, you had one huge fan," my daughter says. "That little old guy we saw at half-time. He came up to me and said how professional you were, 'the best man on the pitch'." That's nice, but I'm still not so sure. A November feeling hangs over me for the rest of the day — grey, unsettled, melancholy. It feels like the month of gloomy introspection, and strictly limited compassion.

Having someone from the family there while I'm refereeing, though, gives me a warm feeling of security. No matter how bad a game you have and how many strangers yell in your face, there's at least one person there on your side. When you're feeling the heat and the hate, you can steal a glance beyond the arena of conflict and fleetingly focus on something much more precious.

Final score: 2-3 (6 x yellow)

Hatred on the touchline

When a player swears at someone in the crowd, it's supposed to be an automatic sending-off. Just before half-time in yesterday's game, the away team's left-winger is standing in front of a bunch of kids, aged around 5-12 years old, telling them furiously to "piss off" just before he takes a throw-in. I show him the yellow card, but he barely seems to notice because he's so steamed. Coming off the field at the break, I ask him what the problem was.

"One kid was spouting off anti-Semitic insults," he says. "A 10-year-old kid!" That's problematic, as the home side is ethnically north African, while the visiting side is the city's only Jewish club. I rescind the yellow card. I also ask him to avoid slanging matches and come straight to me if there are any further incidents. Then, together with a reluctant steward, I oversee the expulsion of the kids from the ground.

The game itself is fine, for once — the few moments of tension quickly de-escalate either through my intervention or the conciliatory behaviour of the players. Are they perhaps overtly aware of the potential uproar should there be any nasty incidents between these two particular teams? I don't think it's just that — they all seem to be genuine sportsmen, on the whole. I have to almost apologetically send off a visiting defender for handballing a shot on the goal-line. The protests are courteous and quickly curtailed, perhaps helped by the fact the team being punished is already 6-1 up.

With just over 10 minutes left, though, the winger is about to take a corner when he gestures me over. One elderly spectator, he says, had started calling him a "dirty cunt" and a "son of a whore". I refuse to continue the game until the stewards eject the man, which happens under loud and angry protest from the offender. I make it clear to the home club that if there's another incident, I'll terminate the game.

The coach of the away team is sanguine after the match. "It happens all the time," he says. "Then when we complain, they always say it was just a spectator, and that he was nothing to do with the club. We try and train the players not to react and just get on with it." I tell him it's an absolute scandal, and I repeat that point in my detailed report to the local FA. Reports to the local FA, though, have a habit of being filed away and never heard of again.

I'd returned the day before from a conference hosted by the Football Collective at the University of Limerick — a stimulating two days of exchanging ideas and research, and discussing, among other themes, how football should strive to make the world a better, more tolerant place.

In the sheltered world of academia that's all very well, but the sporting players in this game gave the impression that such a goal is more than idealistic folly. The spectators, less so. For every vile and poisonous insult shouted out loud, there could be several more still lurking in the darker side of spectators' brains. That's why there must be no tolerance for those who articulate their hate.

Final score: 2-7 (2 x yellow, 1 x red)

Snowballs

Last spring at one of our regular referees' meetings aimed at our ongoing edification, I presented a critique of our online test on the Laws of the Game, where the object seems to be not to test you and make you a better referee, but to catch you out and go, "Ha!" As an example of the multiple stupid questions we are obliged to research and correctly answer once a month, I cited the following puzzler: "During a game on a snow-covered pitch with the ball in play, one of the players throws a snowball at the opposing team's coach. What is the referee's decision?"

Why is this such a stupid question? I asked rhetorically. First, there's a long winter break in this country, so you rarely if ever officiate matches in the snow. Second, due to global warming it hardly snows during the winter months any more at all, let alone outside of the winter break. Third, a game on the hypothetically snow-covered pitch would probably be called off anyway. And finally, in the very unlikely event that you ref a game on a snow-covered pitch, what are the odds of a player throwing a snowball at the opposing team's coach?

The answer to the question is clearly 'red card' for the offending player. But the monthly test wants to know more than that. What's the restart? Drop-ball, direct or indirect free-kick? Get that part wrong and you lose both points — you don't even get a single point for getting the 'red card' part right.

The problem with our online test, I argued to my doubtless captive audience of colleagues, is that I will never remember the correct answer to such an obscure question. And should it somehow ever happen, not a single other person present will have a fucking clue if I've re-started the game in the correct manner or not. Unless there's some anally retentive referee in the crowd who pipes up, "Actually, when a player throws a snowball at the opposing coach it should be a direct free-kick, not a drop-ball." At which point, I'd encourage all 21 remaining players to pelt him with as many snowballs as they could physically scoop up, and to keep going until he's been chased out of the ground (it's in the Fifa Laws, look it up — Law 18, Justified Punishment of Pedantic Twats).

I was thinking about all this on the way to today's game, because I was cycling head on into a snowstorm. I'd left the house as late as possible, because I was sure someone was going to call me and say the game was off. They didn't. So, after a three-mile ride across town, I arrived to find an inch and a half of snow on the artificial turf field, but with both teams dressed and happy to play on it.

The groundsman used a snow-blower to blast out some touchlines, which promptly became invisible again. I allowed the players to wear whatever they wanted to keep warm, mainly because I planned to do the same, and asked for the floodlights to be turned on. Once we'd found the centre spot, we kicked off.

It was probably not that clever to go ahead, but I was influenced by the fact that the two teams also occupy the top two places in their league's Fair Play table. I told them that if things started to look dangerous, or if they started playing like cocks, I reserved the right to abandon the game. "Also, you need to be honest with touchline decisions and help me out." They all nodded in agreement.

I'll confess there was another reason I let them play — I've never reffed a game in the snow before, and I was being a bit macho about it by this point, having cycled all that way and now being cold and wet anyway. "Hey lads, we're not going to let a spot of winter weather stop us doughty Sunday heroes playing our football, are we? Eh? EH?" I didn't shout that out loud while thumping my chest, but it's surely more or less what everyone was thinking.

The match was, at best, a bit of a farce, but occasionally the 22 amateur sportsmen managed to string together a few passes with the eye-catching lime-green ball. The players spent a lot of time sliding about on their arses, and a lot of time helping each other to their feet after ill-timed challenges. There were two obligatory square-ups after late tackles, but that's as good as nothing for this league. In general, it was quite a pleasure to ref — there were a few semi-comical moments to enhance the convivial festive feel on the first Sunday of Advent.

Much to my disappointment, though, not a single player took it upon himself to throw a snowball at the opposing team's coach. Then again, I would have had no clue what to do next, so we'd have had to abandon the game anyway. Drop-ball, direct or indirect free-kick? Two points and a pat on the head from the Examination Board for the correct answer.

Final score: 3-1 (no cards)

The odd bunch

The end of the winter break's approaching and the fixture list is gradually filling with friendlies. I return to the club where last time around I sent off the home coach and three players, one of whom threw his shirt in my face and then had to be restrained from attacking me. Has he been banned for life? No, he's in the starting line-up, and is standing at the halfway line with his team-mates having a light-hearted chat with me prior to kick-off about just how nut-shrinkingly cold it is.

"Last time I was here I showed four red cards," I remind them. They smile at this fond memory and tell me there'll be none of that kind of behaviour today. After all, it's just a friendly. The player who threw his shirt in my face and had to be restrained from attacking me looks me in the eye and says, "The guy you sent off that time won't be causing you any trouble. He's not playing today." Either he has two separate personalities, he's thinking of another game, or he's hoping that I don't remember his face (I do), or that I didn't check if his name was on the team-sheet before I left the house (I did).

They're an odd fucking bunch, right enough. They joke with me before the game, and afterwards too. In between, they are almost exclusively unpleasant. There are two borderline red card fouls that I let off lightly with yellow cards and dark-voiced warnings. My friend with the faulty memory gets a yellow for a rash challenge too ("Yeah, but what about that foul back there by the other team that you didn't card yadder yadder" — I get this after every yellow). A forward goes in the book for not once, but twice, deliberately trying to score with his hand — again, in a competitive game that would have been a yellow-red.

And then there's the super-friendly number 9, who's constantly telling his team-mates to calm down as they moan at each other, try to provoke the opposition (who remain unprovoked throughout), and whine at my decisions. He scores two goals right after the break to level the game, and we even enjoy a jocular exchange about what they put in his half-time cup of tea. Then a few minutes later I turn down a penalty appeal for a supposed foul against one of his team-mates, and the number 9 completely freaks out at me. I show him a yellow card. He continues to yell. I ask his captain to calm him down. A few minutes later they sub him out.

At the final whistle, the home team's captain runs over to me, shakes my hand and thanks me for doing a good job. When I look sceptical he adds, "Well, there weren't too many discussions." We both laugh. "There seems to be an attitude problem in this club," I point out. "I know," he concedes. "It's been that way for years."

I go to pick up the key to my changing room from the snack hut and ask for a cup of coffee to warm me up — it's been snowing on and off all afternoon. The player who last time threw his shirt in my face and had to be restrained from attacking me is also in the hut, angrily sounding off. "This team's terrible," he tells the bloke serving the coffee. "All they do is moan moan moan the whole game long."

The bloke serving the coffee agrees. And he should know — he's the coach I sent off last time around for screaming in my face, "You're a coward! You're a coward!" Maybe he's serving a self-imposed touchline ban. Perhaps the snack hut, well away from the field of play, is the only place where he can keep a lid on it.

"Thanks for the coffee," I say when I bring the key back a few minutes later. "It was much better than your sportsmanship." The coach laughs long and loud at this. I suppose it's good that they've acknowledged their lousy club culture, and can even be cheerful about it too. It's also nice to know that I'm not the problem. Rather than being filled with dread next time I'm assigned a game here, I'll be curious (if not hopeful) to see if this self-awareness has translated into better behaviour.

Final score: 4-6 (5 x yellow)

No cards on Valentine's Day

It's Valentine's Day and I have a date after dark, somewhere in the woods in the south of the city, with 22 younger women. Kick-off is 8pm. Mrs Ref is not happy, but it's nothing to do with the 22 younger women. I'm recovering from a heavy cold, and she thinks I'm an idiot for going out to run around in temperatures just below freezing.

She's probably right (she usually is), but I go anyway. It's not that I wouldn't rather stay at home in the warmth, eating the rest of last night's stew and watching Real v PSG. But once I've accepted a game, I dislike turning it back for any reason. The assignors dislike you doing that even more, and I completely understand their point of view. As a coach, I hate players crying off late with weak excuses, and they do it every weekend. If this was a book about coaching, I'd write a list here of all the best ones ("I have to babysit the dog"), while weeping and wondering why people ever bother volunteering for anything at all.

I like the home club — they're one of the few places to always give you a warm welcome and hand you a bottle of water without you having to ask. The long, metal key-grip to the referee's changing room looks like a murder weapon, but you never know when that might come in useful too. I sit down to get changed and am suddenly worried by a thought that hits me way too late. What if Mrs Ref had come home tonight and been hoping to find candles, chocolates, cards and a three-course meal on the dining-room table? The Full Valentine's Bollocks.

We did come to an agreement when we first met 23 years ago that neither of us were interested in all that crap. In fact on our very first Valentine's Day she more or less dumped me (the old-fashioned way — by phone) and I ended up burning a card and an emotional letter, and destroying a love-song compilation tape by jumping up and down on it, vowing that I would never again waste my time on romantic frippery. We've ignored the event ever since (though our daughters find the story of their mum dumping me highly entertaining). Nonetheless, some of us get sentimental as we get older. Perhaps, just this once, instead of watching me pack my whistle, she'd wanted to be wooed and wined.

Well, too late for that now. I head outside and start the game wearing hat, gloves and all the thermal undergarments I could find in my sports drawer. It's cold enough to dislodge the knackers from a rogue Black Angus. And it's quiet. Oh, so quiet. There's not a murmur of dissent at a single decision. The nearest I come to any bother is when I almost run into the home team's number 10 as she shapes up to challenge an opponent. She mutters, "Oh my God!" in much the same exasperated way my 19-year-old daughter does when I say something that clashes with her politically honed world view.

It's so many years since I experienced this that I'm not sure how to cope. Why's no one moaning? The away team's centre-back slices a clearance that goes just wide of her own goal, and the goalkeeper stands looking at her with a huge smile. "You knew where that was going, right?" she says. They both laugh.

The 90 minutes pass in no time, despite the cold (and my own cold). At half-time, someone brings me the most life-enhancing, soul-warming cup of hot chocolate ever. At full-time, the home team thanks me, pays me, and tells me to keep the change. It's not that hard to treat the ref like a fellow human. And although if it was like this every game I'd never have anything to write about, I really wish it was like this every game.

At breakfast the next morning, with some trepidation, I ask Mrs Ref, "Hey, you weren't expecting roses, Belgian chocolates, champagne and a candlelit meal last night, were you?" She looks at me as though the very thought would be enough to make vomit explode from her heart. "Okay, just checking," I say. "All good." No cards all round on Valentine's Day was the best outcome.

Final score: 2-0 (no cards)

Reason vs emotion

Let's say that in theory the referee represents Reason, and that the players represent Emotion. The (uncorrupted) referee has no interest in the outcome of any given game, as it's their job to rationally and neutrally implement the rules.

Meanwhile, the players have only two goals in mind — the success of themselves and their team. The desire to score and win is driven by feelings of loyalty and ambition. Anything that thwarts that ambition provokes frustration and even anger (I know this because I played for 40 years).

A referee must accept that, as the anchor of reason, they are going to come into conflict with the mental tipping point of performers who, in their dreams, imagine themselves as heroes, even if only for a few hours among a small group of people wearing the same coloured shirt. That's an integral part of the game. There are days, though, when the precarious balance between reason and emotion makes no sense at all. Days when I'm pushed to get emotional too.

On this Saturday night it's colder than it's been all winter — minus 7 degrees, with that same persistently penetrative wind that's been chilling our fibres since the middle of the previous week. And yet again I have the immense privilege of refereeing a one-sided U19 boys' friendly match for the vast reward of €14. I'm sure I'm not the only one who doesn't want to be here.

The second half runs to form. The away team falls four, five, six goals into arrears, and start fouling instead of trying to play. They pick up a few bookings and a time penalty. Two opponents square up after a foul and I bollock them, and when they won't shake hands they both get a yellow card. One of them is the home team's outside-right, number 22.

This player is fouled in the penalty area in the 89th minute, with his side leading 9-1. I would blow for a penalty, but before he's fouled he manages to play the ball to a team-mate right in front of goal, so I play advantage. His team-mate screws up the shot and play continues. The number 22 comes running over to me, absolutely outraged that I haven't given the penalty. "Well, as you saw," I explain, "I played advantage."

He's still outraged, and says so, but as there is only a minute left I don't see any point in sending him out for a five-minute time penalty. A few seconds later, his team scores again and I blow for full-time. Everyone hastens towards the warm changing rooms, and I hang back as usual to check there's no idiocy between players still nursing a grudge. Precisely one player thanks me, which seems to be about the norm for youth games.

I'm about to enter the clubhouse when the number 22 comes running up to me and starts to bleat anew about the penalty decision. "I'll explain it again, because it's quite simple," I say. "I played the advantage. What can you not understand about that sentence?" But on he gestures and blusters — penalty, foul, blah blah blah. Emotion now gets the better of me too, so I just stand there repeating very loudly, "I played the advantage. I played the advantage. I played the advantage." A few lingering spectators look at me, slightly alarmed. The cloth-brained number 22 finally turns around and fucks off, possibly worried that I'm losing it.

Which I am. Not just because this moron is still questioning a perfectly straightforward decision in an inconsequential match with the scoreline at 9-1. But also because I am so, so fucking cold, and I am feeling suddenly peeved at the utter absence of gratitude for me coming to ref their shitty match for peanuts on a night when even Amundsen would have hesitated to leave his tent for a piss in the snow.

The desire to win at sport makes no philosophical sense. It's not key to our survival. Winning doesn't much enhance our knowledge of the world or the human condition. Aside from the transitory feel-good sensation, the benefits of success are minimal. And in the case of our number 22, it can even lead to a reckless greed for seemingly limitless victory.

That might eventually lead to trophies, abstract honours and temporary smiles of triumph, but it won't make him a better human being. God forbid. Not many players seem to subscribe to the claim of philosopher and goalkeeper Albert Camus that everything he'd learnt about "morality and the obligations of men", he owed to sport. Reason and Emotion mostly fuse to make competitive sport work. But in cases of rank stupidity, not even yellow and red cards provide a cure.

Final score: 1-10 (4 x yellow, 1 x time penalty)

Teenage kickers

When I was a young father, people used to look at my daughters and ask me, "Don't you ever wish you'd had a boy?" I used to reply with a short and truthful "No," while resisting the urge to tell them to shut the fuck up insulting my children by implying that they're the wrong sex.

"Well, wait until they're teenagers," these fatbergs of wisdom would knowingly fart on. "Then you'll wish you'd had boys." It turned out they were wrong again. And having coached and refereed teenage players of both genders, and having once been a teenage boy myself, I can only feel grateful for having avoided living with these fluid-shipping, hormonal wrecking balls masquerading as the Lord of the Big Fucking Cock.

On Friday, I told three players on my U15 team they couldn't play at the weekend because they had missed both training sessions last week, and hadn't taken the trouble to let me know why. One immediately texted and said he was sorry, but he'd been injured. The second eventually called and sort of apologised. The third one wrote in the team's WhatsApp group that they would surely lose because now "shit players" were getting picked ahead of him, the standby Garrincha.

I deleted him from the group, suspended him for four weeks from the club, and told him that he could play again once he'd apologised in person to the entire team. He replied by asking when he could have his player pass back so that he could find a new club. Yeah, good luck with that. Coaches everywhere just love a 14-year-old who skips training and thinks it doesn't matter because he's better than everyone else anyway*.

By the time I come to referee an U17 game on Sunday, I've had my fill of teenage boys for about the next seven World Cup cycles. I'm ready to pounce. I don't even bother with a pre-game speech, I'm too busy looking like a 19th-century headmaster. It's how I feel too. I can sense the furrows on my face. I get like that sometimes when I ref — once when I was being evaluated in the US, the assessor told one of my linesmen at half-time, "Tell Ian to actually try and enjoy the game. He looks so serious."

Two players start making out with each other at a corner kick. Not actually making out, I'm just interpreting the homoerotic undertones of their mutual shoving and grunting. They've been getting at each other since half-time. I whistle to stop the corner kick being taken. "Is there a problem here?" How I love to darkly deliver that rhetorical query, meaning, "If there really is a fucking problem here, you ain't seen nothing yet." Yeah, you tell them, Mr. Big Bollocks with his little whistle.

It's effective enough. I'd already talked at half-time to the under-handed home team — 4-0 down — about not getting nasty in the second half. They'd taken two yellow cards just before the break, and I could see where things were heading. Whether my lecture makes any difference or not I've no idea, but in the second half they play fair. In fact it's their opponents who pick up two yellows, becoming frustrated that for a while they can't add to their tally, despite being superior in both size and talent.

Two things happen at the end. The home team, having lost 0-7, gather in a post-game huddle. A few seconds later, they break into laughter. And several members of the away team shake my hand and thank me as they leave the pitch (but not the bolshie one I'd booked). Because of course, on the whole, there's nothing wrong with teenage boys. Just my perception of them.

Though I still don't regret the fact that I never had to raise one.

Final score: 0-7 (4 x yellow)

* He apologised several weeks later to the entire team

Strike!

After more than a month off refereeing due to a combination of bad weather, illness and holidays, I was set to return to the field this weekend. Then my refereeing body called us out on strike (youth games only) to protest a violent attack last week on one of our referees during a boys' U17 game (he's bruised, but okay). Nonetheless, I was still in charge of four games this weekend, one way or another, and all of them reflected to varying degrees the still toxic football atmosphere in my city.

I supported the strike and the reasons for it, even though the action was not even discussed (let alone voted on) at our monthly referees' meeting last Tuesday. My view is that it should have been. Not all referees wanted to support the strike, but you had no choice — if you'd been assigned to a youth game, you were now automatically withdrawn.

On Friday evening, before the strike has started, I ref a boys' U17 game. The home coach introduces herself one minute before kick-off, just as she's bringing her team back in from warming up. "Kick-off is in one minute," I say, pointing out that the away team is already out and ready. She shrugs. I add that I have plans tonight, looking at my watch, but I might as well have been reading her the Confucian Classics in their original Chinese. We kick off eight minutes late.

At half-time, though, she's much keener to talk, appearing at my changing room door with her team 0-3 down. "You need to watch out for offside," she says, courtesy still far from her strongest point. Oh, really? Offside? What's that? I never bother with it, you know. Just let the players roam free, that's what I always say. "How about you teach your team how to defend?" I offer back, seeing as this is clearly an exchange of ideas. Then I close the changing room door, which is a shame because it's a beautiful evening.

On Saturday morning it's my U7 team's game — no ref, but as home coach I supervise. Our opponents have two coaches, and they spend the game wholly contravening the league's Fair Play guidelines, simultaneously bellowing at their wee lads, who are strong, tactically organised, technically superior, already know how to foul, and are loudly ordered how to play on a kick-by-kick basis. My lads heedlessly run around like a swarm of bees, as they're supposed to do at the age of 5 or 6, and we get hammered. At 8-1 down, I ask the opposition coaches to stop shouting at their kids every time they make a mistake and they finally quieten down a bit. Is it my business to intervene at all? Or should I have done it earlier? With arseholes like these, there's never an easy answer.

In the afternoon, there's my boys' U15 game to coach. Now, remember that we refs are on strike, but the games are still taking place. The referees have told the clubs that coaches and parental volunteers need to ref the games so that they can see what it's like to be out in the middle. My club asked me to step in and ref several games this weekend, but out of solidarity I turned them down. Still, as a coach, I offer to referee my own game, especially as I know my team has no problem with respecting refs. That's because I hammer it into their heads on a weekly basis. The opposition coach, whom I know, is fine with the idea. I leave all coaching duties to my co-trainer. What could possibly go wrong?

I don't know if it's the unseasonably scorching hot sun, but the opposition coach — who'd already made a snippish comment at half-time — suddenly freaks out after an hour. Now, I've been refereeing this game with particular care, cancelling out several of my own team's attacks with offside calls (even borderline calls), and booking one of my players for complaining about it. Because our opponents are physically inferior, I'm more than lenient in their favour when it comes to calling fouls, but there's nothing you can do about a gaping difference in quality. When we score our eleventh goal, the other team's coach shouts for offside, and when I ignore him he won't stop screaming at me. Eventually I go over to him and appeal for calm.

What can you do, though, when your appeal for calm meets a raging wall of sound and fury? He rants on and on about the 'offside' goal and an apparent penalty I denied his team for handball (I've no memory of this — of a handball, or of anyone even appealing for a handball). Eventually, I send him off. At full-time, he offers me his hand with a sarcastic, "Reeeeeeeally well reffed." I ignore him. Then he comes to my changing room, ostensibly to report an injured player, but when I let him in he's off again, "That offside goal, we should have had a penalty blah blah." I order him out and slam the door.

The fourth and final game of this wearisome weekend is on Sunday afternoon — I jump in at the last minute to referee a men's game (not affected by the strike). I joke with my refereeing boss that he'll have to call Mrs Ref and my mother-in-law to make my excuses for cancelling on them. Ha ha. After half an hour, the home team's number 5 yells at me for not giving a foul after he's been fairly dispossessed. The attack continues and he says, "If this goes in, there's going to be trouble." The chance is missed, and he says, "Lucky for you." Then he points at his eyes and wonders aloud whether or not mine are functional. "You lost the ball fair and square, now be quiet," I counter, waving a yellow.

And he does. So does everyone else for the rest of the game, which is a vast relief. But then I get home to find that the man I joked with earlier about my wife and mother-in-law has responded to my detailed disciplinary report about yesterday's angry coach by saying, "You should have been showing solidarity with us instead of refereeing the game, even as a coach." Yeah, idiot. It's my own fault. There has since been a lively exchange of emails between myself and the two heads of my refereeing body, in which we're all expressing our anger and disappointment.

Anger and disappointment. We're all at it now. All part of the game. Apparently, the lion's share of the game.

Friday: 0-5 (3 x yellow)

Saturday: 14-0 (2 x yellow, 1 x red)

Sunday: 1-7 (2 x yellow)

Come on you reds

It's quiet and sultry in the park, with distant storms in the air. Two teams of men lazily warm up for the 1pm kick-off. Four days earlier, just a few hundred yards from where we're about to play sport, a dog-walker found the brutally battered body of a 29-year-old woman. Life must go on, though — this end-of-season dead rubber at the middle to lower end of the city's bottom league abjures all musings on mortality. There's 13th place to defend.

It doesn't take long for the afternoon to plummet from meaningless kick-about to a prolonged and rabid expression of collective outrage. In the ninth minute, an away defender chooses to upend the home team's forward, who's through on goal in the penalty area and about to shoot. I didn't personally write the rules saying that the denial of a clear goal-scoring opportunity is a red card offence, but you wouldn't know that from the away team's collective reaction. And no, there was no attempt at all to play the ball, which was far beyond the lugging defender's reach. It was a cynical, calculated trip.

The red-carded player and his team-mates surround me, shouting and gesticulating. I've rarely been less moved by such a display of raw emotion. The home team converts the penalty and the away team spends the rest of the afternoon playing the victim, penalised by the mean referee who's spoilt the game. They foul, they moan, they shout all the way up until their third red card in the 85th minute, shown to their sneering, hostile number 6 whose presence on the field at this point is solely thanks to my lenience.

He's been booked already in the 17th minute for dissent, after which I follow him around the field exhorting, "No foul! No foul!" every time he's heading towards a challenge. Not my job, I know, but I also know that if the away team is reduced to nine men while we're still in the first half, the game's already toxic tenor will sink through the bottom of the rotten barrel and deep into the polluted mud below. Two borderline yellow-card fouls exact stern warnings from me, but he doesn't seem to give a fuck. Mercifully, he gets subbed out before half-time.

In the second half he's back, unreformed. He rips the shirt off an opponent at a corner kick, but they're standing on the edge of the area and I'm looking at the six-yard box, so I miss it. The opponent, laughing incredulously, has to change the shredded jersey. A few minutes later — just after his captain has been dismissed for sarcastically applauding and commenting upon the afternoon's second clear penalty — he clatters into the same opponent, then leans over the player, who's shouting out in pain, to let him know that he thinks he's faking it.

When I show him his second yellow card, then the red, he's so outraged that he walks up to me and pushes me in the chest. I take two steps backwards, arms raised. He turns to leave the field, then comes back for more, but is held back by his team-mates. As the downed player gets treatment, there's a noisy exchange of views all round. I blow the whistle, abandon the game, and walk off.

The away coach (a fellow referee) actually thanks me, shakes my hand, informs me that all my decisions were correct, and says that it's "always the same ones" who cause the trouble. Which makes me wonder why he keeps picking them every week, but as he's attempting to be conciliatory I don't say anything. In fact, I'm barely capable of speaking. It's been a rancid 85 minutes of non-stop harassment and I'm absolutely distraught — three red cards is the very least this team deserves.

In the changing room, I talk to the referee who's shaping up to officiate the same two teams' first XIs. "That's not a league, it's a punishment," he says. He's right, but I wonder what I'm being punished for, aside from ordering off a player according to the Laws of the Game. Was I a brutal central defender in a previous life?

On Saturday afternoon I'd reffed a boys' U15 game. Before, during and after the very heated match, two sets of fathers set a wonderful example to their sons by yelling at each other and gesticulating. Just another weekend in amateur football's dark and rancid basement.

Saturday: 2-1 (6 x yellow, 1 x time penalty, 1 x red)

Sunday: 5-0 (5 x yellow, 2 x yellow-red, 1 x red)

Model behaviour

The first half of this boys' U15 game is one of the most peaceful I've refereed all season. There are only two fouls, and a mild query from the away team about a possible offside on the home team's first goal. As is often the case, the defenders have turned around to see that a player with the ball has outsmarted them. I tell them that he wasn't offside when the ball was played, and we get ready for the restart without any further discussion.

Their coach is much more vociferous. I ignore him.

At half-time, with his team 3-0 down, he walks over to me and starts complaining about the offside decision, and not in a civilised way. "It's because I'm a shit ref," I reply mildly. He hesitates for a second, then starts to moan about something else, but I interrupt him and say, "I told you already. It's because I'm just a shit ref. What can you do about it?" Then I walk away to my changing room (broken into during the first half, but nothing taken because I hide my phone well and never take my wallet with me when I ref).

In the second half, the angry coach's previously polite and well-behaved team decides to follow the adult's example and, the more goals they concede, the more disrespectful and insolent they become, especially the captain. He goes in the book, and later — after a clear and deliberate handball from a team-mate — gets a five-minute time penalty for sarcastic applause, an offence I'm always particularly happy to punish. There's also a yellow for another team-mate, for angrily belting the ball away after he's called up for a foul.

Meanwhile, the coach starts up again. After coming on to treat a player for an injury — during which he chunters on at me about something or other — the gentleman remains on the same side of the field as the two home coaches, and they get into a verbal fight before squaring up to each other. I go over, separate them, warn them officially for irresponsible behaviour, and order the away coach back to his side of the field. He keeps on at me about a phantom yellow card I should have given to the home team at some already-forgotten point in time. I give him a second and final warning, to which he responds, "I could already tell before the game what kind of a referee you were." For his extra-sensory mental powers, he's dismissed for good.

All this in a one-sided game without a single controversial decision. At the end of the game (8-0), the away team's goalkeeper comes running up to me, incensed, and squeaks that he's going to report me to the state FA. I'm tempted to tell him that his time would be better spent watching a video called 'The Absolute Basics of Goalkeeping'. Instead I revert to one of my old favourites. "Are you a referee?" I ask him. He looks confused. "No. Why?" he responds. "Because we always need top experts like yourself to become match officials. You should join our next training course." Although I'm also looking forward to his doubtless enlightening dossier to the state FA on my shameful performance.

In the disciplinary report I write: "This was a classic example of a coach serving as a poor role model by having a pernicious effect on the young men he should be influencing in a positive manner. He disgraced himself and his club either because he was unable or unwilling to accept the heavy defeat, or because he is incapable of supervising, in a responsible and sporting manner, a group of adolescent boys." And next season he'll be back there standing on the touchline, waving his arms around and shooting his ignorant gob off.

Sunday's match went well. A closely fought U17 cracker with sportsmanlike coaches and two teams who mainly focused on what was necessary — the game, not the referee.

Saturday: 8-0 (2 x yellow, 1 x time penalty, 1 x red)

Sunday: 5-4 (4 x yellow, 1 x time penalty)

SEASON 2018-19

ANGER, ARSEHOLES, BRAWLING PARENTS AND A LONG AFTERNOON IN HELL

Let the old shit begin

All through Friday night's game I had 'Someone Out There' by Rae Morris going through my head, but it should really have been a much uglier song, by Eels. So instead of hearing a recurrent, "Someone out there loves yoooooo" over 90 minutes, I'd have been mentally singing to myself, "I'm tired of the old shit/Let the new shit begin."

It's a 'friendly' game between a Level 8 men's team and the U19 squad of the city's third-largest club. The lads are a step quicker and smarter than the men, and so the latter — who are knackered after 30 minutes — resort to fouling, and then moaning about the consequent whistle. The game becomes fractious and there are three yellow cards before half-time — one for dissent, and two for players squaring up to each other and rejecting my suggestion to kiss and make up. So far, so predictable.

There are two further archetypal incidents for football at this level. First, the U19 team score their second goal just before half-time from a through pass. The men's team shout as one for offside, except for their number 99, who has been too slow to move up, possibly weighed down by the number on his shirt. I shout "Play on!" and point at the number 99. When the goal has been scored, the men's team moans anyway. They didn't see or didn't want to see where their number 99 had been standing.

Then in the second half, the captain of the men's team trips an opponent right on the line of the penalty area. No one disputes the foul, but they dispute that it's a penalty kick. I tell them this is a law that's not open to interpretation — a foul on the line is inside the box. Several players loudly insist the foul was outside the box. I don't change my mind.

A friend of mine, Joe, had come to watch the second half because we're heading straight off after the game to try and catch the lunar eclipse.

He was standing almost as close to the incident as I was. "It was on the line," he confirms afterwards. He's never seen me referee before. "I have to say," he adds, "I didn't envy you out there."

Indeed, watching the lunar eclipse turns out to be much the better part of the evening. By that time, my right knee is starting to stiffen — the arthritis I started to suffer from a year ago has not benefited from a summer of rest and physiotherapy. After a night of excruciating pain, I call off the rest of my weekend games at 6am on Saturday morning. Then on Monday morning my doctor writes me a note exempting me from sporting activity for three months.

I thought that this would be a mental blow, although all summer long I haven't really been looking forward to the new season. All my first assignments were in the same Level 10 leagues of perpetual crime and punishment. Things were going to be no different this campaign, as the opening game proved. Let the new shit begin.

Final score: 1-5 (5 x yellow, 1 x yellow-red)

Quiet comeback

On Saturday, I think that I've fallen asleep and transcended into a Referees' Paradise. I officiate a game where no one complains. Neither the players, the coaches, nor the spectators. Not even a whisper of dissent aside from a transient gesture of frustration at a called foul. And then, after the game, everyone thanks me for turning out. Because this is U10 boys' football.

I'm officially injured for another two weeks, but I've been earmarked to coach a young referee who, as young referees will, drops out late on the evening before the game. So I step in, happy that I can take such a stress-free game to get back into the swing of whistling. (How that phrase makes refereeing sound like a carefree, happy-go-lucky activity — like chopping fire-wood or going for a country walk on a mild afternoon.)

Before kick-off, I stand waiting with the away team for the home side to come out of the changing room. "Are you lads going to win today?" I ask. "Yeeeeeees!" they all chorus in reply. Then one adds, "Hopefully." Maybe he's had a look at the league table and it's instilled a touch of realism — they're second bottom with just three points, while the home team is safely mid-table with nine.

Once the home team's assembled, I tell both sides that it's a beautiful morning for football, that I expect a friendly, sporting game, and that in any case we should all be in a good mood because the night before our city's main team, Eintracht Frankfurt, had beaten Fortuna Düsseldorf 7-1. Early in the second half at a corner kick, a home player taps me on the arm and wants to know, "Were you for Eintracht or Fortuna?" *For Eintracht,* I tell him. "Me too!" he exclaims, and runs off looking very pleased.

After the match there's a pretzel and a Coke. The whole morning puts me in a damned good mood for the rest of the day. Yet I'd probably be lying if I said, "If only football could be played like this everywhere, every weekend, at all age levels."

Why? Three months off has prompted many people to ask me if I'm missing it. There are two ways to answer that question. The first is to say, 'No, not at all.' I've really enjoyed the free weekend afternoons after coaching in the morning. I haven't been down or stressed out or wiped out in the evenings because I was threatened or screamed at or told to fuck off.

The other answer is, 'Yes, I've missed it.' Not the actual refereeing, as such. But I've missed the social contact, the sporting participation, and I've missed the theatre. Every game tells a story. I'm feeling the absence of those stories.

In two weeks from now, with my knees feeling much improved, I'm scheduled to referee a boys' U14 game. It's probably a bad idea — in the same way that I retired from playing about a dozen times before I could no longer ignore the message my body was sending me. "I don't want to hear any complaints," Mrs Ref has announced. Which means that I'll have to write them all down instead.

Final score: 6-0 (no cards)

I'm not Dr. Felix Brych

After a long period out injured, you lose grip of your confidence. Have I forgotten how to ref? It's not that you can no longer remember the Laws of the Game, but you worry about having lost the feel for officiating. And when players pick up on a referee with no confidence, they will not hesitate to exploit that mental frailty.

So I precede Sunday's game in the Crime & Punishment League with a new, truncated version of my pre-match speech, delivered in a 'we're all in this shit league together' tone: "Lads, my name is not Dr. Felix Brych. I'm not here today to be yelled and moaned at. I don't have linesmen, and I don't have a video ref. So, save your breath, especially on close offside decisions. I want you to enjoy the game, but I want to enjoy it too. Best of luck."

There's always a share of players smiling when I try this 'referees are human too' approach. They seem to take it on board, and there's a short round of applause for my effort. But there's no way of telling whether or not it worked. If the game's quiet, it might just be that these two teams are well behaved. The Fair Play table, however, tells a different story, so as usual I'm prepared for the worst.

It's an intense enough game with a lot of fouls from the home side, who are bottom of the table, but there's not too much moaning. After an early goal for the away team, there are chances at both ends. The away goalkeeper then palms a speculative long shot on to the crossbar, it bounces back out to the home team's number 11, and he heads it back against the underside of the bar. It bounces down again, on or behind the goal-line, and back out into play.

Goal? I don't think so, but really I have no clue — I'm 30 yards in front of the frame. Everyone plays on, so I do too. The home fans applaud the effort, but there are no howls at an apparent injustice. Only the number 11 is trying to convince me that he's scored, and I ignore him by pretending to focus on play.

There's a certain type of experienced goalkeeper in these leagues who can act as your unofficial assistant. They tend to be greying, level-headed blokes in their 40s who try to spread calm from the back, and who will tell the moaners to shut up and play (articulating exactly what I'm thinking). Being the last line of resistance behind decades of ropey defenders has rendered them philosophical. The away team's keeper is just this type, so I walk next to him at half-time (0-2) on our way back to the dressing room and say, "I feel that I can rely on your sportsmanship — that header definitely wasn't over the line, right?"

Of course, this question could go horribly wrong. "Ha ha, you wang-eyed moron," he might respond. "It was in by a good yard. Nay, a country mile! Remember Lampard for England v Germany at the 2010 World Cup? Well, think another arm's length and you're just about there. Hey, need any help finding the clubhouse? Let me take your arm and I'll guide you up the steps, old boy. Don't worry, we'll get my gran to do the second half, she's over there in the wheelchair."

Or they can respond as you probably expect them to. "No question, absolutely not a goal." Which, in this case, I'm fairly sure is the truth. Then again, what goalkeeper is ever going to voluntarily admit letting in a goal you were too blind to see with your naked eye?

The day before, I take a boys' U14 game that actually sees one more yellow card than the men's game, though it is extremely quiet bar the one retaliatory shove ("I should be showing you red," I lie in an educative fashion, "but I'll let you off with a yellow"). At the end, a group of fathers wants a word with me as I walk to the touchline to pick up my jacket. That's rarely a good thing, but I lend them my attention because there's no escape.

"We just wanted to say, your football boots look excellent!" Not me, just my boots. Still, they're right — yellow and black Puma Kings I love so much that I've had one of them repaired at the cobbler's for the price of a match fee. "They're a bit knackered, like their owner," I say, "but we're just about holding it together." As with my ailing knees, I can't seem to find replacements online.

Saturday: 0-6 (3 x yellow)

Sunday: 3-5 (2 x yellow)

My least favourite things

What are the 10 things I least want to see or hear when I'm refereeing a game of football?

1. The shout for *"Offside!"* almost every single time a forward is through alone on goal. It comes from the defenders, it comes from the coaches, it comes from the spectators — a one-word verbal plague of ignorance upon the amateur game. During Saturday's game, a goalkeeper saved a free-kick and then complained that the player who followed it up to score was offside. How did he see that when he was saving the kick? He went on about it so much (and I tried to ignore him, but he ran after me almost all the way to the halfway line screaming, "Offside! Offside!") that he ended up with a yellow card.

2. *"You have to call fouls against both teams!"* Usually from a losing coach or one of his players. Oh, really? I thought I was just supposed to call fouls against your team as a heaven-ordained test of your patience. And because I have a real and vested interest in who wins this U15 boys' district league game. Sunday's choleric coach, with his team several goals behind, bellowed this one at me. The obvious answer — I'm calling fouls against your team because it's mostly your team that's fouling. Perhaps because that's the way you coached them.

3. *"Ref, how much longer?"* No matter how many times you call the answer out loud, there will be at least three players who didn't hear it for every one that did. If you want to know how much longer, ask your coach. I'm watching the game, not my bloody watch. And what will you do with this knowledge anyway? Suddenly start giving 100% for the last 10 minutes after winging it for the first 80?

144

4. *"Ref, their number 10 just called me a pig-shagger."* Or something. What the ref doesn't see or hear, he can't punish. And we're not going to get involved in a conversation that starts with: "Did you just call FC Farmhands' number 7 a pig-shagger?"

5. The half-time walk to the changing room when you see *one of the coaches walking towards you.* It's usually not to see if you want a piping cup of hot chocolate (although — very occasionally — it is). Be prepared to account for a perceived foul you can't even remember. Register the coach's disgust and disbelief when you tell him your mind's blank. Shame on me — another shocking injustice already lost to time and the dark, moist mud of the municipal field.

6. *A straight red-card offence.* You might think it's an existential peak for any referee — the privilege of pompously holding up the plastic signifier for a big dismissal. But it's the moment I hate most, because already I'm thinking, "That's at least one hour of my Saturday/Sunday night gone writing up the disciplinary report for this dickhead."

7. *The off-the-ball shoving match.* This one's a particular specialty of teenage boys, usually when a bulky defender ushers the ball out of play while his skinnier opponent tries to flail and dance his way around him. Then they square up, push each other in the chest, pout at each other, and hope that I get there to intervene before — for the sake of pride — someone feels obliged to raise a fist. Then I give a lecture like a weary old teacher who's seen it in the corridor a thousand times before.

8. *The Parent With An Opinion.*

9. *Serious faces.* I mean it. During the obligatory pre-match handshakes, I've taken to advising players that they are, in fact, allowed to smile. Go on, try it. Enjoy the sport. It's the weekend in a free and democratic country and you're playing football.

10. *The absence of gratitude.* I read an interview recently with an air hostess who said, "All we ask is for passengers to smile and say thank you. It's not much, but it really means a lot to us." Ninety per cent of players and coaches don't bother. But they should. It's not much, but it really means a lot to us. Thank you.

Saturday: 2-2 (6 x yellow)

Sunday: 11-2 (1 x yellow, 1 x time penalty)

Model parents in mass brawl

I'm back at the club whose name translates as 'Friends of Sport', but where I've rarely had a sporting or a friendly experience. Today it's a boys' U17 game, with around 30-40 spectators. Here's a truncated version of my disciplinary report:

"The first half was played in a fair and peaceful atmosphere, but all this changed in the last 20 minutes of the game when both sides — with the score at 2-2 — sensed that they had a good chance to win. In this hectic and niggly phase of the game there were six yellow cards and a time penalty due to reckless fouls, unsportsmanlike conduct and dissent.

"The coaches remained quiet almost until the final whistle. Then, in the 79th minute [of an 80-minute game], there was a reckless foul by the away team's number 23 against the home team's number 7 right in front of the away bench. The number 23 received a yellow card for the foul.

"The away team's coach walked on to the pitch close to where I was supervising the free-kick and started screaming at me. I couldn't exactly work out why he was so aggravated, but I think he was complaining that I had shown a home team player the yellow card twice, without imposing the time penalty (he was wrong — I hadn't). I gave him a double warning — once for entering the field of play without permission, the second for irresponsible conduct. Although his assistant tried to calm him down, he kept on screaming at me, so I ordered him off.

"He took two steps backwards from the field and screamed at me a third time. I ordered him to leave the ground completely, otherwise I'd abandon the game. He complied and the game continued with the direct free-kick.

"After the final whistle a couple of minutes later, the still-exorcised away team's coach approached me on the field and wanted to continue discussing the apparent mistake with the yellow cards. I declined any further discussion because for me he was banned from the ground and was therefore, effectively, not present [one for the existentialists on the Disciplinary Committee to debate there]. Just as I was busy ignoring him, a mass brawl broke out between the parents and the players of both teams off the field, but immediately spilled onto the field of play.

"There was a whole load of shouting and pushing, and from where I had been standing it was impossible to determine who'd incited the whole sorry spectacle. With the help of the coaches, I separated the warring factions and sent the two sets of players to their respective changing rooms. Meanwhile, the parents and coaches continued to propel loud and mutual recriminations through the previously peaceful afternoon air.

"Once things had calmed down a bit, I tried to determine from the away team's assistant trainer what had happened, as she seemed to be one of the few sensible grown-ups present. A peaceful conversation proved impossible, unfortunately, as the home team's trainer intervened obstreperously, along with numerous other parties unknown, and off we went again with the loud, excitable recriminations — this or that person said or did this, that or the other. Like in kindergarten, except louder, longer, nastier and much, much more pathetic. So I went to my changing room, got dressed, then cycled home.

"A shame, because for 70 minutes it was a decent and exciting game. Some players from the away team later apologised to me for their conduct. But from the multiple adults who conducted themselves in a rowdy and irresponsible fashion there came not a single word of regret or apology."

Final score: 2-2 (6 x yellow, 1 x time penalty, 1 x red)

Just a skirmish

A freezing night, a cinder pitch and a relegation battle in the city's A League between two men's teams who are not only low in the standings, but last and fourth-last in the disciplinary table. Between them, they've managed 16 red cards this season (eight apiece), with the home side racking up six straight reds and an almost impressive 57 yellows in just 19 games.

I ride to the ground pondering the best way to broach this in my pre-match speech. Sometimes I think about saying nothing at all, and that instead I should try and come across as silent, stern and unapproachable. I used to know a ref in the US who'd come to games glowering like a righteous preacher at a swingers' club, wearing a hoodie and dark glasses and looking like he was about to discharge a Uzi on both teams. He was told either to quit or drop the attitude — he was scaring the kids, and the parents too.

I'm not much good at looking like the hard man, though. My first instinct when I meet the coaches is always to smile and introduce myself. No one likes an asshole, and why get things off on the wrong footing? So as we line up to take the field I give them my usual speech about my invisible linesmen and add, "By the way, I've seen the Fair Play table and it's an ugly sight. So, for God's sake, try and play football and enjoy the game." Cue shit-eating grins from both teams.

There's one major flare-up in the first half when the home team's number nine, fouled from behind, goes ape-shit at his tormentor. An away player intervenes and shoves him in the chest and there's a wee brawl. I break it up and show them both yellow. The home team's captain later goes in the book for persistent fouling, but otherwise the only incidents are an own goal and a goalkeeping fuck-up to give the visitors a 2-0 half-time lead.

In the second half, it's a case of keeping a lid on frustrations as both teams commit foul after foul. I adopt the approach of the 'calm but firm schoolteacher' ref rather than the bellowing authoritarian, helped by the home coach who — doubtless under pressure from the club accountant to do something about all the fines his team's been incurring — exhorts his players to keep quiet when they're about to moan that I've blown the whistle for them innocently upending an opponent. There are just two more yellows, one each for foul play and unsportsmanlike conduct.

I do get one call wrong — a throw-in close to the away bench. The coach is closer than I am, and throws up his arms in frustration when I give it to the home side. I realise that it was probably a deflection in his favour, but it's hardly worth reversing the decision. One of the away fans takes the trouble to scream out, "You're a shit referee!" At the final whistle, though, neither team seems unhappy, which is about as much as you can ask for.

In fact, despite its disciplinary record, the home team is an impeccable host. When you arrive at a club you instantly pick up on how it's run. Do they offer me water, and do they have the player passes ready? Do they co-operate when you ask them to appoint two stewards in yellow vests? Do they thank me and offer me a beer after the game? All those boxes are ticked.

In short, I really enjoyed this match. At the same time, I was relieved when it was over.

Final score: 1-3 (5 x yellow)

KÖRPER!

It's snowed all morning, and I hold off leaving the house in case there's a late call to postpone the match, a lunch-time kick-off in the League of Crime & Punishment. I don't necessarily want the game to be called off, but the prospect of several hours of unexpected free time on a Sunday afternoon has its attractions.

I leave the house later than usual, and then cycle to the wrong ground, so I end up arriving cold and wet with just half an hour until kick-off. There's an inch of snow on the grass pitch, but both teams are eager to play. "Have you got an orange ball?" I ask after looking at the surface, which is moist underneath. They do. Will they promise to play sensibly? Oh, of course.

Things start gently enough as the players adjust to the conditions. There are numerous short passes that get stuck in the snow, and several players from both sides flail for balance and slide around on their arses. I wonder whether or not it was wise to let them loose. The home team goes 1-0 up after 15 minutes with a penalty for a full-on foul by the away team's captain. He's the only one who bothers to complain, citing the word *Körper!* (body), which you hear a lot. It translates as, "Football is a physical sport, so what's wrong with me recklessly charging into a player and flattening him?"

Then there's another Level 10 staple — the collective roar of outrage at an offside decision. The away team's number 5 screams at me by way of re-interpreting this law in his favour. "Shut your mouths and play football!" I offer as advice, while showing him the yellow card. "He's right," says one of his team-mates, kindly. The number 5 keeps on, though, so I ask his captain to have a word — one more squeak and he's off. He shuts up for the rest of the afternoon.

It's anchored in the Level 10 constitution that things will hot up in the second half, and as the away team serially implodes in front of goal in their almost comical search for an equaliser, we hit peak levels of fouling and moaning. Whenever their number 10 commits one of his niggly fouls or throws himself on the ground for no reason, he whines, "You've got it in for me!" Which makes me want to show him a red card so that I can say for the first time on a football field, "Just because you're paranoid doesn't mean we're not out to get you."

He gets away with a yellow for dissent, while the home team's captain takes an instant yellow-red for a filthy foul and then kicking the ball away to waste time. He goes without complaint, which almost makes me feel bad about sending him off with just three minutes to go. But in the last minute one of his team-mates scores an unlikely free-kick in a rare moment of skill and they win 2-0.

There's a squaring-up of testosterone-driven idiots in the 92nd minute (the number 5 again), so I blow the full-time whistle and everyone eventually calms down after some fascinating exchanges on the socio-economically crucial themes of 'who pushed who' and 'who said what'. I leave the field with frozen feet that don't warm up until I'm back home an hour later in a hot bath. It's time for the winter break, and that makes sense.

Final score: 2-0 (6 x yellow, 1 x yellow-red)

The pensioner's monologue of thwarted justice

There were some regular features in last night's game that anyone who plays or refs in local leagues will instantly recognise. Let's take it from the top:

* Pre-match — the coach who hasn't got his player passes ready. It's like listening to a scruffy schoolboy explain why he hasn't done his homework. "They're in my car," he says. Well, could he go and fetch them, please? "I'm parked way over on the other side of the ground! There are only 10 minutes to kick-off — can't I give them to you at half-time?" No, I want them now, otherwise we don't start the game. "But I'm an old man!" Then send a young substitute with your car keys and I'm sure we'll have them in no time. Eventually I get them, and they've not even been chewed by the dog.

* 'Your mother' insults. It's been a while since I've had one of these staples of the amateur game. The away team's number 8 is chasing down the home team's right-back, who successfully shepherds the ball out of play for a goal-kick. Out of nowhere, the number 8 aggressively squares up to him and I go over to separate the two. "He insulted my mother!" whines the number 8. Yeah, well, I didn't hear it, so tough. And what is it with the enduring macho bollocks about your mum being insulted? Does the number 8 really think the home team's number 2 personally knows his mum? That the number 2 really, really thinks the away team's number 8's mum is a woman of ill-repute who sells her body cheaply to sleazy punters? Or could he just be trying to wind you up so that you slap him and get a red card? We are, after all, in the middle of a football match, not at the 'Who's Got The Most Virtuous Mum?' world championships.

* The tricky number 9 who turns like a barge in a slurry pit. That'll be the lad leading the home team's forward line. He's spent the winter break getting consciously out of shape, and after every passage of play where he's involved I almost call for an oxygen tent. And yet, he's got something. He plays one pass that reminds me of Paul Pogba's lob to Marcus Rashford for Manchester United against Leicester recently. Another time, a defender's grappling him as he receives the ball, he shakes him off and dribbles past him, but then the defender gets the better of him after all, so the number 9 shoves him to the floor. Needless to say, he's outraged by my whistle. I laugh his protest off, in that dismissive and probably quite annoying manner that we refs have. At the end of the night we wish each other well.

* The opinionated pensioner. I love these old cunts. They wait until you're within hearing distance and then they let loose. There's been a recurrent battle between the away team's rugged left-back and a fast young winger the home team brought on at half-time. The winger ends up getting booked after a verbal warning for squaring up to the full-back, followed by a nasty foul a few minutes later. When I fail to book the left-back for an innocuous trip right in front of the pensioner, he lets it all out in a Monologue of Thwarted Justice. What kind of a referee am I that books the young, nifty home winger, but lets the ox-like away defender off the hook? He's still bumping his jaw as play moves on. One of the great things about the opinionated pensioner is the joy you derive from completely ignoring him.

* 'It's still 0-0!' I only heard this inspirational call once last night, but it's a regular in one-sided games from the coaches and captains of the team that's winning, but who don't want to see any complacency creeping in. So, some sleek top-of-the leaguers will be trotting back to the halfway line after stretching their lead to 10-0, calmly congratulating each other, and the captain — always red-faced, with a beard — will scream, "Come on, lads, back to your positions! Let's go again! IT'S STILL 0-0!" God forbid we give the hopeless hackers a second to breathe, even though they can barely walk, and all look like they just want to cry into their post-match beers. There's no Mercy Rule here, it's not the bloody Catholic Youth League.*

All in all, a pretty quiet and very enjoyable game.

Final score: 0-5 (1 x yellow)

* The Catholic Youth League in Maryland, USA, is the only league I've ever reffed in where they had a Mercy Rule, God bless them. Any team that went seven goals up on an opponent had to play a man down. 'Your mother' insults, virgin or otherwise, were rare to unknown in this competition.

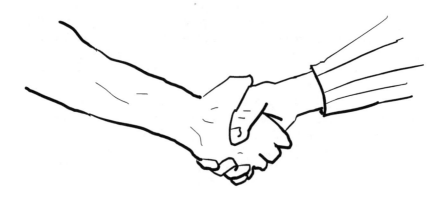

Flood of youthful contrition

It's rarely a good thing when a player you sent off the field three minutes before the end of the match walks towards you at the final whistle. In this case, the number 8 of the home team. It's a U19 game, so it was a time penalty that had followed an earlier yellow card.

What had happened? In the 83rd minute of a most unfriendly and foul-ridden 'friendly' game, he had gone in late on an opponent and left him on the floor, with no apology. He moaned about the yellow card for the foul, and I asked him kindly to keep it shut. Four minutes later he shoved over a different opponent, and complained again when I blew the whistle. This time I invited him to take a break on the touchline. He walked off without further protest.

So what does he want with me at the final whistle? "I just wanted to apologise for my behaviour at the end of the game there," he says. And then he shakes my hand. Fucking hell.

I've barely recovered my balance and my sense of speech when another player approaches me, this one the away team's number 12. In the first half, I'd shown him a yellow for laughing in a loud and sarcastic fashion after I'd called his team-mate offside. There wasn't a single defender anywhere near his team-mate or the goal when he received the ball and scored, so it was hardly a marginal decision.

He also shakes my hand and says, "I just wanted to apologise for my unsporting conduct in the first half." Well, young man, that's absolutely fine.

In an ideal world, I wouldn't have had to caution either player. Still, it's quite something to have not one, but two players say they're sorry. Whether they were prompted by their coaches is neither here nor there. The fact is, they did it and both of them sounded genuinely contrite.

This time last year I was refereeing in temperatures below freezing, with a heavy cold I couldn't shake off, and chronic knee problems. This afternoon it's 14 degrees, the sun is out, I'm in my short sleeves for the first time since last summer, and I'm completely fit and free of pain.

Ambrose Bierce gives the definition of 'apologise' in *The Devil's Dictionary* as "to lay the foundation for a future offence". That could be true, but at least it won't be during my game. Cynicism aside, two young players have said they were sorry for their lack of respect. That makes it a half-decent Saturday.

Final score: 3-4 (5 x yellow, 1 x time penalty)

Oh, beautiful!

Sometimes you know it's going to be a quiet day simply from the coaches' pre-game attitudes. For this boys' U17 match-up, both teams are coached by personable young men who respond with a smile and conversation when I walk up and introduce myself. Much better than the greying, gruff old-timer who won't look you in the eye, and who honestly looks as though he'd rather not be there. These are two strong amateur clubs giving off an air of professionalism.

Since the winter break, the control of player passes in youth games has been reintroduced. It was abolished about two years ago, and was obviously open to abuse. It probably still is in the men's leagues. I confronted one team at half-time after becoming suspicious that a player being passed off as 24 looked to be almost twice that age. "Give us five minutes," they said through a crack in the door of the changing room. When I knocked again they told me he'd had to leave to pick up a relative from the airport — via the back entrance.

Today, I offer both coaches a time and place of their choice so that the pass control doesn't interfere with either their warm-ups or their pre-match team talks. It may not always work, but if you show you're a flexible ref before the game even starts, you might grant yourself a little leeway. I don't hear a word from any of the three coaches throughout the game.

It's a quiet first half, with no goals and no cards. The only incident comes when number 20 on the away team twice pulls a player's shirt in a midfield tussle, holding him back, but I allow play to continue as the home player still has the ball. The away team's 20 then makes a clean tackle, and is incredulous when I blow for a foul. At half-time he wants to know more, so I tell him. "You wouldn't have been able to make that clean tackle if you hadn't held him back to start with — I was playing advantage, but the advantage didn't materialise."

Second half: the home team's captain and central midfielder has been very strong all game. Right after half-time he's fouled once, and then a minute later he's tripped by the visitors' number 20. I guess the players are acting under instruction to neutralise and/or intimidate him, so I show a yellow to 20 on the second foul. There's a short protest at getting a card for a relatively mild infringement, but the card works — the away team stop targeting the home captain. There are two more cautions, both for straight-leg, foot-first challenges.

In the end, the visitors come back from 1-0 down to win 2-1. I'm standing right next to — who else? — number 20 as he shoots from 25 yards out to equalise. "Oh, beautiful!" I can't help but commentate as the ball sails into the top corner, and he drops a smile. I love it when the players and the coaches make it a good game to ref.

Final score: 1-2 (3 x yellow)

Danny (Part 4)

It's been a year or so since I last encountered Danny, the city's moaniest youth coach. He has now coached a team in his model image. Right from the start they foul their opponents, and then complain loudly when I whistle. They are backed up by Danny on the touchline, who screams, "Referee!" every single time. It's an obvious ploy to intimidate both their opponents and the ref. By half-time they have three yellow cards — one for foul play and two for dissent. I've spoken to Danny twice and given him his first two warnings of the afternoon. Does he shut up? Does he fuck.

Half-time: 1-0 to the home team on a straightforward penalty for a trip in the box. Hotly disputed by Danny, as sure as a kettle will boil when you flick the switch.

On the way to the clubhouse at half-time, I take his assistant to one side. I know him, he's a fellow ref. I tell him to please tell his players to stop fouling and complaining. Like Danny, he tries to argue the toss, but I cut him off. Then, joy of joys, Danny knocks on my changing room door for a quiet and reasonable chat. I say not a word as he lists his grievances, and when he comes to the penalty ("It wasn't a foul, and you know it."), I hold up my hand as a signal that he should stop, and try to close the door. He puts his foot in the door and becomes loud, accusing me of a lack of respect and always being biased against him. Luckily there's an inner door, so I turn around and go back through and slam it shut.

I sit on my bench and close my eyes and resolve to try and remain completely calm throughout the second half, come what may.

For the first 15 minutes of the second half there is no sign of Danny. If it's anything like the first time I sent him off, he's off making serial phone calls to my refereeing bosses to tell them what a disgrace I am. I don't care, it's almost idyllic without him. His team stops fouling and complaining and starts playing good football — in this period, they score three goals. True, their celebrations are way over the top, but at least they're smiling.

Danny mooches back into position, but keeps his gob shut until a mass fight breaks out on the pitch — the result of a midfield clash that turns into a wrestling match, concluded when a home player throws his opponent to the ground. Danny and his assistant sprint onto the pitch and right into the middle of the melee. I order them back off the field, and he counters, "I'm trying to calm things down, because you're not capable of it." He's always the man with a pleasant retort. Eventually, things sort themselves out. In the meantime, the two home coaches have arrived on the scene as well. In theory I could send all four coaches off for entering the field of play without permission, but as I've just red-carded a player and cautioned another, I appeal to everyone to play out the final 15 minutes without any further drama. They actually manage to do this.

In the end, Danny's too happy that his team's winning to cause any more bother. I should have sent him off, but I couldn't face the theatrics. "This coach has a knack for drama and making everything about himself, and I wanted to avoid that," I write in the long disciplinary report. "Refereeing his games is like watching a bad comedy where the same terrible jokes are repeated time after time."

Or, as I said to him at half-time before closing the door on him: "It's been three years since the disciplinary panel, and you've learnt absolutely nothing."

Final score: 2-4 (4 x yellow, 1 x time penalty, 1 x red)

The Jules Rimet trophy

Good news for pedlars of anger — supplies are still running high. There is absolutely no shortage. As I wrote in my game report, "For the away team, I recommend an immediate and urgent course of fury control therapy." I'm absolutely sure they will take my advice.

A relegation battle in the League of ragged Reserves, football's abandoned grave-pit where you will find only the cluttered, dehydrated bones of the game's sporting values. Too old? Play in the Reserves. No discipline? We'll drop you down to the stiffs. No fucking use at all? We'll call you when we're short, on a Thursday night at the arse-end of another failed season.

A windless and perfect spring evening under a pale yellow moon, but don't worry — there will soon be some amateur footballers along to rock that temperate idyll. Although, for the first hour there's no problem. The score is 1-1, the game is balanced, the foul count about average, the cards have stayed in my pocket. Then the away team's number 5 fouls the home team's number 7. Number 7 stands up and goes for 5, and 5 goes back at 7, then everyone else piles in. A rank and raucous flange of shrill and indignant knaves.

I've seen this now so often that I can barely get excited enough to run in there, whistle on the blast. Once the collective outrage has begun to subside, I take number 5 and 7 to one side, deliver them a weary lecture, and show each a yellow card. When play restarts, the away team's number 10 then immediately takes out number 7 again, and when I show him a yellow he whines, "But that was my first foul!" Ever since, I've been arguing with myself — should it have been a straight red? Would it have put a stop to the idiocy, or merely inflamed it? Number 7 limps off, and number 10 is wisely subbed out by the away team.

But now the tone's been set for the rest of this ragged, irascible game. Everyone hates each other, there are fouls all over the cinder pitch, the moaning turns shrieky, and I start dishing out yellows for dissent. And then I give a penalty to the home team four minutes from time.

I'm five yards from the play as the home number 10 dribbles through a crowd of three defenders into the penalty area, before he's tripped. The away team disrespectfully does not agree with the call, claiming that the forward had fouled a defender on his way through the melee. I hand out another yellow to the tosser screaming in my face and order a clearance of the penalty area. The spot kick's converted — 2-1.

There are five minutes of injury time because of all the hysterics, during which the away team equalise. They celebrate like someone had brought along the original Jules Rimet Trophy and said, "Tonight, lads, the last team to score gets this." There's still time for them to pick up another yellow for hotly contesting an offside call.

The away team ends up with six of the seven yellows, three for dissent. As they manage a point, they ignore me at the final whistle rather than cursing me anew, although three of their players do shake my hand and say, "Thanks." It's always the quiet ones you don't notice during the game that display a scantling of decency. If only they'd tell their team-mates to stop acting like twats.

Although this wouldn't all be so bad if one or two players, or one of their two coaches, would come up to you afterwards and say, "Sorry, that got a bit out of hand." That rarely happens, though. All I get is the home coach saying, "If you'd shown a yellow card earlier when.... [he cites an incident which already I can't recall], then none of that would have happened."

In other words — all that anger, it was all the fucking referee's fault. I humbly apologise and beg for the forgiveness of all players involved.

Final score: 2-2 (7 x yellow)

Fun and games with Archie of the Arseholes

Another Sunday afternoon in the reserve leagues, choking on dregs from the bottom of the sporting barrel. I look at the 'Fair Play' table. Of the 15 teams in the division, these two are 13th and 14th, with 15 red cards between them. When my phone goes two hours before kick-off, I'm hoping it's to tell me that the game's called off. Instead, it's my niece asking me if we want to hang out and play board games. Sounds like fun. Sorry, I can't make it.

I know the captain of the away team. He's a fellow ref and we get on, so I appeal to him to ask his team to keep it sane. I make the same appeal to both teams as we line up to enter the field. The same old speech about me only having two eyes and no assistants. About not screaming at me every time I whistle for offside. About how we should play in a fair and sporting fashion and actually try to enjoy the game. They all applaud. Sounds like fun. So happy I could make it.

My speech is quickly forgotten by the home team. It's the offside calls that get them going. Their two ageing forwards are caught out again and again, and they're not happy about it. They've been standing in the same offside positions since 1993, but just haven't noticed. The game itself — on a hard and bouncy cinder pitch — has all the finesse of gin-drinking buffalos performing 'Swan Lake' on an ice floe. I've seen more ball control in a teenage country boy making his first call in the back rooms of the *Moulin Rouge*.

The home team's number 19 receives the ball from a forward pass right in front of goal, a good 10 yards beyond the last defender. I whistle before the ball has hit the back of the net and he's incensed. It's so ludicrous to protest this decision that I just laugh and say, "That's the clearest offside decision I've made in a decade of refereeing." He continues to chunter in disagreement.

A few minutes later his midfield colleague, a niggly little number 10 I begin to think of in my head as Archie Arsehole ('Archie of the Arseholes' — a new comic strip about a football team in Germany's worst league?), appeals for a corner when the ball has gone out at least a yard wide of the goalkeeper's outstretched hand. "Why did you even shout for that?" I ask him. He ignores me. Archie *Arschloch* (it has a slightly more alliterative twang in German) appeals for everything in much the same way a dog can not resist licking its own anus after taking a shit.

We get to half-time with the home side 2-0 up, and no cards, but I can feel them in the air. The second half is, as always, worse as tempers shorten and legs capitulate to physical reality. At half-time, I make a bet with myself — I reckon on at least five yellows before full-time. In the second minute after the restart, the home team's number 7 turns a corner directly into his own goal. 2-1. The home team is again outraged because they think he was fouled as he steered the ball home (he wasn't, he was merely under mild pressure from an opponent standing behind him). Archie Arsehole goes in the book for an extended bout of sarcasm. Then I get the satisfaction of denying him a penalty as he throws himself to the ground with a dramatic lunge and a pathetic cry from deep within his tiny, flawed soul.

From this non-foul, Archie fakes an injury to waste time, and when I ask him if he needs treatment, he demands to know why I'm not asking him if he's okay. What I tell him: my only question in this situation is whether or not you require treatment. What I'm thinking: there are around 7 billion people in the world whose health is more important to me right now than yours, ya wee cunt. A frightened-looking youth without any medical equipment comes on to the field to 'treat' Archie. Archie now stands up, miraculously cured, and says he doesn't need any treatment. I tell him he has to leave the field anyway now that someone has come on, and then ignore him for a full minute as he screams from the touchline that he's ready to bring his talents back to the game. I wonder what would come first — self-combustion, or entering the field without my permission and getting a second yellow.

Archie then misses a chance from two yards out. Just thought I'd mention that. I didn't say anything at the time, but now that I think about it: Ha ha ha ha! Archie Arsehole's rubbish! Okay, that's what I was thinking when he missed it too.

The away team ramp up the pressure. In the 87th minute, I book the home team's number 4 for screaming in my face about an apparent offside that

I've seen from an alternative perspective. In the 89th, it's the home team's number 8 who screams in my face about another decision, though I can't even remember what it was. This time, instead of showing him the yellow card, I suddenly lose it. Completely and utterly. I scream back at him:

"WHAT THE HELL IS THE MATTER WITH YOU? WHY ARE YOU SCREAMING AT ME? DO YOU THINK I'M NOT HUMAN? HAVE YOU ALL GOT NAILS IN YOUR HEADS? DID I NOT EXPRESSLY SAY BEFORE THE MATCH THAT I DIDN'T WANT YOU SCREAMING IN MY FACE? AND WHAT DO YOU DO? YOU'RE ALL BEHAVING LIKE ARSEHOLES! WELL, LET ME BE AN ARSEHOLE TOO! IF THAT'S WHAT YOU WANT, LET'S NOT BOTHER WITH FOOTBALL, LET'S JUST ALL BE ARSEHOLES INSTEAD!"

The player I'm screaming at looks genuinely worried. I half expect him to say, "You OK, hun?" He does in fact say, "Okay, okay, calm down. I'm sorry." Everyone else looks half-astonished, half-bemused. I calm down. There's one more yellow card for time-wasting, and four minutes of added time for the same reason. The Arseholes hang on to win 2-1. Several of them come up to me and embrace me and laugh (though not Archie). I start to laugh too. It's like I'm one of them now. Welcome to the Arseholes!

They even give me a €2 tip on top of my match fee. I cycle away feeling light in the head after this cathartic release of pressure. It's not the first time that I've yelled out in anger against poor behaviour, but it's the first time where I felt out of control, that I might have gladly rammed my whistle down someone's throat, walked off and told them to ref their own shitty fucking game.

Back at home, the extended family's sitting around the table playing board games. I submit the match report, half-tempted to write everything you've just read, but I'm too knackered. Cards, substitutions and goal-scorers — then I hit the button. I take a shower, watch Scotland struggling to beat San Marino. I sit down at the table to eat. Finally, my sister-in-law asks, "How was your game?" I start to laugh. I tell the story. My daughter laughs too, while Mrs Ref says, "I don't think it's bad you yelled at them. Maybe they'll start to realise how their crappy behaviour affects other people."

I doubt it. It will go down as, "Hey, remember that day we had that ref who completely lost the fucking plot?" Ah dammit, someone will respond. I wasn't there that day. Sounds like fun.

Final score: 2-1 (4 x yellow)

Take me to Nagoya

A couple of years back I refereed two games in one weekend involving ethnically-based teams from the following four countries: Greece, Morocco, Bosnia-Herzegovina and Korea. Ever since, I've enjoyed asking family and friends, "Which team do you think gave me the most hassle?" And every single person gives the Korean team as their final answer, having exhausted any combination of the first three. All wrong. It was the Koreans who picked up more cautions than the other three teams combined. Our pre-conceptions take another kick in the nuts.

On Friday night, I referee a friendly game between one of the city's top U19 clubs and a touring team from Nagoya High School in Japan. I'm intrigued to see how the teams shape up not just in football terms, but in how they respond to my calls. Another test of the cultural archetype.

The Japanese team come bearing gifts. Not just for the home players, but also for the referee. I've never received anything other than a post-match Wurst and a €2 tip when no one's got any change, so in comparison this feels like the big time. Like when teams used to exchange pennants, medallions and memorabilia and all that '70s stuff. So I now own a pin badge marking 130 years since Nagoya was declared a city (I think).

The small but thoughtful gift has no influence in making me think that the Nagoya team is impeccable in every way. They play fast, attacking football while being physically very competitive, and in the first half completely outplay their German counterparts. Better still, they do not utter a single word or noise, or make a single gesture in response to any of my decisions over 90 minutes. Not even a dismissive wave of the hand. Get this — they focus completely on playing football, and their two coaches focus completely on coaching their team. Nor do they moan at each other for making mistakes — there is one whisper of a gesture from the striker when his winger takes a shot instead of crossing to him, but he's soon over it.

The home team, meanwhile, pick up three yellow cards, all for serious fouls when they've been out-dribbled by the tricky visitors. Some moaning creeps in during the second half too, when they come back into it thanks to the Nagoya team having subbed out almost their entire starting XI at the break. Overall, though, it's a pleasant evening of good sportsmanship.

On Saturday, it's back to the coal-face — two U19 teams in league play. The home team dominates and is six up at half-time. At the start of the second half, the visitors only have nine players on the pitch — one's injured, another has had to leave. Strangely, they start to play much better and score in the first minute of the second half. Now that they're putting in much more effort they also suffer more injuries, and it's clear some of their players have started the game not fully fit. With 15 minutes to go, they're down to six men and so I abandon the game.

It's been pretty peaceful up until this point, aside from the home coach screaming on the touchline. I'd heard him yell about a couple of decisions, but just ignored him. When I end the game early, though, he goes nuts all over again, accusing the away team of faking injuries. The (calm) away coach tells me the home coach has called him "a cunt" several times over. The home coach then instigates arguments with several away players, none of whom are interested in sinking to his level, located somewhere between his two arse-cheeks.

Eventually I ask him, "What the hell is your problem?" Which seems to be becoming my stock question these days — I'd asked it of the German players after their third yellow card against Nagoya the night before ("This is a friendly and these are your guests!"). I point out that it's a beautiful day, and that his team will almost certainly be awarded the 6-1 victory. He shuts up then, but I take the trouble to write up a disciplinary report to perhaps save someone else having to do it in the future.

On Sunday, I arrive at my club to coach my U16s to find that the ref hasn't shown up for the preceding U13 game. I stand in, and all's fine and peaceful. I think. The away coach, who had been happy enough to have someone there to start the game, seems less than pleased afterwards. His lads have lost 7-1. Perhaps he thinks I'd been biased in favour of my own club. I go up and shake his hand and ask him if everything's okay, "Well..." he begins, and then I say, "Oh, sorry, got to run, I've got a game to coach myself in five minutes."

I should have said, "Got to run, I'm moving to Nagoya. To Ref In Peace."

Friday: 4-7 (3 x yellow)

Saturday: 6-1 (no cards)

Sunday: 7-1 (no cards)

Glorious rain

A girls' U15 Regional Cup semi-final, played by floodlight beneath an unrelenting rain. A 0-0 draw that goes to extra time and penalties. A crowd of around 80 look on, hunched under glistering brollies as the clouds unleash their loads without mercy for those of us on the ground wearing shorts and nothing to protect our heads.

Both the players and the coaches allow me to focus fully on what's important — the run of play. Almost every foul is followed by a handshake and a hand to help an opponent stand back up. The only slight whine all evening is on a decision I definitely get wrong — two opposing players go in simultaneously studs up for the ball near the halfway line and connect. I instinctively whistle, then hesitate before pointing my arm randomly in one direction, when I should have given a drop ball (or just let play continue — there's no injury). I'm relieved when nothing comes of the free kick.

There's also one major roar of disapproval from half the crowd. Two minutes before the end of extra time, the home captain goes down with a cry just inside the away team's penalty area, her back to goal as three players challenge for the ball. I'm five yards away from it and judge it as a collision, not a foul. The protesting spectators are between 30 and 60 yards away, watching through the rain and not without a certain bias.

After the penalty kicks, the winning team of course celebrates like crazy, while the away team almost immediately forms a line to shake their hands. Then they both re-group for songs and a morale-boosting team-talk respectively, long since oblivious to the rain that's still billowing down. I leave the field as refs should leave — unnoticed, though there are a few thank yous from the spectators, presumably grateful that someone with a whistle was prepared to come out in this weather.

I may be soaked through, but I'm far from sorry to have been here. It's an even, fairly contested match where I've been able to concentrate on the game without a single distraction. I love every last second, and am genuinely sorry we can't just keep playing all night, or at least until someone scores. This, for once, is what I signed up for.

Final score: 0-0, 3-1 on penalty kicks (no cards)

The goalkeeper's tears, and a penalty

"Thrice he assay'd, and thrice, in spite of scorn,
Tears, such as angels weep, burst forth."
(John Milton, *Paradise Lost*)

Just over 20 minutes gone in a boys' U15 game, regional league. The dominant home team leads 2-0. From a direct free-kick just outside the penalty area, the diminutive but agile away goalkeeper makes a fantastic, flying one-handed save up in the top left-hand corner of his goal. Corner kick, and applause.

I stand on the end-line closest to the taker, as I always do for corners. This one swerves in on goal and the keeper, unchallenged, can only punch it into his own net. 3-0. He's angry with himself now — the great one-handed save has been annulled, at least in his eyes. Then two minutes later he makes another save, attempting to turn a shot over the bar. Only, he doesn't get enough of a hand on it and the ball loops behind him into the net. He scrambles back to try and rescue the situation, but he ends up in a heap in the back of the goal. 4-0, and the game's effectively lost with just 26 minutes played.

I run back towards the halfway line, but when I turn around for the restart I notice that the goalkeeper's still lying on the floor, curled up in a ball in the back of the net. I run back to check if he's injured, just as a team-mate is trying to help him to his feet, but he doesn't want any help. He is crying, and crying hard. He hadn't wanted anyone to see, but now that he's getting to his feet there's no mistaking his emotion. He screams in frustration, grabs at the net, and kicks the goalpost. Added to his two mistakes is now the supposed shame of being the boy whose upset turned to tears.

I know how he feels, and I know that there is nothing I can do or say to comfort him. In my book *The Quiet Fan*, I describe how prone I was to crying during my teenage years, and how I sometimes thought that "I should have been born a girl. They got to cry all the time and no one seemed to bother. On the contrary, girls were expected to cry. It's what they did. Shakespeare's embittered King Lear called tears 'women's weapons'. For boys, they were more like inviting, open wounds."

The goalkeeper is 14 years old, and I want to lay an arm around his shoulder and tell him that everything's going to be alright. There are several reasons why I don't, inappropriate conduct being the principal one, but almost as important is the knowledge that the last thing the goalkeeper wants or needs right now is empathy from the referee. Might as well just send his mum onto the pitch with his blanky and a cuddly toy.

Notably absent, though, is the player's coach. There's not even a call from the touchline to ask him if he's alright to continue, let alone a request to enter the field of play and check on his welfare. I ask him if he's okay to play on, and he nods furiously, wiping away the moisture. In his red eyes and raging cheeks I see everything that I dislike about competitive sport — the pressure, the disappointment, the grief and the anger. All for a game which, beyond the artificial context of this 70-minute face-off, has no real consequence.

The game turns dirty and a little bit nasty in the second half. There's a double time penalty when two opponents square up after a straight-legged foul. Moaning is kept to a minimum thanks to an early yellow at the first complaint. After the final whistle, one of the home coaches walks over to thank me, but with the usual proviso — he wants to complain about a penalty, a call that should "never" have been given (his team were 6-2 up at the time). I tell him that his player clearly and deliberately shoved his opponent over in the box, and the coach shakes his head, like I'm making that part up.

On the changing room door is a sticker that says, "Danke, Schiri" ("Thanks, Ref."). It's a nice touch, but all I can think of in response is, "Oh, just fuck off."

Final score: 6-3 (5 x yellow, 3 x time penalty)

How I knocked Ajax out the Champions League

It's half-time and the home team in this boys U19 game is 3-0 down. My changing room's across the corridor from theirs, but I can hear the coach through two brick walls. He's demanding to know what the fuck they are playing at, because it's certainly not football. He wants some extra effort, he wants them to show that they really want to be out there, otherwise what's the point of being here at all. COME ON!

You could call this place the archetypal city club. I've been here plenty of times before, and to plenty of clubs just like it. It's tucked into the allotments, a stone's throw from the Autobahn. You can see the towers and lights of the city centre to the east, and on a clear day you can see the hills of the wealthy satellite towns to the north. Both feel beyond reach of a club which, unless you were looking for it, you'd never know was here.

There are certain other staples. In the clubhouse there's an elderly woman in charge of everything. She's civil but she's not over-friendly — after all, how many referees pass through here every week? She's the one who gives you the key to your changing room and a bottle of water. She tells you that if you need anything else, just ask. What else would I need, apart from protection if things go bad? After the game she pays you and wishes you a nice night. If you linger and look thirsty enough, she'll offer you a beer and a snack, but it's not something you should take for granted.

Also at the bar is The Bloke Who Stares. I swear he's part of a firm of brothers that occupies every one of the city's 70-odd football clubs. I don't know if he stares at everyone, or just referees, but it's definitely possible he's there especially to stare at match officials, and no one else.

While you can chat and joke away with anyone else in the clubhouse — about the weather, about the game they're watching on TV, about the fact you'd rather be sitting where they are with a beer than going out now to ref for 90 minutes in the rain — The Bloke Who Stares will be silently psyching you out. You don't belong here, he wants you to know. Don't even fucking think about sitting down for a Pilsener. All referees are wrong-eyed, officious, game-spoiling scum who deserve a severe kicking, he wants you to know. If only he were 40 years younger he'd do it himself.

Beyond the main pitch on a weekday night you'll always find the old men's team at 'training', which consists of nothing but the most laborious six-a-side game it's possible to execute without standing still. This is the only point in any player's career where football is actually fun. There's much laughter, because no one harbours the energy any more to get mad — wisdom has caught up with them at last. When the rain starts to lash down upon their grey heads, they move as one towards the bar, bald spots glinting beneath the floodlights. They'll buy a pint for The Bloke Who Stares while pulling his leg and ignoring his manic eyes.

The coach's half-time pep talk works for about 15 minutes as the home team pulls a goal back. "Come on, we've got them now!" roars the number 10 who scores it. The away team then net three times in five minutes and the contest is over. There's a food and drink break at sunset for Ramadan — not that you can see the sun, it's been raining all day. It's the first time I've ever eaten dates in the middle of a game. Neither the players nor the two coaches complain about a single decision all night long, and there's just one yellow card for a midfield clattering, which the player accepts with a raised hand of acknowledgment.

The away team is bottom of the Fair Play table, so the coach looks genuinely surprised when I hand him back the player passes and say, "Please thank your team for their sporting behaviour tonight." He thanks me in return for the praise. It was a good, hard game with fewer fouls than usual, and barely a hint of aggro. True, it was an end-of-season encounter between two teams in mid-table, but that's no guarantee of sanity.

I'm home in time for the last half hour of Ajax v Tottenham. Just as I walk in, Tottenham score their first goal. "It was all going so well until you arrived," says Mrs Ref, who wants Ajax to win because she thinks two English teams in the final would be "boring" (how right she turned out to be). She and my daughter blame me for Ajax going out. Bloody ref, turning up and spoiling the game again.

Final score: 3-7 (1 x yellow)

Hidden key

There's a momentary tentacle of hot lightning followed a few seconds later by a sonorous groan of thunder. It's as though the very heavens are exhorting me to call an end to this shockingly poor boys' U17 game. We're only 22 minutes in and I've already shown three yellow cards, all for nasty fouls. I blow my whistle to interrupt play, secretly hoping that the skies will roar, burst and electrify, and then we can all go home.

"It's not even raining," moan some of the players. I tell them that if a fork of lightning hits the field, they'll know about it. Neither they nor their coaches care, and they all stay out on the pitch while I retreat to my dressing room. After a few minutes I check the radar on my cell phone, and as the storm appears to be moving slowly off to the west, I risk resuming play. It hovers close by, rumbling and threatening like the home team's coach, who's already been warned for encroaching onto the field of play to confront an opposing player about a challenge.

At half-time, the teams stay out on the field. I seriously consider walking back to the dressing room, getting changed and cycling away from it all. Right into the storm, if necessary. I've lost all desire to whistle another dirty challenge. Barely any of these players seem willing or capable of playing football. Why am I even here on a Sunday evening when I could be reading Hálldor Laxness, listening to Epic 45, drinking dark beers, or just staring out the window at the storm clouds?

There's a foul within about three seconds of the restart. "For God's sake, stop fouling and try to play football!" I yell. It doesn't work. There are further yellows and time-penalties for unsporting conduct, petulance, moaning, and so on and on. The home team loses 1-0 and seems to think that I'm responsible for their chronic inability to create even half a chance.

They take the key to my changing room (which I'd left on the home bench) and hide it for 15 minutes, claiming they haven't seen it. Sneaky little bastards. As if I'll have forgotten that next time we meet.

The club secretary happens to be there, a decent lad I've met several times before. "That was a horror game, from both teams," I tell him once I've finally got changed. "One of those matches where you spend the whole 80 minutes wondering what the fuck you're doing wasting your Sundays refereeing. The home coaches were no better than the players." He apologises. It's the same with teenage teams all over the city, he says. "Better that they're playing football here than hanging around where they shouldn't be."

I suppose so. The home team in the U15 game the day before back up his theory. There's always a bloke at this club there who shouts "REFEREE!" all afternoon, no matter which age group is playing. They might as well install an Automated Arsehole whose screams are triggered every time it hears a whistle. The home captain is a sour-faced brat who spends most of the game fouling and trying to intimidate opponents. Isn't the captain meant to be the sporting example to the rest of the team? Well, given the culture at this particular club, that probably makes sense.

There are three penalties, the first one after just 30 seconds for the home team. I'm glad I'm in the right position to see it, and that I don't hesitate to whistle, because the other two later spot-kicks are for the away team. One comes from a corner kick when the home goalkeeper, standing two yards in front of me, shoves an opponent in the back and to the floor as the ball's floating over them. Then he moans like hell that I've given it. It's like dealing with a kid caught with a fistful of sugar-cubes in the larder. The kid stands there and denies that he is stealing them, or that he even has a fistful of sugar-cubes. Because bare-faced denial of the blatant truth is still all the rage.

So, to the stats. Number of players and coaches combined who shook my hand and thanked me over the weekend: 3. Total earnings: €26.

Saturday: 1-3 (5 x yellow, 1 x time-penalty)

Sunday: 0-1 (6 x yellow, 2 x time-penalty)

The game from Hell
(Danny, Part 5)

Danny's the home team coach. I resolve to remain absolutely calm, no matter how much shit this U19 match-up propels in my direction. By the end of the afternoon, I am indeed in faecal heaven.

The away coach tells me that when the two teams met earlier this season, Danny hounded and intimidated the young referee throughout the game. It's the same story I've heard now from three other coaches in this league. Just to recap, it's been more than three years since Danny and I sat in front of a disciplinary panel, where he was fined €150 and told they didn't want to see his face there again. Yet to no one's surprise he's not changed his behaviour in the slightest, a malignant cancerous growth on the city's already diseased amateur football scene.

I gather all four coaches in the centre circle to remind them of the punishment process for irresponsible behaviour. First warning, then the second and final warning, followed by dismissal. They all nod, except for Danny. "Did you get that, Danny?" He gives a token gesture of the head, but I can't read his expression — he's wearing reflective sun-glasses to go with his hipster beard, giving off the usual air of 'I don't give a fuck'.

Neither do the teams, who go at each other right from the off. There are obviously numerous scores waiting to be settled from the first game. Although, compared with what's to come in the second half, the first 45 minutes are an absolute chill zone. There are two yellow cards for each team, all for foul play. Danny shows up way outside of his technical zone, moaning and gesticulating about an offside decision. First warning. He should have received a second warning a few minutes later for screaming at the opposition's number 10, who'd just committed a foul that I'd immediately called. The home team takes a quick free-kick, though, and I leave it.

I can only guess what the two teams talk about at half-time. "We're not kicking and fouling enough. I told you to play ugly, and right now it's just vaguely unattractive. Come on, what's wrong with you, get out there and show me what a nasty bunch of fucking pricks you really are!" If that's the speech, then it works. In the first 15 minutes of the second half there are five yellow cards and two time-penalties. Meanwhile, a crowd has gathered, as it always does at this ground, consisting mainly of teenage boys who are either looking to watch a fight or, failing that, to start one.

In the 63rd minute, with the score at 3-3, Danny makes his stand, enraged about a challenge against one of his players that I've already called. A challenge no more or less iniquitous than any other on this sticky, tense afternoon. I indicate his second and final warning. This causes him to yell at me some more, so I order him off.

Danny then does what he did the first time I sent him off in early 2016. He goes and stands behind the barrier, one yard back from where he's been all game, insisting that this is his right, and that he's now "a spectator". And just like last time, I tell him to leave the ground or I will suspend the game. This time, however, there's no club official to escort him away (that team threw him out years ago). He refuses to move, so I blow the whistle and start to walk towards the changing room. I'm immediately surrounded by very emotional home players, and then all kinds of spectators who have an opinion as well. For 25 minutes I stick to my stance — when Danny leaves the ground, the game will resume.

As well as being head coach, Danny is listed on the team sheet as being 'responsible for order' on the day, and that means there is not (and there never was) anyone present who's actually in charge. I stand there like a cop, and play judge, jury and executioner too. Can't he stand 20 yards back from the field? No. What if someone stands next to him and keeps an eye on him? No. But in the Bundesliga the coach gets sent to the stand and watches the game from there! This is not the Bundesliga and there is no stand. Besides, I know him. He won't stay where he's told.

Danny finally leaves, though not before telling me what a shit ref I am. I gather the players and tell them all that the game's a disgrace and has nothing to do with football. Perhaps they could play the last 27 minutes without seriously hurting someone. After the restart it's quieter, but still plagued by fouls. In the last minute, a home player headbutts an opponent in the stomach as they're both getting up off the ground following what feels like the one thousandth foul of the day. He goes without complaint after seeing the red card. At the final whistle (it ends 4-5, but that seems almost irrelevant) there's the obligatory mass brawl involving both teams, lots of screaming and shoving, and several of the aforementioned young fans. I stand and observe it until some adults from the away team intervene and everyone finally clears the field, two and a half hours after kick-off.

Danny's back from exile. Oh joy! "Every time you ref us it's the same shit," he says. I ignore him. In fact, by accident, he's spoken the truth. Even though I know that's not how he means it.

The home team's assistant coach refuses to pay me, "because you sent our trainer off". He's a fellow referee. I say nothing in response. Then one of his players knocks on my changing room door and asks me if it's true I haven't been paid. I confirm that's the case. He lays a two cent coin down on the table then leaves. I get changed, go home and — for once after such a game — manage not to sink into an immediate state of melancholy. I don't feel at all unhappy with the way I ran the game, given the circumstances. Mrs Ref asks me if I'm okay. I tell her that I feel fine. "Then why are you shaking?" Probably because I need a beer.

On Sunday morning, I wake up early and spend three hours writing up the disciplinary report. I round it off by wondering why I spend so much time composing these meticulous reports, yet trainers like Danny continue to stride the touchlines, and the standard of sportsmanship out on the field continues to stink like a sewage pipe blocked with the rotting corpses of a dozen syphilitic skunks (though I don't use that exact phrase).

Later that day, I ref a men's game. It's the final match of the season and they're in a good mood. The smell of barbequed meat drifts across the field from the clubhouse. Behind one goal a very small but rowdy group of away fans is drinking heavily and protesting my calls. In the second half, the unmistakable smell of weed comes from the same group, but the goalkeeper says it's not a problem. The next time I look, they're all flat on their backs, fast asleep.

In the final minute, I stand right in front of them at a corner kick just as they're waking up and getting to their feet, all red eyes and lamb's legs. "You lads have a good nap?" I ask them. They laugh, and one says, "You know what it's like — last game of the season." Thirty seconds later that game's over, and the season too. Handshakes all round. I get a beer and a sausage, and I get paid as well. Next Saturday I'll re-certify for another year. Why the fuck would I do that? Because an afternoon like this is just enough to help me keep the faith.

Saturday: 4-5 (12 x yellow, 2 x time-penalty, 2 x red)

Sunday: 5-1 (no cards)

SEASON 2019–20

PUDDLES, BAGPIPES, MOTHERS AND MITHERING

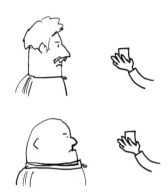

Cards for coaches

My first game of the new season coincides with my 54th birthday, accentuating the sense of another cycle that may turn out to be the same as the last one, and the one before that. But wait, I hear you say. That can't be true. Fifa has introduced several new Laws! Ah, so the game of football matures a little every year. Fat chance of that happening with me, as Mrs Ref might observe.

One particular change should make a difference to referees at the dog-scrap amateur level. Now we can show yellow and red cards to team officials, and no longer have to follow the laborious process of a verbal warning, followed by a second and final verbal warning, concluded with a straight-arm dismissal and a further verbal justification. This not only required a lot of effort to explain three times to coaches that they are "behaving in an irresponsible fashion", but also allowed them room to disclaim and involve the referee in an always-unhelpful discussion. Plus, in amateur football, showing a red card is much more effective and straightforward than pointing to a non-existent stand.

The head coach is now also responsible for the behaviour of everyone on the bench. If you can't identify which one of half a dozen substitutes or team officials screamed at you, you just caution the coach, who carries the can of conduct for those in their charge. That's a significant and beneficial change to those of us alone on a field with 22 young male players and a dozen more potentially temperamental time-bombs planted along the touchline.

It's only fair to warn them of the new laws, though. Today I make the mistake of not bothering. It's a relaxed friendly between two women's teams, and the coaches are very friendly prior to kick-off. Nothing at all controversial happens during play, until close to the end, when I'm unsighted for what was probably a handball by an away player with her back to me. The home coach screams for it, then at me. A few minutes later he does the same, just before the final whistle, when he thinks one of his players has been fouled, when in fact she's just knackered (like everyone else). This would have been the perfect time for an experimental yellow, but I let it go and ignore him. A small birthday gift in recognition of the fact it's a meaningless game at 36 degrees centigrade, and thus hard for everyone to stay cool (though I still think, "Shut up, you arsehole").

My second game is another friendly, but between two teams who — by a delightful coincidence — last season each accumulated 88 yellow cards in league play (plus nine and three red cards, respectively). I gather both coaches and deliver a spanking new lecture about what will happen if anyone on either bench yells at me — there will be cards, but no warnings and discussions. They both say that they have read the new rules, and have briefed everyone concerned. There's not a coo of dissent from the benches all afternoon.

On the field, though, there are nine yellow cards, a statistic that can no longer be a surprise to anyone who referees in this city. It's a typically dirty game, and the cards are divvied up as follows — dissent (one card — the first yellow, in the 19th minute, part of my now established policy to try and snuff it out at the first sign); foul play (four cards — as usual, it should have been more); and unsporting behaviour (four cards — two for a flirty wee couple who push and shove and square up to each other; and two for deliberately delaying restarts).

You could have added at least four or five more for delaying restarts, including two players who belted the ball away in frustration at their own crapness. But again, the temperature was somewhere in the mid-30s, and there comes a point where showing a card for every little infringement — no matter how justified — just becomes depressing.

That hour and a half of concerted quiet from the benches, though. I'll take that every Sunday afternoon, thank you very much.

Saturday: 1-2 (no cards)

Sunday: 3-5 (9 x yellow)

Ref-in-residence

If you whistle for a penalty that no one's appealed for, does that mean the foul really happened? In the fourth minute, an away team defender shoves over the home striker as the two compete for a bouncing ball. It seems so blatant, yet there are none of the familiar shrill cries of "Referee!" before I make the call. Is it because it happened so early in the game, and no one quite expects to yet see such an unnecessary infringement?

Even more uncanny is that no one complains. There are not even any groans of exasperation at my decision. Not a single away team player tells me that I've got to be joking. The defender does not stride over and insist that he was only a. playing the ball, b. just shielding his space or c. didn't even touch the opponent! They just accept it. The number 9 steps up and converts. 1-0. And after that early setback, there's still not a breath of dissent.

It worries me for a while. Let me repeat: no one appealed, and no one complained. It maybe happens in the U15s and below, now and again. Never in the men's leagues, not even during a friendly. I'm simply not used to refereeing two outstandingly sporting teams. There is only one slightly unpleasant incident in the whole 90 minutes.

After an hour, with the home team leading 3-0, the away team pulls a goal back. The number 6 first of all swipes at the ball on the edge of the penalty area and completely misses it. By this time — it being July and still around 30 degrees in the evening — most of the players are knackered already, and no one's quick enough or motivated enough to close the midfielder down. So he gets a second swing at the ball and this time connects well enough to score. Then he squares up to the home team's captain and does some sort of male pre-mating dance by sticking out his chest and grunting.

The home team captain and I have the same reaction — what the fuck? The captain wants to know if the number 6 would like to make something of it, so I separate them and ask the number 6 what the hell he's playing at. He just looks at me like a scolded schoolboy who didn't know, sir, that cock-roostering was against the spirit of the game. I toy with a yellow card, but end up telling him just to behave himself and stop being a moron. His team-mates chastise him for acting like he's in kindergarten.

Aside from a sole caution for a pulled shirt when the home striker is almost through on goal, everything else is wonderful. No hysteria about offside calls, just a couple of polite queries I can answer with a quick shake of the head. Afterwards, there's food and drink and a chat. I praise the club for their hospitality and friendliness, and they say that's how they always treat the referee, no matter what happens on the field. I almost ask if I can set up a tent on the grass field next door and become their in-house referee. Ref-in-residence. Between games I'll write poetry about the reserve team's chunky right-back.

By the time I cycle home, the air has cooled and there's a raging orange backdrop behind the hills north of the city. Twilight couples linger on benches by the river, kissing or smoking or staring at the sky. What a sweet and perfect night.

Final score: 4-2 (1 x yellow)

Club linesmen

Unless they find a way to reverse the ageing process, I will never again referee with 'proper' linesmen. I don't miss running the line myself — too much quiet time, and you get to hear too many comments from spectators who think they're being funny when in fact they're just being twats. There are times, though, when I wish that I could still referee as part of a qualified threesome. That is, almost every time I have to deal with a club linesman.

Quick recap — club linesmen have only one job. To indicate when the ball is fully out of play. Just that one job. Despite that single, simple task, sometimes it's easier to do without them. Not tonight, though.

I'm refereeing a men's friendly on a manicured grass field, but the lines are marked in a fading white. It's a 7pm kick-off, and the descending sun's rays slant across the pitch to make them even less visible. We start the game with a sub from the home team holding a flag on the bench side, but leaning back against the dugout with his arms folded. The other side of the field is unmanned, and the line is almost entirely invisible. After 10 minutes, I ask the away team to send someone over, so one of their subs hunts down a flag and reluctantly traipses around the sideline to take up position.

In the second half, the line's vacant again. The flag lies on the grass, just beyond the halfway line, as though its previous operator had hoped it might be technologically capable of doing the job on its own (I'm sure someone's working on this idea). Inevitably, one player on the home team at some point claims the ball's gone out, while the away team player continues to run with it. I let play continue until he's fouled just outside the penalty area. The first player's outraged that I didn't call for a throw-in.

I get quite tetchy for the only time. "You're the home club. It's your responsibility to provide linesmen. I already asked in the first half because I can see fuck all over there." I point over towards the home bench, where the other linesman has now been subbed in, and no one else has taken over his heavy duty task. "You want to complain, go speak to your coach." His team-mate tells him I'm absolutely right and that he should shut up.

We're expected as referees to concentrate fully for 90 minutes on numerous infringements that any one of 22 players could be committing at any time. But raising a flag to indicate that the ball's gone out? That seems to be an incredible ask for your average club linesman. They can spend half the game lifting the flag with studied diligence when the ball's catapulted 20 yards beyond the sideline (thanks for the signal, but I got that one). Then the one time you look around for help on a close call, it's guaranteed that you will see them either:

- talking to someone else behind them and not even looking at the field of play
- looking at their mobile fucking phone
- disappeared. Gone. The flag is on the floor. It was time for a beer/cigarette/wank in the club toilet, who knows?

Their other tendency is, despite my pre-match instructions, to flag before the ball's gone completely out. Then they whip the flag back down again as a player gets to the ball after all. Often I'm already in the process of whistling. Cue grief in my direction from the player. I just point at the linesman and say that he signalled, what can I do? Nice to deflect the blame for once. This gets especially lively if the linesman is one of the player's team-mates.

Ten minutes before the end, a long, counter-attacking ball is played out to the home team's right wing on the unmanned side of the field. The number 8 sprints after the ball, there's no sign of a defender. Instead of running after him, I dash over to the touchline instead, at least 40 yards behind the play. Sure enough, the ball goes out two feet just as the number 8 gets to it, but he flicks it instantly back into play and heads off towards the goal. I blow the whistle, and he belts the ball away in anger. Then he turns round and sees where I'm standing. There's general laughter.

The lack of capable club officials is just a minor quibble with this game, which is quiet and sporting throughout. "I always like it when you ref us," says one player from the (heavily) defeated away side at the final whistle. Dude, you don't know how much that means to me. Way, way more than having a competent linesman.

Final score: 7-1 (no cards)

Blocked pissoir

"This isn't a football game any more," states the home team's captain as he leaves the field. I've just shown him his second yellow card after he pulled back and brought down the away team's swift outside-right as he was haring towards the penalty area. The score is 0-4. Five minutes earlier I'd shown him his first yellow for his sullen, sarcastic query of, "Are we not playing offside today?" after the away team's fourth goal.

No, it's not a game of football any more. It's a forum for petulant whiners. It's a maelstrom of bleating, skill-deprived tossers in acrylic uniforms. It's a platform for snorting, righteous, hot-eyed wankers viewing every call against them as a heinous affront to their human dignity. This has nothing to do with football. Especially not among the home team, most of whom are shit at it (five minutes in, I predict to myself a scoreline of 0-4).

Both teams are the same, though. All afternoon. Every foul called is not a foul. Every foul not called is, by contrast, a foul. Every offside decision called is not offside. Every call of 'play on' after an offside appeal is — you've guessed it — horrifically erroneous too. Of course it's offside. Four slow, stubby and rubicund defenders are screaming that it's offside, so it must have been.

Last Sunday's game, at the same level, went without a hitch. This week, I make the same speech to the players and coaches as I made then. The coaches are fine. The players, though, instinctively react to each call expressing the shock of an innocent man tasered with 50,000 volts. "Referee!" Out of the seven cards I show, four are for dissent.

One away player screams at me for what he considers to be the wrong call for a throw-in. His team's 5-0 up at the time, and five minutes earlier he'd received a yellow for foul play. That's not enough to stop him yelling all over the shop. I ask him about this, and he calms down and runs away. That final warning? You're welcome.

At one point in the second half, I start to imitate the players, repeatedly calling out, "Referee! Referee! Referee!" in a series of braying, child-like accents. Things calm down a bit after that. As noted before, it can pay off if they suspect that you might be a little unhinged. No one wants to have to deal with the fallout if the ref has a mental breakdown right here on the field.

Inside, though, I've long since had it with these two teams. I'm running around in the second half thinking, "Maybe I'm having a shit game today. Maybe I'm getting every single decision wrong. Maybe I get every single decision wrong every week, but other teams are too polite to moan. Maybe I should quit."

Yet I can't think of any major calls that either team could have complained about, where they could have said with absolute certainty, "You screwed that up, everyone could see it, you ruined the game." The sending off is beyond dispute — the second yellow alone almost qualifies as a straight red. At 0-5 I give a penalty to the away team when their forward is simultaneously fouled and crushed by three defenders — the home team doesn't complain specifically that it isn't a penalty, they just let out a moan of grief. Typical of this fucking ref to give a penalty against us. Like I am responsible for the tri-partite offence.

And that "offside" on the fourth goal? It came from a cross, the attacker was left completely free in front of goal, in line with — and neglected by — the captain who disputed it a few seconds later. If he's offside, it's by the kind of margin that only video technology can measure. Sadly, in the blocked-pub-pissoir of a league these two teams play in, we don't yet have that luxury.

At 0-6, a home forward blazes an easy chance high over the bar. "Was that my fault as well?" I enquire. "No, not this time," he says, and pats me on the back. It's a rare light moment on the kind of afternoon where I cycle home with lead in my legs and a black cloud above my grey head. Less a game of football, more a complete waste of human energy.

Final score: 1-6 (6 x yellow, 1 x yellow-red)

C level

There's a new underclass in the city's football scene. Sensing that there's room to sink even further, a new City League C (Level 11 of the German pyramid) was created out of the bottom-feeders of last season's B divisions. I'm fully expecting us to plummet through to X, XX and triple X as we cascade on down to the ultimate basement — the Z League. No ball, just 90 minutes of swearing, fouling and fighting.

After 40 minutes of Class C sport, I stop the game and instruct both captains to huddle with their teams and tell them: "Either you start playing football, or I'll call the game off and recommend that both sides face lengthy bans." We've just seen the game's fifth and sixth yellow cards after a second mass confrontation. It's nothing to do with me. They just seem to genuinely hate each other.

The home team's been banned before, so they take notice. At half-time I chat with their trainer on our way to the locker room, and he promises that he will make the need for discipline clear to his players. It helps that they score three quick goals right after the break to go 5-0 up, and then they start to relax.

An away team player moans half-heartedly about a foul in the lead-up to the subsequent sixth goal. There are still plenty of poor challenges, and a home team player goes in the book for the now almost obligatory scream of, "Never! Never!" after an offside decision he's seen with alternative eyes. I should really send the away team's captain off for his second cautionable foul with five minutes left, but he apologises to the fouled player and I let it go. After all, they're already 8-0 down.

But then, with two minutes to go, the away team's number 18 — booked in the first half for a nasty foul that was borderline red, and which had set off one of the shouty, testicle-swinging, multi-player square-ups — takes out an opponent in midfield for no good reason, so they go down a player after all. Upon seeing the red card, he squares up to me and yells in my face, "You wanted that, didn't you? You wanted that!" Dude, not as much as you seemed to. I just look past him and point to the touchline, while his team-mates tell him to stop being such a twat (good luck with that).

Many of the away team's players had shaken my hand just before we ran onto the field. "Whether you shake my hand again at the end is still an open question," I say, and how we all laugh. After the final whistle, not a single one of them shakes my hand. It requires a tiny wee bit of character to take three seconds to thank the ref after a defeat, and these lads are not up to it. See previous games.

On Saturday, I ref a boys' U19 match with no trouble, apart from one sarcy dissenter who wants to know after a challenge that I let go if "we can all break each others' knees now". It's his tone that sees him booked, rather than what he says, not helped by the way he'd chewed out a team-mate for a minor error earlier in the half. His coach subs him out immediately, bollocks him, and then keeps him on thsideline for the next 25 minutes. Once back in, he behaves.

That's proper player management, and if coaches dealt with all dissenters in this fashion from an early age, we wouldn't be facing the recruitment crisis in refereeing that could eventually mean the end of Class C down to Z. Unless they downgrade even further by playing without a ref. There's a dark, voyeuristic side to me that thinks such games might almost be worth paying to watch.

Saturday: 1-8 (1 x yellow)

Sunday: 8-0 (8 x yellow, 1 x yellow-red)

Why am I so shit?

One of the reasons I love refereeing is the number of philosophical discussions it leads to about the game, both off the field and on. At the end of 90 minutes in last night's City Cup game, for example (score: 1-1, with extra time about to be played), a defender on the away team came up to me and asked, "Why is your refereeing so shit tonight?"

Good question. Am I having a bad day? Am I biased against his team for reasons real or imaginary? Am I just in general not fit to arbitrate the game of football due to a lack of knowledge, experience and temperament? Or does the player hold a distorted view of my officiating skills because five minutes earlier I'd sent off one of his team-mates for his second yellow card offence, and now they had to play extra-time one man down?

Correction, two men down. Insulting the referee is a straight red card.

The player is astonished. What was the red card for? Well, I explain, you just insulted the referee. No I didn't, he maintains. I didn't say you're a shit referee. I just said that tonight your refereeing is shit.

His team loses the game 4-1. At the end of extra-time, he comes up to me in order to maintain again that he had not intended to insult me (though he didn't go so far as to apologise). He reasons that if I, as the referee, had said to him that he was having a shit game, then he would not have seen that as an insult. Only if I'd said he was a shit player.

I reply that first, in my role as a referee I would never tell him that he was having a shit game (I reserve such judgments for here — my therapeutic trough). Second, if I did tell him that he was having a shit game, then that would indeed qualify as an insult. He begs to differ, then walks away by reiterating his view that I'd had a shit game.

190

On the way back to my changing room at the end of a fraught and intense two hours of football (most of which I actually enjoyed — it was a fast, skilful game between two good teams, despite many fouls and much verbal unpleasantry, especially from the touchlines), two officials from the home team ask me what the red card was for. I tell them what happened, and about the player's justification. They both burst out laughing. I start laughing too, so that when the away team's coach (yellow-carded for persistent moaning during extra-time) twice comes into my changing room to complain loudly at length about his player's yellow-red card, I'm utterly sanguine. When he's done the second time, I wish him a nice evening as he slams the door shut.

I'm sure he doesn't think that I'm a shit ref. Just that, on this particular night, my refereeing was shit. My view of him as a coach and a human being? I couldn't possibly judge. If you can't say something nice ...

Final score: 4-1 (8 x yellow, 1 x yellow-red, 1 x red)

My last promotion

Why are some players quiet throughout every game of their career, and some just cannot stop their gobs? They yell at team-mates, they yell at opponents, they yell at referees, they'd probably yell at Jesus Christ if that spiritual entity floated down on the pitch for a Second Coming half-way through the second half. "Not now, Jesus, we're 2-0 up with 20 minutes left. Come and save us after the final fucking whistle, Christ almighty!"

I reffed the home team a few weeks ago in a pre-season friendly that ended up with nine yellow cards, four of them for this particular team. I check the game report to see who offended, and what the offence was. I take note of players cautioned for unsporting behaviour and, even more so, dissent. That would be the diminutive number six, a central midfielder.

Last time around I showed him a yellow after just 19 minutes, which ensured that not only he, but everyone else too, stayed mostly quiet for the rest of the game. This time, he starts up again not long after the opening whistle, moaning about every call. I reach for my pocket and his captain comes running up between us, exhorting his player to shut the hell up, and promising that from now on he'll be quiet. I lecture the number 6, and he nods, and for now I withhold the caution.

He seems to think that his captain's instructions are only valid up until half-time. After the restart, with his team 2-0 down, he resumes mouthing off at every call. I show him the yellow card, reminding him of our deal that he was to keep his chops sealed for the rest of the afternoon. I also ask him, "Why do you do that? Why do you dispute every single call? What do you get out of it?"

He looks at me as though he doesn't understand what the hell I'm on about. Or maybe he's worried that if he answers back, I'll take that as dissent and show him a second yellow. It's a trap! A few minutes later he's out of the game, injuring his hamstring after fouling an opponent, a call I'm sure he'd have quibbled about if he hadn't been clutching the back of his thigh.

The home team are second, the away team is top, but there's a gulf in quality between the sides. When the away team scores on a through ball to go 2-0 up shortly before half-time, the outfoxed centre back raises his arm and yells for offside. The keeper's screaming about offside as well, but his ire's aimed at the defender for trying to spring the offside trap, and failing. The gist of the goalkeeper's message is: try getting to the fucking ball instead of hollering for offside. I wish more goalkeepers would stress this to their defenders.

There's something else unique about today's game, at least for me — in summer I was 'promoted' and can now referee games at Level 8 of the German league system (the *Kreisoberliga*' — the highest level I can ref at my age). Today's my first game at this level. It's faster, and there are some extremely good players, but there's still a lot of fouling and moaning. The main difference is a crowd of around 300 who have actually paid to get in.

The home spectators, of course, are like their number 6 — they contest every call against their team. There's a difference, though, in 300-odd people complaining about your calls compared with a lone loudmouth or a habitually foul-tongued partisan pensioner. I like it — it feels natural. Of course they're going to moan about every decision. That's what they're here for.

"That was never a penalty," a home player informs me in the bar while I'm filing the game report. The away team's number 10, who'd tormented the home defence all afternoon, was on his way past an opponent and almost at the end-line, ready to cross for a lurking team-mate, when he was shoved to the ground. "Were you the defender involved?" I ask him. Yes, he says. "Well, of course you'd say it wasn't a foul," I reply, but he doesn't think it's funny, just walks away shaking his head.

A heavy defeat, in which his side were outclassed and created maybe two or three decent chances. Hopefully their goalkeeper will focus his team on that stat, rather than entertaining conspiracy theories about offside calls and apparently dubious penalty decisions. And maybe the captain will tell the little number 6 that, if he wants to keep on playing for the club, could he please keep his dumb mouth shut.

Final score: 1-6 (4 x yellow)

A captain in control

It's been a quiet Sunday — I'm almost an hour into my second game of the day and I've yet to show a card. The away side's number 10, however, has been in my field of vision since a series of fouls in the first half. Now he trips an opposing player a few yards outside his own penalty area, then kicks the ball away when I whistle for the foul. I show him the yellow card.

His captain asks me politely if a yellow card is not a bit harsh for the offence. I reply that the player had already committed three fouls in the first half, and that I'd had a word with him about his conduct. The captain says, "Ah, I see. Okay, that's fine." And moves away.

A few minutes later, one of his own players is clattered in central midfield, and stays down briefly injured. The home team's player apologises and tries to help him up, but the player's not ready. The fouled player's team-mate marches over from his position at right-back and loudly starts a sentence aimed at me with the words, "With all due respect ... "

His captain's there again and cuts him off. "No!" he orders. The full-back starts to speak again, and the captain says, "No! Not to the referee, and not to me either. Not to anyone!" The full-back makes what is clearly a super-human effort to shut the fuck up, then turns and walks away. I can see it's killing him. I make a brief thumbs-up gesture to the captain and move away, as the fouled player is back on his feet and ready to continue.

This was model leadership, and all the more conspicuous because of its rarity — often captains think they have more of a right to rag on the ref than their charges. It's also worth noting that his team were 7-0 down at the time. Frequently in such games, a trailing side will resort to niggly fouls and other illegal methods to take their frustration out on a better team. There is absolutely none of this today.

In fact, the game is petering out on a hot afternoon when, out of the blue, another unexpected event occurs. It's the 84th minute and the home team is 8-1 up by this point. There's a hard but fair fight in midfield for the ball between the home team's number 10 and the away team's number 7. The latter comes away with the ball and starts to run towards the home goal. The number 10, for reasons only he can know (and don't forget, his side is leading 8-1 and there are only five minutes left), chases after the number 7 and, without any hope of catching him, wildly swings his leg and takes the opponent out completely with a hack to his left ankle.

There's an understandable roar of outrage from the away players and a collective "Whoo!" of surprise from the few dozen home spectators, casually drinking beer right next to the incident (they've been making good-natured quips to their own players all afternoon). Before anything escalates, I blow loudly and show the player a straight red. He looks genuinely astounded, but not a single team-mate protests the call. He walks off and gets involved in a few discussions with the away team on the way.

The number 7 is in some pain and rolls off to the sideline for treatment. After the game, I ask him if there'd been any previous between himself and the number 10 that I'd missed, and he says absolutely not. It was just a moment of utter stupidity at the end of an uncontroversial and very sporting game. The number 10 does come and apologise to him about five minutes after the final whistle, but for me that's way too late for contrition, so I don't mention the gesture in the match report.

A few hours earlier I'd refereed a boys' U17 game with little fuss. After the game, I enjoyed a sanguine chat with the away coach — we talked about a non-call for offside on one of the goals conceded (he accepted my explanation), then about the game in general, and also about youth football in the city. It was a Sunday of calm coaches and responsible captaincy — it makes such a difference to the tenor of a game, and puts me in a mellow post-match mood. More days like this, please.

Sunday morning: 3-0 (no cards)

Sunday afternoon: 8-1 (1 x yellow, 1 x red)

Unplayable, but we play on

A Sunday afternoon men's game in the arse-end of a satellite town attached to our city. It's raining, so I take the train rather than the bike, then walk two miles to the ground alongside a busy four-lane road, passing petrol stations, dubious car dealerships and repair shops, and a lone bar incongruously called the Bistro Royale, with brown cafeteria tables and a sparse, all-male clientele. I reach the ground an hour before kick-off and inspect the compact cinder pitch, bordered by a huge car park, a faceless housing estate, and a grass field that looks in much better condition, but has already been closed off by a protective groundsman.

The pitch is playable at 2pm, but by kick-off at 3pm it's already developing puddles, and the rain's getting worse. Amazingly, people are actually paying to get in at the gate and watch this. Around 50 in all, most of them equipped with umbrellas. A van pulls up in the car park and its driver starts hooting and screaming out the window. When the home team goes 1-0 up after 20 minutes, he does it all over again, but after that he's mute — within another three minutes, they're trailing 2-1.

It gets chippy for a while. The away team's number 8 goes down in an aerial challenge, but his team gets the ball in a promising position and I play advantage. They lose the ball and, as the number 8 is still lying in a heap, I stop play. He peels himself out of the slime and starts to yell at me for not calling a foul. I tell him that I played advantage. "Advantage?" he repeats, incredulous. "Advantage?" Like he'd ordered and paid for champagne, and I'd just served him up a jug of steaming rat's piss. "Yep, it's part of football," I say and run off, because he's back on his feet and remarkably unhurt.

At the break, it's still 1-2. The home team are in the changing room next to me and discard a half-time tactical talk in favour of yelling at each other. It doesn't help. By the 47th minute they're 1-4 down, and they're still yelling at each other. The bloke in the van's driven off. The away fans sing a short but quite cheery song after every goal. The home team is probably wondering why it didn't accept my offer to call the game off at half-time. There's now a two-inch deep puddle reaching a few yards onto the field on the far touchline, stretching in length about 50 yards.

The spectators on that side of the field have a great time of it. Inevitably, the ball gets stuck a lot, and players start splashing about helplessly like in pro games from legendary times before stadiums had proper drainage. No one suggests packing it in, so I let them play on. We're all soaked and spattered. The home team only have 11 players, and after losing one to injury they more or less give up. The away team hammers in goal after goal, the keeper doesn't even bother diving any more. I blow up a couple of minutes early.

The screaming in the home changing room much louder after the game than it was at half-time. The defence feels let down that the midfield didn't bother covering back. The midfield wants to know why the defenders insisted on trying to dribble the ball out of defence time after fucking time. It sounds like a club on the verge of folding. They only run one side, with a squad of 18 ageing players. And there seems to be something of an issue with team spirit. The coach at least thanks me and says I had a good game, which you don't often get from a coach who's lost by 11 goals.

On Saturday, I ref a boys' U19 game on what is probably the last golden evening of autumn. A mainly peaceful encounter, except just before half-time the home team's assistant coach screams loudly in protest at an offside call against his striker. I turn towards him and make the 'stop-that-shit-now' gesture, with the appropriate facial expression.

A minute later, as I'm coming off the field at half-time, he jogs up to me with a rueful smile. "Really, really sorry about that," he says. "I shouldn't have yelled that out. And it absolutely was the correct call, he was definitely offside." Blimey. Well, thanks in return for the unqualified apology, it's very much welcome. Aside from some brief minor league macho twattery from the home team's number 14, the rest of the game is as quiet as a game should be.

Saturday: 6-2 (2 x yellow)

Sunday: 1-12 (4 x yellow)

Red or yellow?
You have two seconds to decide

The away team's number eight, a midfielder, goes in way too hard and late on an opponent, about 40 yards from the home team's goal. It's a foul, no one's going to dispute that. The 100 or so home fans dutifully roar in outrage at the challenge, while the fouled player goes down with a cry and clutches his thigh. Part of me thinks it should be a straight red. Another part of me instantly counters that a red card would be too harsh.

In the few seconds I have to make a decision, I try to take into account the temperature of the game. The home team's second from the bottom, the away team second from the top. The score is 1-1 and there are 15 minutes to play. It's been an intense, hard-fought game, with lots of shouting and what we are now obliged to call "emotion" (but which I'd more often than not classify as stupidity). The underdogs have come back strongly in the second half after going in at the break 0-1 down.

The number eight has not committed any other fouls this game, at least none of them bad enough for me to remember. He also stays close to the scene of the foul, although it's only when I prompt him that he offers the player a helping hand and an apology. The fouled player is pissed off at him, but not furious, and accepts the hand. "It was deliberate," he says to me, tentatively getting to his feet and rubbing his leg. It was, but was there really "excessive force" involved? And if I send this player off now, will it have only a negative impact on the game? Will I just be making myself the sudden centre of attention?

When it's borderline, I err on the conservative side. I go for the yellow card, wondering if I've bottled it. But no home players have demanded the red, or even suggested it. Ten minutes later, they deservedly take the lead, and the ground goes as nuts as any ground maybe can in a tiny town at Level 9. As I walk off at the end, one of the ever-present wise old men stops on his way out and says, "You had that game well under control, ref." No one mentions the number eight or his nasty foul.

There were, however, eight yellow cards in all, including three for dissent. One of those went to the away team's coach on the cusp of half-time. The ball went just out of play over on his side of the field, but although the club linesman (from the away team) didn't raise his flag, I whistled for the (home) throw-in. This prompted my linesman to start yelling at me, and when I told him to desist, the coach joined in yelling at me too, and then pretty much the entire away contingent of subs and travelling fans. Over a fucking throw-in. So I told him to calm down, and when he didn't (after all, this was a throw-in near the halfway line — really worth losing your rag about) I showed him yellow and yelled a little bit back at him. At that point, his own players started telling him to shut the hell up, and he finally did.

One other moment worth recounting — in the second half, with the home crowd pumped at having just equalised, one of their forwards ran down the left too early, and I knew before the ball was even played towards him that he was offside. I also knew what was going to happen when I blew the whistle. Yes, the obligatory roar of wronged outrage from the home support. "Refereeeeeeeeee!" Maybe at one time I'd have cowered. Now it's so predictable that it's all I can do to stop myself from laughing. All in all, though, I enjoy the feisty, challenging game.

On Friday evening, I ref a boys' U19 game in steady, cold rain. My feet turn into two barely functional ice blocks at some point in the second half, despite an infusion of hot orange juice from the concessions stand at half-time. There's not a murmur of dissent all night, and just one yellow card for a tactical foul, followed by a self-conscious grin and an apology. At the end I thank both teams for their sporting behaviour. They give me food and more drink before I set out into the soaking dark, braced for five more months of long-sleeve refereeing on bone-numbing nights like this.

Friday: 5-1 (1 x yellow)

Sunday: 2-1 (8 x yellow)

"Thank you", he whispered

I look at my watch — we've played 45 seconds of this boys' U19 game, and I've already shown the first caution. The away team's number 10 barrels in to a challenge with no intent to play the ball, and every intent of sending the home team a signal. His opponent goes flying. Number 10 gets a bright yellow signal in return, along with a roar from my mouth that this is not how things are going to play out this afternoon. The home team's captain, shaping up to take the free-kick, whispers, "Thank you."

My dad always used to say to me, "Make sure your first challenge counts. Go in hard so your opponent knows you're there and that you're serious." These were wasted words on me, unfortunately — as a lad I was built like a beanpole and tackling wasn't the strongest point of my game (my team-mates at the time said it wasn't part of my game at all). I wonder if the number 10 has a dad who offers him similar advice. He looks momentarily amazed that I've shown him a card so early on in the game, but then accepts it.

The rest of the half is peaceful, until the same player picks up his second caution for a nasty foul, just before half-time. He takes the five-minute penalty without dissent, and I ignore his coach who's jumping up and down on the touchline screaming that the player can't be given a time penalty because he hasn't yet had a yellow card. Presumably he hadn't taken his seat by the game's start, and missed the early caution. His player corrects him as he leaves the field and the flapping and honking abates.

In the second half, it's instructive to watch the number 10 after he's sat out his five-minute punishment. Twice he wants to dispute my calls, and once he almost gets into a stramash with an opponent after a midfield challenge. On all three occasions he pulls himself together, keeps his mouth shut, and walks away. He knows that with one more transgression, he's off. So there's concrete proof, as if it's needed, that cards and cautions are an essential part of keeping the lid on games being contested by 22 physical and motivated young men.

On Sunday, in a level 8 men's game, there's an entirely different discussion point. The away team gets a free-kick in front of goal, 25 yards out, about 20 minutes in with the score at 0-0. There's a three-man wall. As the kicker runs up to take the kick, one of his team-mates suddenly sprints up and stands at the end of the wall. I've no idea why. I blow the whistle as the ball's in the air. Its perfect trajectory takes it into the top corner of the goal — a quite beautifully executed set-piece, cancelled out for a quite unnecessary transgression.

There's a lot of confusion. What have I blown for? The home team seems astounded that they've got away with not conceding, and now have an indirect free-kick instead. The baffled away team asks for the reason, though they are very civil about it. It probably helps that they're completely dominating the game, and they know this won't be their last opportunity of the afternoon. They take the explanation well, and the captain yells at the player who joined the wall for not knowing the new rule — which is not so new given that it's now been in place for over five months.

At the end of half-time, as the players are returning to the pitch, the scorer of the disallowed free-kick approaches me and says, "You were absolutely right on the rule there. But ... you know, it was such a great goal!" I tell him that I've every sympathy. I once had a referee blow the final whistle after I'd shot from 30 yards out and the ball was still in the air. It went on in the top corner, but the goal didn't count and we lost 3-2 (the opponent next to me shook my hand and said, "Hard luck, mate."). But, I tell the disconsolate Messi of the Kreisoberliga, at least your team will all know the rule from now on.

I do wonder if anyone would have protested if I'd let the goal stand, but that's not a risk you can take. If I'd signalled for the goal, then any home team player — assuming they were clued up on the laws — would have been well within his rights to protest. While I would have demonstrated that, as a referee, I either didn't know the new law, or that for some reason I was not prepared to implement it. I'm not sure which of those two truths would have been more damning.

Saturday: 4-1 (4 x yellow, 1 x time penalty)

Sunday: 0-7 (2 x yellow)

'You're acting like a bunch of fucking wankers'

The weekend before last, just south of Frankfurt, a 22-year-old referee was knocked unconscious by a player who'd just received a red card in a Level 10 game. The referee had to be air-lifted to hospital. Thankfully, he recovered physically, but it made the national news and — as always with an incident like this — caused a lot of (temporary) agonising in the media and the football community about the way that referees are treated. Again and again the figure is quoted that over the past few years the number of registered referees in Germany has gone down from around 80,000 to 58,000. That's a massive and significant drop in numbers. There have been similar worries in the UK about the decline in the number of officials, and it's all for the same reason — who in his or her right fucking mind would want to spend their free time refereeing amateur football games in the current climate of General Anger About Everything?

I don't quote this exact statistic while shouting at the home team coach and the players of both teams in general during this (Level 9) men's game. But I do forcefully make the point that "soon there'll be no one to referee your shitty games because we've all had enough of your shit behaviour, so shut your mouths and get on with the game, for Christ's sake." Still mad, I break into English: "You're acting like a bunch of fucking wankers." (I don't know if anyone understood this or not, but they'll have got the gist. I feel it's legit — I get sworn at in a multitude of languages in this city, but of course I can't put into the match report, 'Player number 16 said in Serbo-Croat, You're a turd-faced twat whose whistle should be shoved up his arse,' if I don't understand Serbo-Croat. Though the time an Italian player called me *bastardo* I was pretty sure of his meaning, even though I don't speak Italian.)

There are 20 minutes left, and I've no desire to complete the game. For a while I stop running, and whenever anyone looks like they're about to protest a decision (it's a seemingly automatic reaction, especially for the players on the home team), I stare at them and they keep quiet. Let them think I'm nuts. Let them think there's another level of worryingly unhinged pissed-offness I haven't yet stepped down to. I no longer care.

"You were absolutely right to shout what you did," says a non-playing member of the away team's entourage after the game. "I couldn't agree with you more." The assistant coach says I had a good game, so I point out to him that his team moaned almost as much as the home players. "It's true," he concedes. "That's something we need to work on."

It starts, as it so often does, with offside. On a short field, the home team plays the offside trap, and the away team's forwards are caught time and time again. Their bench roars in outrage until I go over and tell them to quit the protests. "Yell at your players for getting caught offside, not at me," is my instruction, and they do at least take it on board. As long as there's someone to yell at, right? We're not talking about close decisions here, by the way — we're talking about two, three or even five yards offside.

The home team thinks I'm having a great game at this point. "Good call, ref," they say. Until the away lads start to time their runs much better and beat the offside trap. The home defenders are so used to shouting "Offside!" by now that they can't believe it when I wave play through, even though I'm standing level or almost level with the last line of defenders, because it's become the key place to be. By half-time, they're 3-1 down and disgruntled. In the second half, I turn down a home team penalty appeal for a supposed point-blank handball which from my viewpoint didn't even hit the hand (and even if it had, I wouldn't have given it from that range), and then for not whistling what they see as a foul on their number 10, but which to me looked like both players going for the ball and colliding. That's when the home coach — the man who'd introduced himself before kick-off as "a member of the board and responsible here for order, so come to me if there are any problems" — starts going off at me. And when he won't shut up after two appeals for calm, that's when I go off back at him (see my sweary wee outburst above).

I'd been telling a colleague just the evening before at our monthly referees' meeting how I'd been having a mainly peaceful season, and was really starting to enjoy refereeing again. More fool me for tempting fate. I'd only been offered the assignment on the morning of the game, and had seriously thought about turning it down given the notoriously bad nature of Level 10 football in this city, and given that the temperature's just above freezing now, with an added wind-chill. I'd been planning to go to the pictures with Mrs Ref. But I didn't, I went out to get yelled at by grown men in shorts on a really cold November night.

Some home team players are more conciliatory after the final whistle. The number 10 comes and shows me the stud marks on his shin from the foul that I didn't call, though he's not being aggressive about it. I explain to him what I thought I'd seen and then add, "But, you know, I could well have made a mistake, so if I did then I'm genuinely sorry." He's okay with the apology. I do actually feel like I let him down, and that the game slipped out of my control. I should have shown yellow at the first dissent from the away team bench during the first half. Four out of ten.

I try to imagine what it would be like working in an office and all your colleagues surrounded your desk and started shouting at you whenever they thought you'd made an error. I think it would make you quite depressed, and then you'd quit. That's the simple answer to anyone wondering why refereeing numbers continue to plummet.

Final score: 4-6 (5 x yellow)

Every game an epic drama

The home team's coach has been trying to get my attention to make a substitution, but there's a lot going on so I haven't noticed. When I see him waving his arms at me and yelling, I signal for him that it's okay to make the substitution. "I've been standing here for two minutes trying to get your attention," he screams. I don't like his tone, so I walk over to ask him to calm down. He continues to yell, so I show him the yellow card. Then he starts to yell about the yellow card.

I could show him a red now, but instead I fight back. "I couldn't hear you because there are 22 players out there all yelling at the same time — perhaps you should yell at them to shut the fuck up. I come all the way out here to ref your game for fuck all money, and you expect me to put up with you screaming at me?" He claims now that he wasn't screaming, he just wanted to get my attention. You were screaming, I counter, and you were completely lacking respect. His assistant coach chimes in with, "He's right, you know." Which, for once, is a very welcome intervention.

After the game, the coach approaches me again to "explain" why he was upset. His player had gone off injured, and he'd been eager to get a replacement on to the field. That's still no reason to scream at me in a disrespectful fashion, I say. He makes a dismissive gesture and cites the now standard excuse for bad behaviour: "You have to remember that football's a game of emotions."

Oh, that's alright then. You were just expressing your emotions. Sure, I'm willing to be the sponge for your frustration. That's what referees are here for, we just soak up all your aggression, your bile, your seething rage that not everything is going exactly as you planned, and not all the decisions are being called in your favour. No problem, mate, whenever you want to emote, just take it all out on me. That's why I get paid the big bucks, to be your psychological trampoline — just bounce up and down on me until you've got it all off your chest, and I'll continue to spring back up every time.

It's the only thing to be in football nowadays — *emotional*. If you aren't, you don't care enough about your team and the game. All the TV adverts for the weekend's Huge Game are showing us The Emotions again and again. Then during every single televised game there are the multiple slo-mo close-ups of players, coaches and fans showing us their tears, screams, tantrums, fists raised, fists being thumped into the ground or thrown through the air. Oh, the agony! You can't just enjoy sport any more, you have to express intense feelings about it. If the referee gets in the way of your explosive outbursts, there's nothing that can be done about it. You just happen to be a very emotional person, in touch with their deepest inner feelings.

The only player to come and shake my hand after the final whistle also wants to talk about his yellow card for dissent. He too had screamed at me, about one of his players lying injured in the penalty area. He wants to explain that. I tell him that I have no problem with him bringing something like that to my attention, but that he doesn't need to bellow it at me as though I had not only injured the player by going in studs up, but was deliberately leaving him to die in a heap on a cold November afternoon. "Why can't you just tell me in a normal voice?" Well, I know the reason. His team had wanted a penalty, and I hadn't given it. Frustrating. Enough to make you come over all emotional.

Before the game I'd specifically warned both teams that I would show yellow cards for dissent. Out of the eight yellows I show, four are for exactly that. Every time, the player seems surprised, like the law on dissent was only introduced last week and nobody had told him.

There are other areas of disagreement, in particular when the home goalkeeper scores a bizarre own goal. After a corner, he's waiting for a botched clearance to come back down out of the air, facing his own goal. The ball hits his nose, he fumbles the catch, and it bounces into the goal off his chest. The away team celebrates, and six home players surround me and proclaim that he was fouled. The goalkeeper makes a mistake in his own penalty area, and it's always a foul, right? Another Law you may not know (Law 18 — The Right To Make It Up On The Fucking Spot).

I'm standing right in front of him at my usual corner-kick position on the touchline. There is no attacker anywhere close to him, let alone a foul. When it's clear that I'm not going to disallow the goal, the goalkeeper falls dramatically to the floor, clutching his nose. The coach comes on and puts an ice pack over it. I walk over — there is no swelling, no bleeding, no mark of any kind. I invite him to play on, and he does so, heroically cured.

There's a lot of this from both teams, though it's mainly the home side trying to waste time and hold on to a one-goal lead. Again and again there's a clash, and a player goes down with a theatrical cry and a roll for good measure, holding some part of his body and ready to die for the cause. Perhaps I should be more tolerant of this; maybe these young men are just expressing their emotions. Even at Level 9, it's an epic drama.

Final score: 3-2 (8 x yellow)

'Do you play the bagpipes?'

There are some days when you don't feel like leaving the house. It's getting late on a dark Sunday afternoon and the Scottish League Cup Final's just a click away. Everyone else in the family is on the sofa in the warm living room, a plate of Christmas sweets on the coffee table alongside the remote control. It's been raining for the past three hours. And I have a 5pm kick-off — boys' U19, preceded by a cycle ride up a rutted, puddle-pocked and very busy road.

Many, many people ask me, "Why do you bother?" I should point out one thing that's maybe not always clear in this book. I love refereeing. On a good day. In that respect, I'm like almost any fan. Some days I want to write a love letter to the sport that I coach, that I ref, and that I played for over four decades. And there are days when I want to sign off from the whole thing: 'Dear Football, It's taken me a long time to reach this conclusion, but it's finally time we went our separate ways ... ' It's always enticing to imagine the potential freedom that lies on the other side of such a break. Yet the fear of a head-fucking, latter-life crisis in the resultant void always prevents me from having the guts to take that ultimate leap.

And as Mrs Ref says, "You'd be back out there four weeks later anyway." And no one knows me better than the person who lived through my three previous attempts to retire from playing, and twice from coaching.

Sure enough, two hours after moping around the flat — staring through the window at the puddles on the roof of the building opposite, and half-hoping for a cancellation — I'm out on the field living the highlight of my sporting week. I'm running into the rhythm of a frantic but flowing 90-minute battle for the ball. There are fouls to call, players to calm, a rigid arm in the direction of the penalty spot, and almost no dissent.

We're into first half stoppage time before the first yellow card, a tactical foul by the away team's number 10 on the home team's number 17. The latter follows through and lashes out at the ball in frustration (his team are 0-2 down), but misses it completely and instead kicks the opposition's number 7 hard in the shin.

There's much excitement at this, and I immediately show the miscreant a yellow card too, accompanied by a lecture. On my way back to the dressing-room at half-time, though, I already regret this decision. It should have been a straight red for violent conduct. The number 7 went down, and was then subbed out, limping badly (though he was thankfully healthy enough to return right after the break). I was too lenient because, up until then, it had been a sporting game, and the number 17 had not committed a single foul.

Coming back out for the second half, I apologise to both coaches of the away team and tell them that I think I made a mistake. They both immediately tell me not to worry about it, that the game's going fine, and assure me that they weren't expecting a red card. Out on the field, the away team's already waiting for the restart. Their number 13 wants to discuss another call from the first half, where his team-mate was, in his view, body-checked by a home defender. "You know, it's possible I made an error on that call," I say and his expression changes for the better. More players surround me, as we're still waiting for the home team to come back out. They ask me if I'm from Holland (my German accent apparently sounds Dutch.) No, I say, Scotland. Do I play the bagpipes? No, I hate the bloody bagpipes. But surely I drink whisky? Oh yes, no problems there. It's a light, welcome exchange that makes it clear no one's pissed off about my failure to show the red card, and that it needn't hang in my head for the second half.

This plays out much like the first, only with more fouls and more yellows, including a lone caution for dissent. The rain is now coming down like it's making up for last summer's drought in half a day. I don't think players or referees ever notice bad weather once play starts, but I do have an unsubstantiated theory that it helps to suppress moaning because almost everyone has the attitude to just muck in and get on with the game. The home team improve and twice pull within a goal of taking a point. It's an exciting and well-played match. At the end, we're all utterly soaked, and — depending on shirt colour — either disappointed or exhilarated.

Count me in the second group. Neither players nor coaches have any complaints at the final whistle, just warm words. I'm in severe need of a hot bath, but stupidly happy that I had the opportunity to leave the house and run around in the rain. That I'm still lucky enough to be part of the game.

Two weeks ago, the spritely ref in the game before mine told me that he was 82 years old. I reported this back home. "So," says Mrs Ref, "assuming you don't croak in the meantime, just another 28 years to go. At the least." Let's hope so.

Final score: 2-3 (5 x yellow, 1 x time penalty)

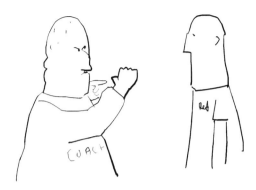

'Watch out or I'll smack you in the face'

The good news first — the weather's turned mild and it's stopped raining. It's my last game of the year, a men's mid-table clash, Level 10. I'm warming up next to the pitch, where a boys' U13 game is coming to a close. There's a very young ref in charge, so I already have half an eye on the game, but there's no major excitement from the touchlines and he seems to be fully in control.

Then, the away team coach starts yelling at him. I'm too far away to work out what it's about. There's no one down injured and there hasn't just been a goal or a penalty awarded, so there isn't any obvious cause. The coach is gesturing and shouting and he doesn't want to stop, so the young referee goes over to talk to him. I break off my warm-up and walk towards the field, though I'm still a few dozen yards away. The teenage ref is trying to talk to him, but the coach — a man of around 40 — is talking back over the top of him, loud and vehement. The young referee eventually gives up and goes back to re-start play. If this had been my game, the coach would have been red-carded, but I can see why a young ref might feel too intimidated to follow through in the face of such an aggressive performance.

Seconds after the game has resumed, I walk up to the coach and ask him why he's screaming at such a young referee. He looks at my warm-up jacket and sees the pennant of the city's refereeing association. Then he says, "Have you got a problem?" I tell him that as a referee I most certainly do have a problem with his touchline behaviour. His response is: "Well you'd better watch out then, or I'll smack you in the face."

The trainer of the home team hears this, as does the away team's co-trainer, who comes over and orders his colleague off the field and behind the spectator barrier. He's thankfully ahead of the situation, so this prevents me from immediately calling the police. There have been enough violent incidents in the past few weeks to warrant it, though. I talk with the home coach, and we agree to meet again once the game's over about what we should do. She says that the coach's first outburst at the young ref came out of nowhere, that she has no idea what might have set him off. I walk away and continue warming up, feeling shaken.

When the boys' game is over I approach the young referee and tell him what happened. We identify the aggressor from the initials on his tracksuit. The home trainer adds that she was called a "cunt" by one of the away team's players as they came off the field. The away team's co-trainer, meanwhile, tries to reason away his colleague's behaviour and to play the incident down. I understand why — it's because finding youth coaches is becoming as hard as finding people to referee youth games.

Look, I tell him, we have to report this. If I don't, then next week he goes one step further and throws that punch. Right in front of two teams of 12-year-old boys. He reluctantly assents. So when I get home, I write up what happened, with a lurking sense of melancholy at the whole incident. I get immediate messages back from both the league's admin and my refereeing body thanking me, and promising immediate action.

After the coach's threat, which was not an idle one, I don't much feel like refereeing a 90-minute men's game, but it goes okay. There's the requisite amount of complaining, but a couple of funny moments. One player yells loud and hard about an offside call, until his own fans on the touchline tell him that his team-mate was at least two yards off. I was thinking about a yellow for dissent, but before I can pull out the card he breaks into a smile and apologises. Then a defender screams at me for awarding a corner instead of a goal-kick, until his goalkeeper informs him of what the rest of us already knew — he'd clearly saved it and turned the ball around the post. "Oh, really?" says the defender, all mild manners now. Yes, really.

There's a row about a throw-in at one point, between two opposing players. I call them over. "Do you really want to have a fight about a fucking throw-in?" I ask them. They agree that would be stupid. They shake hands. See, it's not so hard.

After today, it's the winter break. Next year, everyone, please try to stop screaming at other people during football matches. And if you can't do that, try quitting the game and leaving the rest of us in peace. Your toxic aggression, your idiotic posturing, your egotism, your self-exposed ignorance, your choleric "emotions" — they're useless to me, to you, to your team-mates, to the players in your charge, to your family and friends, and to everyone who cares about football too.

Final score: 1-1 (4 x yellow)

Punishing dissent

During the winter break, the German FA issued a set of instructions to its top flight referees regarding dissent, diving, time-wasting and aggressive behaviour towards referees. It reiterated that each offence on its long list was to be punished with a yellow card. The instructions were passed down the chain of command to all amateur referees. And so to my weekend.

Saturday afternoon: A boys' U19 game between the second-placed team (at home, in white) and the third (away, in black), separated only by goal difference. As we line up, I mention the new guidelines, and warn them that any kind of dissent will be punished with a yellow card. But these are teenage boys, and they probably need to be told at least 15 times before they take the information on board. In the eighth minute comes the first caution, for the forward on the white team who protests loudly about me calling his foul on a defender. In the 12th minute comes the second yellow card, for a defender on the black team yelling at me for not giving what he insists was an offside call. The rest of the half is quiet.

In the second half, the game heats up. With the away team leading 2-1, I whistle for a penalty when the home team's goalkeeper comes off his line, clears the ball, but takes out the attacker (who needs two minutes to recover). I know there's going to be protests, because all players and coaches believe the goalkeeper has an inalienable right to do whatever he likes in his penalty area. The home team loses 2-3 and the white team blame it all on me because of the penalty call. Final tally — eight yellow cards, four of them for dissent.

Saturday evening: I'm at home watching Leipzig v Borussia Mönchengladbach in the Bundesliga. Borussia are leading 2-1 when their forward Alassane Pléa protests loudly and gestures at referee Tobias

Stieler for not calling a foul. Stieler whistles to stop play and shows Pléa the yellow card. The striker looks aggrieved, makes a comment and two further dismissive gestures. Stieler shows him a second yellow card and he's off. I am on my feet applauding. Leipzig equalise and Pléa's stupidity has cost his team two points. And, who knows, possibly the Bundesliga title or a place in the Champions League.

Sunday afternoon: Men's friendly. Same speech as yesterday. The first half is peaceful, aside from the away coach once screaming out "Referee!" I ignore it. As we're lining up to start the second half, the home team's striker asks me if I watched the Leipzig-Mönchengladbach game. I tell him I did, and that Stieler's double-carding was exactly the kind of leadership we amateur referees have long been seeking from the top of the game. He smiles and nods and says he agrees.

In the second half, the away team's striker goes in the book for yelling at me after I've called a foul on him. "He's two metres tall!" he says, by way of justifying a deliberate elbow in the back of the player he fouled. You probably know this already, but there is nothing in the Laws of the Game that says you can foul a player just because they are two metres tall.

Then the away team coach screams at me again, while I'm on the other side of the field, having just called a foul in his team's favour. He wants a yellow card too. I walk deliberately across the pitch and show him one, seeing as he wants it so badly, and tell him to calm down. Then I turn around and walk deliberately back (his team is losing). At the end of the game, though, he doesn't mention it — just shakes my hand and thanks me.

Weekend tally — 12 cautions, six for dissent.

Monday morning: Tobias Stieler says that Uefa has demanded punishment for disrespectful gestures for years, "but in Germany, we've been a bit lenient. There has to be a change in behaviour." Because in amateur football, he adds, there have been too many attacks on referees, and the Bundesliga has to set an example.

Predictably, the Bundesliga's coaches are moaning about not being allowed to moan. The same dullard's arguments about "emotions" are aired once more. The sparrow-brained "TV expert" Lothar Matthäus demands that referees show more tact and restraint, but as the *Süddeutsche Zeitung* points out in its commentary, why is it always the referees that have to show tact and restraint? Why must football's anger and 'emotion' always be directed at the referee?

"For there to be a change in behaviour," the paper concludes, "a lot more referees have to be similarly persistent in applying the law — and then presumably a lot more players will be sent off. Unless they too can learn tact and restraint."

I hope that the rest of us referees — at all levels of the game — can follow Mr. Stieler's excellent example.

Saturday: 2-3 (8 x yellow)

Sunday: 3-0 (4 x yellow)

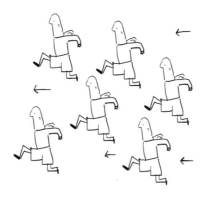

Chicken rush

As teams warm up for the resumption of competitive league play, there's a rash of men's friendlies as the players try to get back into shape following the winter break. Many coaches seem to have spent their break studying the masters, and have decided that the best way to approach the second half of the season is with a spanking new tactical system they ripped off an Internet Chalkboard of Football Wisdom.

In practice, this currently means following the vogue for Pressing and Gegenpressing. Game pattern: for the first five minutes, let the opposition pass the ball around the back four. Next 40 minutes, yell "Pressure!" and send the forwards and midfield into hectic spoiler mode. There follow about 600 changes of possession, and almost as many fouls, as decidedly amateur players attempt to implement The Klopp Doctrine. Instead of looking like European champions, though, the teams look like decapitated fowl in the farmyard after the puddles have frozen overnight. It's not so much Kick and Rush as Chicken Rush.

By half-time most of the players are knackered, and in the second half we see something approaching a normal game of amateur football, with space opening up, more chances created, and much less charging around like under-sexed hares on the first day of spring. I'd suggest that instead of playing the first half, both teams are sent on a 45-minute run to wear themselves out, then we just play the second half as normal. Let us pray that the Pressing Trend will soon suffer the same fate as Level 10 teams' poorly attempts at tiki-taka a few years back.

Wednesday's game was a classic example. The home side were clearly pumped up and full of a desire to prove ... something. What, exactly, I don't think even they were sure of. That the laws of physics still dictate if you run like a drunken buffalo into the back of another human being at speed, he will almost certainly be knocked to the ground? And that the person/buffalo who knocked him to the ground will then turn around to the referee with his arms outstretched to make the case for having made no contact at all?

I'd been assured before the game from both sides that "we all know each other", so there would be no bother, which is the equivalent of a huge red flag in a ring full of seething bulls. That is, thanks for the warning that I'll have to be on my toes for the whole 90 minutes. Sure enough, there are five yellow cards and shitloads of bad blood and even worse football, and that's just before half-time. "What's wrong with trying to play the ball? Why can't some of you at least try to do that?" I plead as we walk towards the dressing rooms. After half-time it becomes more of a game (see pattern above), and almost enjoyable. It's still a dirty game, right enough, but there's plenty to do, a couple of cracking goals, and virtually no dissent.

On Saturday, I referee two teams I've met before. After five years refereeing in the same city, faces become familiar, with the notorious Danny often the point of comical reference. On this day there are no cards, very few fouls (and certainly no bad ones), some jocose exchanges between players and referee, and absolutely not a hint of moaning about my decisions. It's a complete pleasure to run this game, but only an idiot would fool himself into thinking it can be like this every weekend.

Ten minutes before the end, the away team's right-back commits a tactical foul with his team already six goals down. I wave play on for advantage, but the attack eventually comes to nothing. The right back gives me a shit-eating grin as I turn to give him a reproachful look. "Surely a yellow card," murmurs a home player. "Definitely," I concur. "But not today."

Tuesday: 7-1 (4 x yellow)

Wednesday: 2-3 (7 x yellow)

Thursday: 1-3 (1 x yellow)

Saturday: 7-1 (no cards)

How to revolutionise the offside law

For amateur games where there are no neutral and qualified linesmen/ assistant referees, I propose that the International Football Association Board (IFAB) add the following clauses to Law 11, Offside:

- Any team that attempts to influence the referee's decision by appealing for offside, either verbally or through gestures such as raising an arm, automatically renders the opposing player in an onside position. In this way, the unsportsmanlike conduct of the defending team directly benefits the attacking team.

- All attempts to influence the referee's decision with regard to offside decisions shall be classified as unsporting conduct, and be punishable with a caution (or a ten-minute time penalty in leagues that operate sin-bins).

- Any protest from an attacking player deemed by the referee to be in an offside position will likewise be punishable with a caution.

This would be a radical change to the law, but it would make an immense difference to refereeing at the lowest levels of the game, where there is a serious lack of the necessary three match officials for the following two reasons:

- an increase in the verbal and physical abuse of referees, leading to a drastic fall in recruitment numbers

- the clubs themselves are not willing to pay for qualified ARs

Therefore, the clubs and players who have a direct influence on the number of available officials can not complain about such a law change.

They've brought it on themselves. Which brings me to last night's game, a classic example of players from both teams constantly leaning on me to give (or not give) offside decisions in their favour.

It was a friendly between a Level 8 team (a league without ARs) and a Level 7 team (a league with ARs). The former team should be used to playing without ARs, and behave accordingly. The latter can perhaps be given some leeway, as they would normally expect a linesman to be making the calls, but should still have been aware of the (for them) exceptional situation and granted *me* some leeway.

It's worth reiterating that a centre referee without ARs can only do their best to make a judgment call without being in line with play. You have to be looking in two directions at once — at the player with the ball, and at the last line of defence. In most cases, this is a physical impossibility. If the player with the ball is not being challenged by an opponent, it's much easier — you can already anticipate when they will pass and turn your head in the direction of the back line just as their foot is about to make contact with the ball. If they're being pressured, though, you have to focus on the player with the ball in case of an illegal challenge. In narrow situations, I lean towards giving the benefit of the doubt towards the attacking team, no matter how many lumpen centre-halves raise their arms and yell, "Offside!"

At times, there's a whole dialogue going on out there. Defenders are loudly yelling for offside, opponents are shouting back, "Never! Never!" Most of the time, they haven't a clue. Defenders are hoping I'm going to bail them out for their lack of speed and dodgy positional play, attackers of course want me to believe that their through-pass or run was perfectly timed. In the end, at least one party is going to be unhappy, and they will always let me know about it. Offside is the mother of amateur football's perpetual frustration.

At one point in the second half, I'm perfectly in line with the away team's defending line when the home team's number 24 receives the ball in an offside position. When I blow the whistle, he screams in my face, "What?!?" I show him the yellow card, in line with the new German FA guidelines on dissent. He's baffled by this. "But I only asked 'What'?" he says. "I didn't insult you." Gee, thanks. And by the way, insulting me would have been a straight red.

When shite teams started playing the offside trap in the 1970s, it was considered a tactical development. What a beautiful sight it was — four line-dancing, mud-spattered heifers moving forward as one, their arms in the air, negating entertainment and emptying stadiums. The IFAB could have snuffed it out back then by classifying such shenanigans as unsporting behaviour (and I'd love to hear anyone argue that this is not unsporting behaviour). It's thankfully no longer prevalent in the professional game, and VARs have rendered dissent on the matter almost obsolete at the top level (aside from the ludicrous micro-decisions made by computer — but that's another issue).

At the game's arse-end, however, we still have to put up with its inharmonious legacy. For the sake of peace and more advantage to the attacking team, we should at least experiment with the suggested law changes above.

As we come off the field, I explain to the number 24 why I showed him the yellow card. "All I did was ask," he reiterates. "Yes," I say, "and you did it in such a mild and polite fashion." We both laugh, and then embrace. I wish more games would end that way.

Final score: 5-3 (4 x yellow)

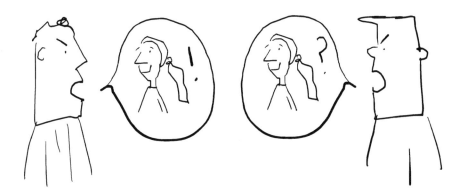

Your mother (yet again)

"If the poor, insulted mothers only knew how many fights they were responsible for instigating on the football fields of Germany every weekend … " So began one of my paragraphs in the disciplinary report that followed Sunday's U17 boys' game.

Call someone a 'bastard', and they might get shirty, but they don't scream, *"Are you saying my mum and dad weren't married when I was born?"* Call someone a wanker and they might be pissed off, but they don't get right in your face and yell, *"Are you implying that I indulge in acts of sexual self-gratification? ARE YOU?"* Yet call someone a son of a whore, and they immediately think that you are insulting their mother and freak out in her defence. This insult is apparently personal in a way that being a bastard or a wanker is not. I'm not saying any of these terms are acceptable on the football field (they're not), but this last one really seems to set the place on fire.

It's a relatively normal teenage boys' game. A bit of fouling, a bit of moaning (two yellows for dissent), millions of errors, and the occasional flash of football. With two minutes to go, the away team's leading 2-1 and on the attack. The home team's number 4 fouls the away team's 17, but not quite as heavily as the number 17 makes out when he goes down exclaiming and clutching his ankle (don't worry, dear reader, he's able to play on). A foul, but no yellow. At this point, though, his team-mate, the number 11, sees fit to start loudly reproaching the number 4 for his foul. I intervene, tell him that he has no business getting involved, and show him a yellow card for unsporting conduct. I suspect it's all a ruse to waste time while defending a narrow lead.

The game ends with no further goals or incidents, but right after the final whistle the dispute between the home number 4 and the away team's

11 escalates with a cascade of indignant shouts. I'm too far away to hear exactly what's said, but 'the mother insult' is in there somewhere (which party directed it, I've no idea), and before I can intervene for a second time, the number 11 hits the defender in the chest and knocks him to the ground. Both furious players are then held back by their team-mates, I show the number 11 a red card, get the number 4 to calm down, and eventually everyone returns to their changing rooms, all chuntering about how badly the other team has behaved.

All of this has become so routine now that it seems hardly worth recording. It's as tiresome and predictable as a toddler howling in its high chair and swiping its unwanted soup to the floor.

I know and like the away team's coach, and he's duly subdued and apologetic after the game. I'd spoken with both sets of players before kick-off about respecting my calls, and for the most part they'd kept it in check aside from the two flashes of dissent. But it seems there's nothing you can do when somebody insults somebody else's mother. The family honour must be defended. I can't help but feel, though, that most of these players don't really care that much about their mums, they're just using it as an alibi to behave like posturing, brainless cockerels.

"I recommend," I pompously conclude in my disciplinary report, "a lengthy ban, so that this young man can take his time to reflect on why he plays football at all." I'm sure that he will. While baking his mum a cake and treating her with the respect she deserves.

Final score: 1-2 (4 x yellow, 1 x red)

The art of communication

"Communication is the most important aspect of refereeing." It's an old guy, leaning on the surrounding barrier of the field where I've just reffed. We're watching the game following mine. I don't know if he's making a general comment, or if the comment's specifically aimed at me. Either way, I spent a lot of Sunday's game talking with players, right from the moment I arrived at the clubhouse. Here are some of the different ways that an amateur referee communicates with the two teams over the course of the three hours spanning our arrival to an occasionally embittered departure.

Pre-game

1. *Introduce yourself.* On arrival, seek out both coaches, shake their hands and smile. Greet players just arriving or already warming up, strike up a conversation if the chance arises. No one wants an aloof authoritarian in charge of their game. As a player, I hated refs who thought they were too good for Sunday league. Let the teams know you'd very much like their team line-ups confirmed online 30 minutes before kick-off. If they're having problems, especially before evening kick-offs when many players are rushing to arrive from work, show that you're flexible, but start to look less flexible as kick-off approaches.

2. *Make known your expectations.* Chat with the players about what you expect from today's game as they line up to run out on to the field. You are naturally anticipating a fair and sporting encounter. You do not want to hear any loud yelling and dissent in your direction, especially with regard to offside decisions (dream on). On Sunday, I told the teams that we would not be shaking hands before or after the game due to an official directive on Coronavirus. That led to grins

all round. When this happens, smile back and show you think such directives are just as ridiculous as the players do. Even though you think the directive is the very least we should be doing ahead of a looming pandemic.

At the centre circle, you and the two captains are the three adults in the room. Inform them that if there's a major outbreak of trouble, you'll be talking to them and asking them to help calm any given situation. (This brilliant policy only breaks down when it turns out that the captain is a bigger arsehole than all his team-mates put together.)

During the game

1. *Talk, but don't dominate the conversation.* A small handful of refs are a real pain and never stop talking during the game. Again, from a player's point of view I found this really annoying. Don't make yourself the centre of attention. It's important to let them know you're there, though — tell them that you're not happy with that early challenge, and that's not the way things are going to be today. The same applies to dissent: "Hey, what did I tell you just before kick-off?" No need to show a card straightaway, unless it's a really extreme case (an absolute gift for refs that helps them set the tone) — just remind them of your guidelines.

2. *Pre-empting dissent.* Explain decisions, either verbally or using hand gestures, to pre-empt, for example, the indignant right-back's incredulous question, "What was that for?" after he's just brutally up-ended the other team's tricky left-winger. One of my favoured responses to this question is, "You fouled him three different ways, which one do you want me to give it for?" An exaggeration, but it always ends the discussion.

3. *Admit your errors.* In the first half, the home team played a ball towards a forward who was clearly offside. He looked like he was going to play the ball, but then left it for an onside team-mate running through, but I'd already whistled — too early. Cue much shouting (though the first forward was arguably interfering with play), so I apologised for whistling too early and owned the error. This led to immediate de-escalation. When it doesn't, you can say, "I already said sorry, what more do you want?" The 'more' being a yellow card for dissent.

4. *Chat with players*, without getting involved in long conversations. On Sunday, the home team's number 19 was pushed over near the sideline and I whistled for the free-kick. As he stood up, he remonstrated loudly about the player who'd fouled him. "I whistled and gave the foul, so get on with the game," I said. He still moaned on, so I said, "You've not exactly been an angel today, have you?" He smiled for the first time all afternoon and said, "That's true."

Like the player who'd fouled him, he'd already had a yellow card. His team-mate in the centre of defence also complained about me not calling a foul after a tussle with an opposing forward who then narrowly shot wide. "I'm sorry you lost out in the fight for the ball," I told him. (There's a 50-50 chance that any defender who's just been outplayed will claim that he was fouled.)

5. *Involve the captains.* Remember that centre-circle chat at the coin toss? In the second half, I asked the away team's captain to have a word with his number 2, who'd already been booked, and was sailing close to a second yellow. I'd talked with the player myself, but the captain backed me up and told him to cut out the fouls. Which he (just about) did. I really don't like sending players off, especially in a game that — while feisty — didn't turn nasty.

Post-game

1. *Don't seek out conversation*, especially with the losing team. Wait for players to approach you, for whatever reason, while noting down the game score and the time of the final whistle. A rarity in this game, though — the away team forward on the losing side, who'd also seen a yellow card for delaying a restart, congratulated me on a good game, and he wasn't even being sarcastic.

2. *In the clubhouse.* Once you've filed your game report, showered and changed into civvies, then 20-30 minutes distance can be a good time to chat about the game if there are any issues. As it happened, I picked up my expenses from the home team player who'd got clattered at the halfway line five minutes before the final whistle. I hadn't called the foul, because I'd played advantage — his pass went to a team-mate, who in turn played his outside right through on goal, and he finished in the far corner. This turned out to be the winner in a seven-goal thriller. I went back and apologised to the player, and said I had been so intent on following the play that I'd missed who'd fouled him, even though the foul had been worthy of a yellow card. The goal salved his hurt. After the game, we laughed about the incident, and then talked for a long time about the ethics of amateur sport and the thankless task of refereeing in general.

All in all, an enjoyable afternoon using language to try and tread the fine line between showing all involved that, while you are a legitimate member of the human race, you're not going to take any shit either.

Wednesday: 0-3 (4 x yellow)

Sunday: 4-3 (6 x yellow)

Is it too late
to say we're sorry?

"Boys, every manifestation of dissent and unsportsmanlike behaviour will be punished with a yellow card, in line with the new German FA guidelines." All four teams nod — two on Saturday (U17) and two on Sunday (U19). Neither game is especially well or poorly behaved. The fact I barely notice a total of 13 yellow cards across the two matches (two cautions for dissent, two for foul play, nine for unsportsmanlike conduct) perhaps reflects how immune I've become to this city's lousy sporting culture.

I reffed Sunday's home team last month, and it didn't end well (see 'Punishing dissent'). I gave a penalty against their goalkeeper when he charged out of his goal in a one-on-one with the opposing team's striker. He cleared the ball first, laid out the striker second (he needed treatment). Despite the screams of, "He played the ball!" I stuck with the decision and yellow-carded the keeper (one of the few who didn't protest). The penalty was converted and the home team lost 2-3, and for the remainder of the game they moaned and fouled and then deliberately left the key to my changing room out on the field, so I had to walk back for it.

Imagine my delight when I'm assigned to officiate them again just a few weeks later. The two adult coaches must have discussed this too. They had also been vociferous on the touchline both before and after the penalty, but I'd ignored them. Today they are much more conciliatory, and before the match offer me a full, unreserved apology for both their own and their team's behaviour at our last meeting. I thank them for the apology, but also reiterate why I gave the penalty, and why I'd give it again. I do concede that it was a tight game at the top of the table, that emotions were running high, and that not every referee would have awarded the penalty. "That's no excuse," says one of the coaches. "We should be better than that." Indeed.

226

I wonder when I'd have received their apology if I hadn't been refereeing their team again. Only a cynic, though, would question why they've waited five weeks until today and then, half an hour before kick-off, become contrite enough to express their regrets at having been such shitty, unsporting role models last time around.

The team's captain also apologises after the coin toss. During the game, you can see what an immense effort it's costing them to keep quiet every time I give a decision that doesn't go their way. They concede another penalty, this time it's two defenders hacking away at an opposing forward, and there's no quarrel with the call because there's nothing to dispute (not that this will necessarily stop someone moaning). However, the number 14 who was carded for dissent last time around comes on as a sub and can't stop himself from whining yet again when he flattens the away team's right winger. Another yellow for yelling. They play very poorly against a team they beat 8-0 earlier in the season and lose 3-1, and only the captain shakes my hand at the final whistle. Rather than shouting at the ref, they'd ended up moaning at each other.

Saturday's game starts with a quiet first half and no cautions, but — as happens again and again — the second sees a dramatic upturn in mediocre conduct. No fewer than three players are booked for kicking the ball away to prevent a quick free-kick from being taken. You'd think after the first time that players would take this on board, but apparently not.

The great thing about giving a yellow for this offence is the indignant reaction of the player. Along the lines of, "But all I did was kick the ball away!" Absolutely, you chump, what a stupid fucking thing to get a yellow card for. Now, who was it who kicked the ball away? Was it me, the referee, or was it you, the player?

On Saturday morning, I was coaching my U9 team. Three fathers of players on the opposing team were standing behind the goal their sons were defending, bellowing useless instructions throughout. Their coach was a quiet type. "Quite some extra backing you've got there," I said after a few minutes, hoping he'd go over and tell them to shut the fuck up. "Heh, yeah," was the response, and that was it. One of my own dads was 'coaching' there too (though not so vehemently), perhaps encouraged by the three idiots, until I walked across and said, "Remember, no instructions." He apologised and moved away. He tries it every game, like he thinks I'm not going to notice.

Oh, Gods of football, please give me the strength to continue. Or, even better, the strength to give it all up.

Saturday: 3-2 (8 x yellow)

Sunday: 1-3 (5 x yellow)

Note: The 2019-20 season was cut short in March due to the first lockdown of the pandemic. The following season began on time, but was suspended at the end of October 2020 and only resumed the following June, when pre-season friendlies for the 2021-22 season were officially classified as being part of the season, which ended on June 30. Got that? Okay, back to the cut and thrust.

SEASON 2020-21

CACOPHONY, REVENGE AND GETTING BOOED OFF THE PARK

Captain Opinion

It's the first half of my first game for almost six months, and the away team's captain is yelling at me. He went in late after an opposing defender cleared the ball upfield, and as the pass went astray, I blew for a free-kick. I don't know why the captain's so mad at the call and I don't much care, but I tell him firmly that there's no point in dissent during my games. It should be a yellow, but it's a friendly and we've all been out of action for a long time, so I leave it at a lecture. Call it Covid-related leniency.

Around 28 players take the field for tonight's game in all, and only one has a problem with my refereeing. In the second half, it's the mouthy captain again who complains at great length that a goal his team just conceded was "clearly offside" (it wasn't). As usual, his authoritative view of the play comes from the other side of the field. This time, I show him the yellow card and he can't believe it. He's the captain, for goodness sake. He's allowed to criticise the referee, and the referee has to be man enough to take his criticism on board.

While writing his number down I tell him that the rules explicitly state the exact opposite — namely, that there's no special dispensation for the captain when it comes to poor behaviour on the field*. This is underscored five minutes later when he goes in late on an opponent with a straight leg tackle. Second yellow and off, and his protests are even louder. My refereeing's laughable, I'm a joke, etc. He gets into a verbal spat with an opponent who tries to reason otherwise. Eventually he leaves and his tired team collapse and lose 6-1. He sits in a sulk on the touchline glaring at the game. It's possible he's reflecting on how he let his team down, both as a captain and a player, and promising himself to be more disciplined in the future. But it's much more likely that he's blaming the shit ref for ruining the game and his team's no doubt otherwise meticulous pre-season preparation.

The next evening, I'm reffing a fast and exciting boys' U19 game. Again, there's very little trouble all night except from another captain — this time on the home team. At the coin toss he'd refused to say a word of welcome to either myself or his opposite number, let alone crack any hint of a smile or even meet my eye. Fine, he's obviously psyched up for the game and very intense. Yet that intensity translates into a moaning monologue when his co-defender goes in hard on the opposing winger and brings him down just outside the penalty area. I blow for the free-kick, no one else even blinks at the call, but Captain Opinion has to have his say until I interrupt him and tell him to zip it.

How did I shape up after the six-month enforced lay-off? I've been running plenty, but haven't sprinted for a long time. In the first game, I notice that I'm off the play a few times, caught out by the long ball tactics of both teams, who are lower-division hackers. The second, where the technical and fitness levels are much higher, is easier to telegraph and keep pace with — it's faster, but more enclosed. It's no profound revelation to say that it's fantastic to be back out on the field. A couple of captains aside, most of the players obviously feel the same way.

Tuesday: 6-1 (3 x yellow, 1 x yellow-red)

Wednesday: 0-3 (2 x yellow)

* Law 3, Clause 10: "Team Captain. The team captain has no special status or privileges but has a degree of responsibility for the behaviour of the team."

The revenge foul

Wednesday night: Sometimes you know when a player is out to get back at an opponent. The 'revenge foul' is a particularly hard one to prevent, and short of following the aggrieved player around and shouting 'No foul! No foul!' as they head towards the play, there's usually not a lot you can do. In my first game of the weekend, there's a brutal revenge foul that comes out of nowhere, conducted with the efficiency and cynicism of a Kremlin-backed assassin.

Early in the second half there's a tussle in midfield, and a home player comes away with the ball. The away team's number 9, who's just come into the game at half-time, complains that he's been fouled, but I see it differently and let play continue. A few seconds later I have to stop play as the number 9 is now in a shouting match with several players from the home team. I don't catch exactly what's said, but I show him a yellow for unsporting conduct and invite him to keep his mouth shut for the rest of the game and play football instead (which, to be fair, he does).

A couple of minutes later, the same number 9 receives a pass in the centre circle. The home team's number 11, presumably upset by whatever the number 9 had said to him, rushes in at him from behind with a straightened leg and takes him out at the ankles. The number 9 falls in pain to the floor (he goes off for treatment, but returns to the game later). I blow with all the authority vested in me by the powers of Fifa, pull out the red card from my back pocket, and the number 11 turns and leaves without the hint of a complaint. Honour satisfied, or something, though it could easily have been a broken leg.

There are four further yellows in a nasty, foul-plagued game where the home team launches a thousand long balls high into the sky, with no appreciable result. They sub out seven players at half-time and I say to the new players lining up to give me their numbers, "I'd have done the same the way your team's played so far." They don't seem to find that very funny — critical comments are a one-way street, apparently, mainly directed at my offside calls. Most of the spectators opt to turn their backs on the second half and watch the Inter Milan-Sevilla game on the big screen outside the clubhouse. Good choice, and I wish I could join them.

Saturday: I coach a young ref doing his second game, at U13 level. He's an ambitious, bright and communicative lad who's extremely keen to learn, and already comfortable with a whistle in his hand. Both sets of coaches behave impeccably, and the home club is very welcoming. The afternoon is an absolute pleasure.

Sunday: Another pre-season friendly. On two occasions, opponents square up to each other, about nothing much, nose to nose, eye to eye. One's about a throw-in. Both times, I yellow-card both players. The second time, I'm busy noting down the players' names when the home team resumes play without waiting for my whistle. I give it a blast and yell, "Hey, we had to stop play because these two idiots behaved like morons, and now I have to write their numbers down, so can you just wait?" Play stops and they all look suitably sheepish.

The home team go ahead when I play advantage following a late tackle in midfield. It's always the same — the fouled player yells 'Hey!' as he goes down, gets up, and then starts remonstrating with me even as I'm waving play on towards the goal. Then, GOAL! "Well fucking played, ref! You absolute God of the fucking whistle!" In my fantasies, but in reality they're too busy congratulating the goalscorer, who was one of the players booked for idiocy.

I talk to him after the game. He concedes the yellow card was correct, and that the advantage call was a pretty damned good one. He's a nice bloke. Off the field, they nearly always are.

Wednesday: 0-3 (4 x yellow, 1 x red)

Saturday: 2-2 (no cards)

Sunday: 3-1 (4 x yellow)

Offside by a whole Peter Crouch

There's an old fellow behind the away team's goal during Saturday's game, and he's angry at me about an offside call. How he could see that the call was wrong from behind the goal is anybody's guess. He shouts that I'm a waste of time, and backs up his conviction with dramatic arm gestures. There are three ways to respond to this: 1. Ignore him. He's obviously craving attention, so don't grant him the pleasure of thinking you're bothered. 2. Move towards the moron, kneel down and then blow him an extravagantly choreographed kiss. 3. Move towards the moron and say, "I'm standing on this side of the barrier because I love football. You're standing on the other side of it because all you've got is a big trap."

I only thought of options two and three after the game, but that's probably just as well. Ignoring him was the best policy. After the game I walk right past him to see if he has the courage to berate me face to face, but he's gone all quiet. Perhaps his anger has dissipated and been replaced by the gnawing existential dread of his own mortality, fuelled by a sense of futility at the idea of protesting offside decisions during a boys' U15 football game. Whatever it is, I reserve the right to engage options 2 and 3 at some future point of conflagration.

There had been a loud yell from the spectator area during the first half about a different offside situation — one where I'd allowed the away team to play on after a well-timed through ball. After the play was over — it didn't result in a goal — came the after-shout that the player had been "two metres" offside. The next day, during a men's game, I hear the same claim in an identical situation that leads to the only goal of the afternoon.

This time it comes from a defender. "He was two metres off!" This is the default length for offside rebuttals — it's never 10 centimetres, or even half a metre. It has to be two metres, to stress the utter gaping wrongness of the decision. As if, when the ball was played, you could have perfectly slotted Peter Crouch into the space between the attacker and the second-to-last defender.

In Sunday's case, the away team's red-faced number 3 had been lagging, and so he played the attacker on. The same defender loses possession a few minutes later, but is bailed out by his keeper diving at the feet of the forward. Then his keeper rescues him a second time with a fingertip save from a miscued clearance. He is having a bad afternoon, and it's clear whose fault this is - the referee's. Every foul he commits, he bellyaches. Every time he's dispossessed or loses out in a challenge, he claims that he was fouled. Every denied offside appeal is disputed until he talks himself into a yellow card — the only one of the afternoon in an otherwise manageable game.

"When the ball was played, the attacker was still onside," I explain to him with a hint of impatience. He gives me that ironic smile, like I can't possibly know what I'm talking about, then shakes his head and refutes the call anyway. "Really," I say, "that's a law you should probably know as a defender. If you don't, then you're in the wrong position." Like most lumbering back-liners, his constant offside appeals are merely a cry for help in the face of his declining pace. Or a denial that it's time for him to step down to the reserves.

Sunday's host club treat me like all home teams should — the coach greets me by name, makes sure I have coffee and water, and asks me several times if I need anything. We have a nice pre-game chat about the club and its place in the medieval wine town on the banks of the Rhine where we're fortunate enough to be playing football on a beautiful afternoon.

At half-time, the same coach asks me if I have everything I need, in the same friendly tone. "I'm fine, thanks," I say. "But I could do without the hysterical screaming from the touchline — once about an offside, another about a handball." Honestly, you wouldn't think he was the same man who'd just been doing that. He mutters an apology and says, "Okay." In the second half, he yells one more time about a corner kick call (undisputed by any players), and I turn to him with a WTF shrug. He stops himself, smiles and makes his own mouth-zipping gesture, and all is good.

Afterwards, there's a bratwurst and some post-game analysis. Aside from these superfluous outbursts and the bullish number 3, a perfect afternoon's sport.

Saturday: 0-2 (3 x yellow)

Sunday: 1-0 (1 x yellow)

We need The Slits and The Raincoats

I've reffed two boys' U19 games over the past few days — one cup tie, and one league game — and have finally come to realise that these games will never be quiet. I took a friend, Frank, to the first game and said to him, "The chances of there being no cards tonight are about one per cent." As a former player in the GDR youth system, Frank was not at all fazed by the intensity of the game, and thought the seven yellow cards plus one five-minute time penalty and a red card were just about right.

Putting 22 adolescent boys on a limited rectangle of ground and letting them all compete at the same time for a single round leather ball is never going to lead to group yoga and 90 minutes of wellness therapy. As the sole controlling factor, the referee has to reckon in advance with high testosterone levels and inevitable frustration, aggression and foul play. The trick is always finding the balance between lenience and punishment, as well as hitting the right tone when it comes to keeping the players in check and focused on the game

In these two games, I was gifted ideal situations in the first half that allowed me to assert my authority — both times, two opponents squared up to each other following a battle for the ball and exchanged words, while around them team-mates began to yell and join in the excitement and general shoving. There's nothing in the rule book about dealing with such situations, and all refs will have their own way of de-escalating the stramash. Here's my own guide:

1. Don't run towards the conflagration, unless you're really far away — it gives the impression that you're part of the general panic and not

really in control. Walk up firmly and wait until you're close by before blowing your whistle, very loudly. In 99 cases out of 100, that will be the signal for the peripheral players to peel back and for the nonsense to be curbed. It's actually what they're waiting for.

2. Separate the combatants, if they haven't already separated themselves (often they'll run off, so keep a close eye on their shirt numbers). Take a few steps back and command them to come towards you for a short audience, away from all the other players. What's going to be in your short lecture? I've tried various things down the years, but my current favourite is this: "So, are we done with all the macho posturing now?" The players nod, and may even apologise, as they did in yesterday's game. "Pack it in and play football if you want to stay on the pitch." Firm tone, no yelling, then a yellow card each. Get them to shake or bump hands.

The two incidents didn't make the games any less aggressive in sporting terms, but certainly stopped any further squaring-up and chest-beating. Of course, there's nothing you can do if it *does* all kick off on a grand scale (apart from abandoning the game and walking off). Most of the time, though, you're in that crisis prevention mode. When 17- and 18-year-old boys are running full pelt into each other while disputing possession of an elusive object, there will be collateral grievance. Our job is keeping a lid on that, and now that I've worked out how, I've mainly come to enjoy reffing these matches.

Some other takeaways from Games 8-10:

* *Noise from the bench*: There was a lot of moaning from the away benches during both games, but also quite large crowds for this level (60-70 spectators), so I opted to tune out the complaints. A couple of times there were lengthy questions from the bench as I was waiting for free kicks to be taken close by. There's a feeling of liberation when you ask yourself, "Do I bother trying to answer that, or just ignore it?" — and then you just ignore it and run away with the action. Sorry, mate, I'm concentrating on the game.

* *Coaches don't know the rules 1*: One assistant coach (claiming to be a referee too), after his team had won 6-2 and been awarded two penalties, came to complain that they hadn't had a third penalty. Indeed, his player had been fouled, but the ball ran straight to a team-mate in a prime scoring position on the edge of the six-yard box. He then hesitated for too long and his shot was blocked by a defender. Did I not know that in the penalty area, when you play advantage and no goal occurs, then you have to call back the play and still award a penalty? No, I did not know about that rule, mainly because that rule does not exist.

* *Coaches don't know the rules 2*: In Sunday's game, the away team's number 7 is on a yellow for having deliberately upended the home team's

tricky winger in the penalty box. Later, he charges from the wall at a direct free-kick well before the opponent's kicked it, and thus blocks the shot with his arse. I blow for a re-take, and he complains, so I send him out for the five-minute time penalty. His coach wails that you can't send someone off the field for a time penalty "just" for blocking a free-kick. Yes, I can, and if you add the dissent then it would be a third offence — consider yourself lucky it's not a red.

* *Disrespect*: On Saturday evening I ref a women's game. The club's over-30s team (men) have just finished and head straight for the bar behind the goal, blasting out shite techno music and sing-along *deutschrock* for the next two hours. There's sarcastic cheering and comments when the ball's down that end. As they drink more, the comedy scale sinks from 'desperately unfunny' to 'fucking depressing'. None of the players or their coaches complain, though, so I ignore them — I've no desire to interact with two dozen inebriated twats on top of my other duties. I just hope that the women show up at one of the men's games soon and start getting wasted while cranking up the speakers to The Au Pairs, X-Ray Spex, The Slits and The Raincoats. I'm sure the lads wouldn't mind.

Wednesday: 2-6 (7 x yellow, 1 x time penalty, 1 x red)

Saturday: 0-4 (no cards)

Sunday: 9-1 (6 x yellow, 2 x time penalty)

Straight red, no complaints

I don't want to show the away team's right-back the red card. It's the 93rd minute, the game's as good as over and his side is leading 3-0. Prior to that, he'd been one of the few players to show that it's possible to defend well, but without fouling your opponent in every second challenge. Frankly, there are half a dozen other players on the field I'd rather see head for an early shower.

But, but, but ... a few seconds earlier he and the home team's number 11 had been chasing a long through-ball played out to the left. The winger had, for once, just beaten him to the ball and poked it ahead, ready for a clear run on goal. The right-back arrived a second too late and clattered the number 11 to the ground. Brutal foul play and the denial of a clear goalscoring opportunity — take your pick. With a rueful expression, I pull out the red card and he accepts the decision without any protest at all.

Afterwards, he comes to the changing room to apologise, and to tell me that he's already said sorry to his opponent, who was injured but — thankfully — not seriously. I tell him that I was sorry to show him red after he'd had such a good game, and that I knew the foul was not intentional. That would all be reflected in the disciplinary report, as well as his apology, with a recommendation for the shortest possible suspension. It's one of the evening's more pleasant verbal exchanges. Because the home team are what we in refereeing circles call a BOMB — explosive, and a Bunch Of Moaning Bastards to boot. As I was writing up a disciplinary report anyway, I decided to give them a special mention:

"The home team spent the entire game complaining in almost knee-jerk fashion at every single decision that didn't go their way. Three players and the coach saw yellow for dissent, and that was lenient. It's as if the only fun they get out of football is to moan at or yell at the referee. Although the club officials are amiable and friendly, the players seem to follow the poor example set on the touchline by their hysterically screaming coach."

An example — following a long goal-kick taken by the away team, a home team player close to me screams that an opponent is offside. I point out that you can't be offside from a goal kick. His reaction? To laugh out loud and call my refereeing pathetic.

Second example — an away team fouls a home player, and I immediately whistle for the free-kick. A home team player just yells, "Heeeeeeey!" right in my face, as though I've either fouled the player myself, or refused to recognise the blatant foul. I show him the yellow card, and one of his team-mates yells, "But we all want to go to work tomorrow!" I ask him how that justifies his team-mate screaming in my face. He calms down and runs away. In football, when you peel away the anger there's never any substance beneath the bluster and rage.

All in all, it's a vile game with little decent football played, on one of those old plastic pitches with no give and more bounce than hailstones on a rubber roof. I go to pick up my changing room key from the drinks stand. "Thanks, ref, sorry it was a bit stressful," the club official says with a cheery smile. It's such a breezy under-statement that I can't help bursting into laughter, along with all the men of a certain age who are hanging out there. Despite a shit evening, I immediately feel a lot better and snicker all the way back to my changing room.

My bike's got a puncture right now, but it's a mild evening so I walk home listening to the new Throwing Muses LP. An away team player spots me from his car and stops to offer me a lift. I thank him and politely decline — with games like this I need an hour to decompress. I know I didn't have a good game tonight, and need to get my head together for the next one in just 24 hours. Same city, same division, same kind of young men in their 20s. But hopefully no more BOMBs going off ...

Final score: 0-3 (7 x yellow, 1 x red)

Noisy neighbours

There are three kinds of neighbours: 1. the ones you get along with, maybe even become friends with 2. the ones you ignore, and who ignore you in return (maybe they're weird. Maybe you're the weirdo) 3. the ones you fall out with over some issue (loud music after 10pm, a barking dog, a dog that shits on your lawn ...) that seems trivial to outsiders, but which possesses you more than you'd be prepared to admit. Neighbours are like relatives — you can't choose them, and there's only a certain number you're going to get along with.

These teams are neighbours. They share the same pitches, while their clubhouses lie 50 metres apart, separated by the changing rooms and the toilet block. It doesn't get more 'derby' than this. Do they get along? I check the records for the last time they met, late last year. There were 11 yellows and a red card. So, probably not much.

I talk to the home team's chairman before the game and ask him how things stand in the hood. "Er, not so good right now. We took three of their players over the summer." Spectators will be segregated down separate sides of the field, with two stewards on each touchline. I tell the stewards before kick-off that I want to know about any kind of insult or swearing aimed at anyone on the field. The only problem, though, is the smell of weed coming from three young lads on a bench that wafts across the field during the first half. Smoking's supposed to be banned at the ground, so I point it out to the stewards and they take care of it.

Maybe a bit more intoxicating smoke from the touchlines would have chilled the players. There's no trans-club loving in this game. After a fairly mild first few minutes, things start to escalate. Between the 23rd and the 28th minute, I show five yellow cards (four of them either for squaring-up, or for angry off-the-ball shoving of an opponent), and deliver two stern lectures about the downside to idiocy. It just about works and I manage to keep the game under control. It's a good game, too. At half-time the score stands at 2-2, and the 100 or so fans are vocally involved, but not in a bad way.

The difference between this and last night's game is the level of dissent. Tonight there's almost none, and I can sell my decisions even when there are instinctive protests. When there's constant moaning, it grates on your confidence and leads to bad calls — the players can probably sense your insecurity and exploit it without mercy. But when the players accept your decisions and get on with it, you feel vindicated and on top of things. Although there are five more yellows in the second half, and way too many fouls, it's a really enjoyable, fast game with some decent football amid the general animosity.

The home team wins 4-2 thanks to two late goals, and they're suitably triumphant. There's a post-match dispute on the field, but the players take care of it themselves just as I walk over to check what's happening. Ten cautions (five for each team), but that's a decent price for successful management of the game.

After filing the match report, I go to the home team's clubhouse and ask to speak to the number 10, who scored two goals — including the go-ahead goal at 3-2. He also received one of the yellow cards — a likeable but quite volatile character. I'm pointed towards the home team's changing room, where he's sitting with a beer, still in his kit. Everyone looks very serious when I come in. What can the referee possibly want with us now? "I just wanted to say that I put your second goal down as an own goal, is that okay?" I tell the number 10. His face contorts, he lets out a yell of protest and demands to know why. "Well, it took a deflection," I say with a straight face (it did, but only a minor one). His team-mates catch on, though, and start to laugh. His relief allows him to break into laughter too. Party atmosphere restored.

On my way out, I cycle past the 'away' team's clubhouse. The lights are on, but it's extremely quiet. Despite the noisy neighbours, it looks like they're ready to turn in for an early night.

Final score: 4-2 (10 x yellow)

Ejecting an adult
from a youth game

At all games, the German FA requires that the home team names one person who's responsible for order and civilised/sporting behaviour. Most of the time, thankfully, it's not an issue. Just occasionally, though, that person needs to step up when there's trouble among the spectators. Except that they rarely do, unless you specifically instruct them. Sometimes even then, as on Saturday's game at the 'Friends of Sport', they still do nothing. Here's a redacted version of the disciplinary report I sat up typing until 1am on Sunday morning:

"In the 75th minute of an extremely quiet game, the home team's number 7 was attacking the ball in the away team's penalty area. The away team's goalkeeper reached the ball first and cleared it out for a throw-in. The number 7's momentum caused him to collide with the goalkeeper, who was briefly injured, but able to play on.

"A number of home team spectators were standing in this corner of the field, directly in front of the action [it was the only shady spot]. During the game they'd protested loudly about any decisions given against their team — superfluous hysteria with its base in ignorance, but all part of the game. After the collision described above, some of these fans believed the home team was due a penalty. A man around 40-45 years old, of normal build and wearing jeans and a white t-shirt, began to loudly swear at and threaten the away team's goalkeeper. There was talk of a fight after the game, and something to do with the keeper's father — I didn't catch the exact words because I was ordering the home team's trainer and his assistant (listed on the team sheet as the chief steward responsible for keeping order), who were standing next to the spectators, to eject the spectator from the field.

Because they declined to take any action at all, and because the situation was urgent, I myself ordered the spectator to leave. He walked towards the ground's exit, but while walking behind the away team's goal he continued to swear at and threaten the young goalkeeper.

"The game continued with a throw-in, but a minute later I noticed that the spectator in question, instead of leaving, had walked around to the spectator area in front of the clubhouse. Here he greeted an acquaintance and then stood with two other men behind the spectator's fence, again insulting the away team's goalkeeper. I stopped the game, walked over to him and ordered him to leave the field a second time. Now it was my turn to be on the receiving end of his insults — I was a shit ref etc. While walking towards the exit, he repeatedly flipped me the finger. Then he started to head back towards the away team goal but I followed him and insisted he completely leave the premises, which he finally did.

"During this entire episode I received not a breath of support from the home team. The steward responsible for order, Herr Hxxxx, remained completely passive. The game was stopped for three minutes, later added as injury time.

"The away team's coach told me after the game that the ejected spectator was notorious for causing trouble at this club. It was clear that he is well known at the home club. But nobody there wanted to let on that they knew him. The home coach wanted me to believe that he 'hadn't noticed anything was happening' (!). Standing in front of the changing rooms, I asked the two home team coaches if the man was the father of one of the players, but they both refused to look me in the eye and answer the question — there was just silence. Feeling extremely annoyed, I returned to my dressing room — five minutes later, the coach came and told me that he'd 'asked around', and then gave me the spectator's name. He was unwilling or unable to give me more details.

"I am still angry, shocked and baffled that a spectator at a youth team game could conduct himself in such a crass, unsporting, insulting, slanderous and threatening manner, and not a single club official or grown-up intervened. For me, that is an absolute disgrace."

Sunday's game was a complete contrast. On the last day of summer, I cycled out on one of the ancient European trade routes (now a cycle and walking path) to a village where the club immediately welcomed me, and continued to make me feel welcome until I left several hours later. It was a hard-fought Level 8 men's game with 95 paying spectators in a woodland setting on an actual grass field. The players got on with the game instead of moaning at me. Spectators sought me out afterwards to thank me, and to chat about the game and refereeing in general. I cycled home with a view of the sun setting in the west.

Saturday: 1-5 (2 x yellow)

Sunday: 4-1 (6 x yellow)

Cacophonous flak

"Why on earth didn't you award us a penalty when their goalkeeper fouled our forward?" I'm chatting with the home team's coach after the game. He's smiling, he's friendly, and it's a perfectly reasonable question. If his team had been given the penalty and converted it, they'd have likely taken all three points against the league leaders, instead of just one.

I tell him the truth. That I didn't see it. That at the exact moment the forward was dribbling around the goalkeeper, my view was suddenly blocked by a retreating defender. The next thing I knew, both keeper and forward were on the floor, the ball had rolled out of play, and the home team and all their fans were appealing for a penalty. Although, it has to be said, they weren't appealing for the penalty with 100% conviction. I pointed towards the corner flag. Cue much jeering from the crowd, incredulity from the 'fouled' forward. A corner kick may have been the right decision, but it may well not have. It could have been a goal kick. Or it could have been a penalty.

"Hey, it happens," he says, patting me on the back. "You had a great game anyway." Which is nice of him to say, but it isn't true (more on that later). Even if that had been my only error, it was a match-deciding error. While running towards the away team's goal, I should have been able to get myself into a position to see what was about to happen. I should have taken into account a retreating defender suddenly blocking my view.

Still, telling the home coach what really happened is good for my conscience, rather than making up some bollocks that I had definitely seen the goalkeeper play the ball. I immediately feel better after the confession, helped by the fact that the coach is so nice about it. The home team then offer me food and drink, and I hang around to watch the first half of the next game — a Level 6 encounter, staffed by the full contingent of three referees.

I look at the two linesmen with some envy. The other reason I feel like I had a poor game today is down to offside — the away team's bench and its forwards screamed in outrage at least four times during the second half about offside calls. At first, you just think it's their frustration. Then your confidence is undermined and you severely start to doubt yourself. Am I getting these calls wrong?

The home team's forwards generally timed their runs from deep, and were running through on to the passes after the ball was played. The away team forwards were standing in offside positions when the ball was played, waiting for it rather than running on to it. Yet so loud and indignant were their protests that I began to wish for only one thing — assistant referees whose main job it is to make that judgment. When that flag is raised, they take all the attention, all the cacophonous flak.

I mentioned this to the away coach after the game, but he's less accommodating than his counterpart. He's also not having my explanation about how the home team beat his team's offside trap. One call, he claims, was "five metres" out. That is, he wants me to believe that his forward was five metres onside when the ball was played. If that's really true, I should probably quit refereeing altogether.

After a couple of these mass tantrums, the temptation is just to let play run, even though I was sure that the player receiving the ball was offside. But I wasn't going to succumb to that kind of pressure and so braced myself for the collective outrage each time I blew the whistle. Appeasement in the face of intimidation would be another reason to quit refereeing altogether.

As I'm leaving the ground just before half-time of the Level 6 game, there's a ball played forward to the home team's winger down by the corner flag. The linesman raises his flag for offside. And how do the home fans around me react? They're mad as hell, all yelling at the linesman that he got it wrong. So in fact it makes no difference having linesmen. It just means that somebody different gets the abuse of the players, coaches and crowd — all of whom, of course, have seen the situation much clearer and more correctly than the one person actually qualified to judge.

Final score: 1-1 (7 x yellow)

Ejecting a coach
from a youth game

Boys' U19, City Cup, quarter-final. It's as fast and physical as you'd expect, but a good game. I'm enjoying it, until the home bench starts up, shouting about every tiny decision. I raise my fingers to my lips to make it clear that I would like them to pipe down — their conduct is completely out of place. The players are not fouling much, and not complaining at all. Still things escalate, and once again I'm just going to translate the (redacted) disciplinary report, which not only describes the behaviour of the home coaches, but explicitly asks when the state FA is finally going to fucking well do something about it:

"In the 34th minute there was another loud protest from the two home coaches after one of their players was called offside. The incident was down the left touchline, on the same side of the field as the coaching benches, at least 40 yards ahead of the home bench — from their position it would actually have been physically impossible for the coaches to have accurately determined that their own player was clearly offside when the ball was played to him. From the players themselves there were no protests.

"As the unnecessary protests continued I walked over to the home bench and said in a calm but firm manner, 'Please, stay calm over here so that it stays calm on the field.' Head coach Rxxxx responded in a harsh tone, 'Oh, I should spend the rest of the game with my mouth sewn up, or what?' [Yes! - Sporting Conduct Ed.] I ignored this remark on the grounds that there was no point in starting a stupid discussion, but then the coach yelled at me again regarding the offside call, so I showed him the yellow card for irresponsible behaviour.

"In the 43rd minute, there was a midfield duel for the ball in the home team's half, which cannoned off the home player and went out for a throw-in near the home bench. When I indicated a throw-in for the away team, coach Rxxxx again completely freaked out and screamed at me for several seconds. I approached him anew and once again asked him to calm down, telling him that this was his final warning. His angry fit inexplicably continued, so I was left with no other choice but to show him a second yellow card (and thus a red) for irresponsible behaviour, and to dismiss him from the playing area.

"Coach Rxxxx however refused to leave the field and just continued yelling at me. What was he supposed to have done, he wanted to know? I explained in a normal voice that he was being dismissed for irresponsible behaviour. "What?" he barked. "I didn't understand you! What am I supposed to have done?" I replied, "You know exactly what you did, now please leave the field." But he wouldn't, so I suspended the game and went to my changing-room, saying that the game would resume once he'd accepted the red card. (As his equally agitated assistant was listed as the team official responsible for order, I didn't think it was worthwhile asking him to appeal to his colleague's reason.)

"The home team's captain knocked on my door shortly after and informed me that Coach Rxxxx had indeed left the field and would spend the remainder of the game outside the technical zone. The game was suspended for around five minutes. It continued with a throw-in for the away team.

"There were a couple more short outbursts from Coach Pxxxx in the second half, but otherwise the rest of the game was peaceful on the touchline. The behaviour of the players on both teams was, with one exception (a yellow card for dissent for the home team's number 7 in the 84th minute), sporting and exemplary.

"I received no apology for these incidents from Coach Rxxxx, nor from Coach Pxxxx, nor from anybody else at the home club. That's a shame, because I've broadly had positive experiences with this club in the past. I was a member there for three years before becoming a coach at my current club in 2017.

"Analysis: I would rate all the decisions I made in this game as uncontroversial. As the two 'controversial' decisions were for an offside and a throw-in, I believe that the only point of the protests was to intimidate the referee. Of course there can be no tolerance for such conduct. As a referee without linesmen, I have to completely focus on 22 athletic, highly motivated young men throughout the game. It does not help the players or the referee when two coaches on the touchline are constantly out of control of their emotions.

"Something else I don't understand — how can a coach greet me before the game in a friendly manner and treat me like a human being, and then right after the whistle's blown start cursing me like a stubborn mule? More questions: how can people who have no self-control be in charge of a youth team and serve as an example to teenage boys? How can a club tolerate its coaches treating the referee in such an abrasive and disrespectful manner?

"As coaches Rxxxx and Pxxxx were so kind as to advise me on my 'impossible' decisions, I would like to offer them some advice as a licensed coach myself: concentrate on the game and your players, not on the referee. Thanks to your crass behaviour, you unnecessarily ruined a beautiful evening of football.

"And finally, a couple of questions to all those reading this disciplinary report, whether it's the league director, the state FA, the disciplinary panel or the Referees' Association. When will this unacceptable behaviour finally be punished as it deserves to be punished? At every ground I see the 'Fair Play' signs, but they're paying nothing more than lip service. When will you all finally understand that the standard of sporting behaviour in this city is to a large extent fucked? (See, for example, my disciplinary report from last week on fan behaviour at the 'Friends of Sport'. Or numerous other reports from previous seasons.) That the referee, working alone for 90 minutes for the laughable remuneration of €14, at some point will no longer be arsed to come and be barked at by aggressive and choleric adult men, all in the name of sport?"

Final score: 0-4 (6 x yellow, 1 x time penalty, 1 x yellow-red)

Jeers and loathing

Referee training courses often emphasise that we "must have the courage to make the big decisions". That is, making calls at crucial points of a game that we know are going to be very unpopular. This happened to me twice at the weekend, and both times my whistle prompted a whole world of pain and unhappiness. Both involved penalties that influenced the outcome of each game. I am happy with both calls, as I was perfectly placed to see both offences. I'm less happy with the aggressive consequences and what they say about the human ability to accept unhappy truths.

Saturday night: Boys' U19 league game. The away team is leading 1-0 with four minutes to go, but the home team equalises on a breakaway. The away team is claiming a foul in the build-up, but there was no foul in the build-up, their central defender was merely outmuscled by the goalscorer. Two minutes later, the home team's captain is tripped in the box, five yards from where I'm standing. It's not a hard foul, just a clumsy one, but it's an irrefutable one. I point to the spot.

Away team players surround me, yelling. I send them sharply away. After the penalty's converted, they do the same, but then realise they don't have long to try and claw the goal back, so they disperse quickly. Upon the final whistle, though (the score remains 2-1), the collective tantrum is so loud, unpleasant and insult-heavy that I red-card their number 14, who had already seen yellow for dissent in the 66th minute.

A group of away team parents had been allowed to attend a supposedly spectator-free game, as long as they stood far behind one goal while socially distancing. By full-time, though, one of them has made his way around the field in order to catch me on my way to the changing-room.

His opinion of my refereeing will have reached several surrounding towns. I wonder if his son was proud of this paternal performance.

Sunday afternoon: Men's league game, level 9. The home team is 2-1 up after leading 2-0 at the break, but under heavy pressure. This is a game with a lot of melodrama — players going down under challenges with loud cries of agony, clutching ankles or faces, only then to re-join the game like hyper-doped greyhounds two minutes later. There was one such case when a defender lost an aerial battle to allow the away team's number 5 to get his side back in the game at 2-1. The home team would, of course, have preferred a free-kick for themselves rather than having conceded a goal.

There's a home crowd of around 150 egging them on (no masks, no social distancing), greeting every whistle against their team with rousing howls of scorn and disbelief. The home team starts to believe its own crowd and the cards for dissent zip out of my pocket like wasps heading for a kids' picnic. The goalkeeper fails to claim a corner, the ball bobbles around the six-yard box, a defender fleetingly, deliberately brings it under control with his hand and then wallops it clear.

'Handball!' the away team chimes, and for once this appeal is spot on. I whistle and point for a penalty. The crowd is collectively and totally outraged, several home players surround me and start screaming that there was a foul on the keeper (I'm starting to sense a pattern ...). Again, I loudly order them away, but one gets a yellow when he really should have had a red, so loud and up close does he get to my face. The penalty's scored, and for the rest of the afternoon, I'm the idiot. At the game's end, several home players let me know that I cost them the game (and not the player who handled?), while the assistant trainer twice asks me sharply, 'What did you take at half-time?' (I'm tempted to answer, 'A shower, with your missus — didn't you hear us?' But it probably wouldn't have helped.)

The referee's changing room is in the main stand, right next to where a vocal group of home fans are waiting to serenade me off with a chorus of jeering, catcalls and critical evaluation. A cheery home official assures me that I shouldn't take it personally because "they're like that every week. In 20 minutes they'll have forgotten all about it." I'm not sure whether that makes the situation better or worse.

We have been told that if we're concerned clubs are not properly implementing Covid-19 distancing and hygiene rules, then we can withdraw from refereeing until the health crisis is over. It's a very tempting offer right now. Aside from the obvious health dangers faced by referees when clubs are not following the rules, every game is throwing up players, coaches and spectators utterly incapable of accepting straightforward decisions, and reacting like I have torn their world in two. Some of these people seem unhinged, possibly borderline psychotic.

And there was me post-lockdown, like an evangelical grandma, thinking teams would be so happy to be out on the field again that we'd experience a new era of tolerance, fair play and exemplary conduct. Those fans were right — I really am the idiot.

Saturday: 2-1 (4 x yellow, 1 x time penalty, 1 x red)

Sunday: 2-2 (7 x yellow, 1 x yellow-red)

The Alpha Wanker

I lost a lot of sleep last weekend because of the theatrical scenes that followed the penalty awards in the two games I refereed. I woke up in the night and started replaying the scenes in my head, several times over. It didn't help. Through Wednesday, I wasn't much fun to be around (even less than usual) — I was tired and irritable, while wondering how bad my refereeing must be if it causes such extreme emotions in so many people. If you're thinking, "Jesus Christ, mate, it's just amateur football, don't let it get to you," then I concede that you are completely in the right.

What also retrospectively bothered me was the health danger — players coming up close and screaming in my face in the Covid-19 era. I didn't even think about it at the time, although I was instinctively backing off and demanding they keep their distance. The leagues where this happened in Sunday's game — to the south of the city — have in the meantime been suspended. Which on one level is a shame, but in the case of the home team that couldn't accept a clear decision that went against them, I can't help but think: tough shit, lads, but it's no bad thing you were sat at home all afternoon yesterday glaring at the walls.

In Frankfurt, games are still on for now, despite soaring Corona stats. This past weekend, I made a simple speech before the Friday and Saturday games. "If a single player comes and screams anywhere close to my face, I'm ending the game and fucking off home. Is that clear?" Everyone nodded, some even applauded, and best of all — it worked. Friday's game (men's Level 10) drew a single yellow card for a bad foul, and just one bout of bad temper from the touchline aimed at the player who committed it. Afterwards, I was given a tip on top of my match fee and offered a beer by the cheery home team, who had just lost 5-2. I was quite choked up.

It also helped that I shunned the referee's changing room, turning up with my kit already on, and changing my footwear on the subs' bench. That I was concerned enough about the virus to reject the comforts of the dressing room in favour of sitting out in the rain helped get across the message that for me the virus is very real, and that for men of a certain age it represents a genuine health risk.

On Saturday afternoon, I reffed a U19 boys' game with 15 goals and six yellow cards, but again the atmosphere was good — just one yellow for moaning, and otherwise the behaviour was fine despite the home team getting comprehensively walloped. And finally, a girls' U14 game on Sunday morning where the only bench available for me to prepare for the game was where the away team's parents were standing. This led to a normal, adult conversation about refereeing, youth football and the current pandemic, and possibly stopped any of them from moaning at me during the actual game. It maybe helped that I held out my reading glasses and said, "If my reffing's shite, feel free to run onto the pitch and bring me these."

Of course, there's always someone around to behave like a twat. The assistant coach on the home team is sure that he's seen a foul on his goalkeeper when the away team go 2-0 up from a rebound (in fact she drops the ball from a shot and goes to ground to try and retrieve it in the ensuing scramble — she's in tears at her mistake, but unhurt when I go to check if she's okay to continue). After an hour of peace, his moment has come to yell at the ref, at length, because of course he has seen the situation better from the touchline. I decide it's best to ignore him. Let him scream away, while everyone else wonders why he's being such a cock. A few minutes later he freaks out again, about a perfectly normal trip against one of his players (again, no one's hurt). I call the foul, then call at him to calm down.

Again, the attention's now on the assistant coach, the blaring moron, an arm-waving, barrel-bellied bell-end of rotten sporting morals, a superfluous, blunt-ended floppy prick raving into the gorgeous Sunday lunchtime sun, failing to spoil the game, but successful in making it known to around 50 fellow human beings — I am the Alpha Wanker here. While the rest of you may regard this as mere recreational time for teenagers, I stoop lower to make this all about me, Franz Fuckwit, an embarrassment to myself, to my team, and to my club, without even the grace to apologise when my tiny cantankerous mind has finally calmed itself down.

That aside, a great weekend. Which is good, as it may be the last with any amateur football for quite a while.

Friday: 2-5 (1 x yellow)

Saturday: 4-11 (6 x yellow)

Sunday: 0-3 (no cards. Although AWAC — Alpha Wanker Assistant Coach — deserved a red, I didn't want to distract any more from the game, which the players were enjoying just fine.)

Danny (Part 6)

I get a call at 4pm. Can I referee a men's game at 8? It's raining and cold and it's almost November, and I'd planned to be on the sofa watching Rangers v Lech Poznan in the Europa League. I know, the wild life I lead. But I say yes because I'm useless at saying no. After I hang up, I get the email and I see the teams, and there I see his name. He's listed as a substitute, assistant coach and team manager for the away side. Oh joy, oh joy, it's my lovely Danny boy, back from a lengthy ban imposed by the disciplinary panel after 'the Game From Hell'.

I haven't seen Danny since I sent him off in that game last year. Also in the team tonight are four players from that U19 line-up he was coaching, including the player red-carded for head-butting an opponent in the gut, and the defender who came in to my changing room to put a two-cent coin on my table in lieu of full payment (I've still not been paid for the game). Tonight they are all standing outside the changing room when I arrive, and break into exasperated laughter when they see me. Good to know they haven't forgotten that game either.

As I did at the weekend, I speak to both trainers about the need for absolute peace on the field, and that I will call off the game if a single player screams anywhere close to my face. At the toss-up, I check with both captains that the teams have got the message. They have. Off we go.

Those lads who were so bolshie, macho and aggressive in the U19s are remarkably quiet now that they are playing with men, not boys. They are also getting spanked. By half-time, they're 4-1 down, troubling the scoreboard only thanks to a clumsy own goal from the home team. So, at half-time, three players are subbed out. Danny's time has come to turn the game around as a striker.

It might be tough, though. The past year has not been kind to his figure. He's 31 now and has developed what might kindly be called a low centre of gravity (think Granit Xhaka, then double it). His first contribution is to blaze a rebound wide and high from six yards out, in front of an open goal. To be fair, he does play one lovely through-ball that his fellow forward hits against the crossbar. Otherwise, though, he can't get into the game. When he passes to a team-mate who's offside, his reaction to my whistle is as inevitable as tomorrow's sun rising in the east. He moans, but I ignore him, just as I do when he sarcastically laughs after I whistle for a clear handball he commits at the halfway line. I'm following a policy of no drama, denying him the attention he seems to crave as a prelude to his own martyrdom at the hands of the evil referee.

The lad who laid down the two-cent coin? He gets murdered at right-back, over and over again. He also gets a yellow card for a deliberate foul when he's been dribbled past for the 11th time. I'm wondering if I have a two-cent coin in my wallet to give him at the end of the game as an appreciation of his performance tonight. But the best is still to come.

At 85 minutes, with his team now 9-1 in arrears, Danny's night is over. His coach subs him back out. Danny's not in agreement with this tactical move. Perhaps he thinks that he still has time to turn the game around with a late treble hat-trick. He starts to yell at his coach even before he's left the field. They have an almighty row that lasts all the way until the final whistle. In this time, while they're going at it like pneumatic church bells on the last Sunday before the Apocalypse, they don't even notice that their team scores two late but entirely cosmetic goals (see, Danny — your coach was right!). It's all I can do to keep my eye on the game, and to not laugh out loud as we bring the night's action to a close.

I'm still chuckling to myself as I walk to the tram stop. Just around this time, the Hessen FA is announcing the suspension of all amateur football. That's sad but inevitable news. But as a major consolation, I got to referee the most karmic and enjoyable game of the year. Ha!

Final score: 9-3 (5 x yellow, plus a massive portion of internal *Schadenfreude*)

Apology procession

First game for eight months, a boys' U19 friendly. The pandemic's second wave is over, while the third one (driven by the Delta variant) is not forecast to hit Germany for another two months. It's been humid and in the mid-30s all week, the worst kind of weather for outdoor sport. The back-end of June seems an odd time to be re-starting play. But these are odd times. It's still the 2020-21 season, but really we're preparing for 2021-22. In the meantime, I've been 'training' by watching the referees in the European Championships, who — aside from their leniency on dissent — have been doing an excellent job.

The home team wants to play three halves (2 x 45 minutes, plus an extra 30 minutes) because they have so many players. It's okay with me, but their opponents, with a squad of 16, say they'll decide after the 90 minutes. That makes sense, given the weather. Kick-off is delayed because the German FA's software won't accommodate more than 11 subs. When that's finally sorted out, I start the game and soon we're back to normal — two yellow cards in the first seven minutes. The first is for a tactical foul, the second is when the away team's goalkeeper upends a home forward who's about to score. At half-time, the home team's assistant coach wants to know why it wasn't red. "He made an attempt to play the ball," I say. He doesn't think much of that explanation. Some rule changes can take years to seep into the consciousness of players and coaches (and even some refs).

Following a robust challenge, there's also a time-penalty for an away player for the usual adolescent squaring-up and verbal growling. There have been many such challenges, plus holding, grappling, shirt-pulling and ankle-tapping. I don't know exactly when all these infringements were coached into youth football, but it happened at some point in the past 40 years. When I played at this age, at this level, the referee was a barely relevant presence. I hardly recall any fouls at all, let alone yellow and red cards.

The home team, 2-1 up at half-time, completely subs out its A team for its B team, who are better disciplined and far less hectic — they eventually win 3-1. The away team agrees to play for a further 30 minutes. I tell both coaches and captains that this game's off the radar — I'll show no cards and record no goals, I'm reffing as a courtesy. But they should cut out the constant fouling and keep it clean. If there's any stupidity, I'm going home. Nods all around.

Seven minutes into the 'extra' game and the home captain gets into a square-up scenario with an opposing defender. I sharply remind them about what I said before the restart and they back off. Two minutes later, it's the home captain again, this time in a shouty chest-shoving encounter with the away team's striker. I blow my whistle and walk off and wish them all a good evening.

The home team's coaches apologise and thank me for having stayed on. When I'm back in my changing room, I can hear them bollocking their lads for the lack of discipline, and for messing up the chance to play another 20 minutes. A few moments pass, then there's a knock on my door. One of the home team players apologises for their behaviour. Then there's a whole procession of players knocking and telling me that they're very sorry. The last one is the team captain.

Sometimes you meet up with old friends for the first time in years, and after five minutes it seems like you last saw each other just the day before. For better or worse, that's what reffing feels like in this comeback game. I have no problem settling back into the rhythm, such as it is. The game's still there, and those of us who survived are still here to play it, coach it and officiate it. But it will clearly take much more than a global pandemic to change our attitudes about the way we approach sport.

Final score: 3-1 (5 x yellow)

Eye of the fucking tiger

"Nooooooooo!" It's still 40 minutes to kick-off, but already I'm in mental agony. My changing room is next door to the away team, and they're playing motivational warm-up music. There seem to be only two criteria for such music — it has to be blasted out at an intrusively loud volume on a below-par sound system, and the choice of song has to be the most unimaginative shite with the perceived widest appeal. In today's case, *Eye of the fucking Tiger*. They can't hear my *cri de coeur*, of course, because *Eye of the fucking Tiger* is way too loud. I can't stress enough how much I hate this song. That dumb, macho opening riff I've heard 25,000 times too often. The whiney vocals. The asinine lyrics. And everything else about it, which sticks in my poor, suffering head for the entire first half.

If the International Football Association Board gave me free rein to add just one law to the game, then it would be this: "Teams playing loud pre-match motivational music that annoys the ref will be issued with a collective eleven yellow cards prior to kick-off. No exceptions. Should that pre-match music consist of Survivor's *Eye of the Tiger*, those cards will be red, the game will be abandoned, and the opposing team awarded a 25-0 win. The ref shall be permitted to access the offending team's changing room with a heavy hammer to attack the source of the music and render it beyond further sonic re-production."

I think that's reasonable. It certainly makes a lot more sense than the comical handball law the IFAB's now had to retract and semi-restore to its original state.

So, to the game. It's questionable why the away team felt the need to musically pump themselves up for this one. It's a men's friendly, and both teams are playing for the first time in nine months. It's humid and over 30 degrees, and we're playing in the sun. Both sides have enough players to sub out almost their entire teams at half-time. Even then, I agree to a water break, and they need it. The first pause for refreshment is hardly over before they start asking me how much longer to go. Soon players give up moving for any ball that's not directly played to their feet. There are a lot of goals — less down to attacking agility, more due to defensive immobility.

Still, everyone's too knackered to moan about any decisions and it's a quiet afternoon. It's not exactly what you'd call "the thrill of the fight/Rising up to the challenge of our rival", even though there are 11 goals. It's officially the end of the calendar year, and as of next weekend, the 'new' handball law will apply. Though, sadly, not my draft law about pre-match music. The pertinent song is now back in my head thanks to me sitting down to type this blog entry. Survivor fans among you will see that as harmonic justice, but I've got the guts, I've got the glory, I'm going the distance and I'm not going to stop until Fifa adopts the law word for word as set out above. Just a ref and his will to survive and outlaw *Eye of the fucking Tiger*.

Final score: 6-5 (2 x yellow)

SEASON 2021-22

ERRORS, HECKLERS AND DANGEROUS DERBIES

Amateurs on steroids?

In my day job, I've been editing an interview with a scientist who works in anti-doping research. The scientist estimated that the number of young men taking anabolic steroids runs into the hundreds of thousands — somewhere between half a million and 700,000. He didn't say what geographical area that estimate covers, but even if it's the entire world the numbers are still way too high. The damaging and often deadly side-effects of anabolic steroids far outweigh the 'benefit' of temporarily boosting your muscle mass.

One of the negative side-effects of abusing steroids is a marked increase in aggressive behaviour, and I'm wondering if there's a connection between steroid consumption and the high number of young men losing a grip on their tempers during amateur football games. I thought about it even more following an ugly incident just before half-time in this friendly between two Level 8 men's teams.

I like this level, because everyone can play, and there are generally fewer fouls. The players are more skilful, more savvy, and better disciplined. True, the home defence complains loudly about a non-existent offside when they go 2-0 down after 10 minutes, but I nip the dissent in the bud with an early yellow, and that's it for the day. Instead of trying to play a dubious offside trap in a game with no linesmen, they stop moaning and drop a player back into the sweeper position.

Then, with the score at 1-3 on 43 minutes, the home team's number 11 takes out the away team's number 17 with a robust challenge in the centre circle. I'm five yards away, so immediately blow for the free-kick. I'm ready to have a strong word with the number 11 about his challenge, but I never get the chance. The number 17's on his feet and raging in his opponent's face.

They both become loud and push each other in the chest, yelling threats and insults. I whistle like a steam train, to no effect, while their team-mates try to pull them apart.

If the incident had ended there, I'd have left it at a pair of yellows and the customary lecture. But no sooner have things calmed down than they re-escalate, and the two rage-faced miscreants go at it anew. There follows another separation by team-mates, another brief calm, and then a third and final wave of fuck-witted hollering and breast-pounding. By this time, I'm standing and waiting at a distance of 10 yards until they've both calmed down enough to come over for a very short chat, which is: "Not on my football field, comrades. Disgraceful — you're both off."

They go without protest, perhaps having exhausted their supplies of shit-headed behaviour for the day, and there isn't a cross word or a complaint throughout the entire second half from their remaining (and largely sensible) team-mates. There's a fan club of half a dozen lads on the right wing who jeer me every time I give their mate offside (which is four times, and every time by at least two yards), but then I have the pleasure of yellow-carding him right in front of their eyes after a nasty late challenge on the away team's left back.

At the end of the game, the number 17 seeks me out to apologise for his conduct. He agrees that he insulted his opponent, and that things got a bit out of hand, but is able to deliver the heart-warming news that they both hugged in the changing room and made up. I nod, and included a short account of his wee speech in my disciplinary report, but often these apologies are made when their tempers wane and they realise they're facing a suspension of at least three games.

Could I not downgrade the red cards to yellow-red cards, one of the coaches wants to know? That way, the players won't be suspended for longer than one game. He's polite about the request, so I politely reply that it's sadly not possible, and that I hope both players do indeed receive the appropriate suspensions, because that's exactly what they deserve.

"Can't we at least play with 11 each seeing as it's a friendly?" a player asks at the start of the second half. Sorry, can't do that either. Just enjoy the extra space. The sun's out, the game is calm, the storm of rage has passed. What caused it, maybe only science can explain.

Final score: 2-6 (2 x yellow, 2 x red)

When this 'shit job' is a breeze

Before leaving the house, I spend an hour reading the newspaper. The Taliban is marching unhindered on Kabul, taking us back to square one after 20 years of death and futility. The two sides in the Ethiopian civil war are gearing up for the next round of conflict. Floods and serial wildfires around the globe are still not sparking the necessary political will to save our planet. I fold up the paper and cycle off to referee a game between two of the city's diaspora sides, who once formed part of the same country. Within living memory, they engaged in a war that cost an estimated 22,000 lives before two new states were formed — Serbia and Croatia.

There are several teams in our city formed by exiles from the former Yugoslavia. Some were founded by migrant workers in the 1970s, others came into existence later as a result of the various population-shifting conflicts that hit the state during its 1990s break-up. One of today's teams was formed in 1973, and became a go-to club for Serbian immigrants. Their opponents were originally a pan-Yugoslavian side, but professed themselves to be a Croatian club in the 1990s, prompting their Serbian members to leave for the other team. The city's 'Balkan derbies' during that decade could attract crowds several hundred strong.

It's always worth doing your research, but it's even more important to approach a game without expectations, be they good or bad. True, I once refereed a cup tie here between teams from a region of historical conflict that for 90 minutes teetered on the verge of something much more than a game of football (see 'Putting Out Fires'). But the only thing awaiting me at today's game is a journalist from a Serbian newspaper published for the ex-pat community. He wants to know if he can take a picture of both teams together before kick-off. If they're on board, you certainly don't need my permission, I tell him. I also take a snapshot of the two teams, who then all shake hands in the centre circle — which we're no longer supposed to do because of Covid, but this seems like a worthy exception.

There's really not much to write about the game itself, other than to say it was the most peaceful I've officiated in this country since the Japanese high-schoolers came to town. Any fouls are followed by apologies and a helping hand. At one point, the coach of one side quickly steps on to the field to spray the injured foot of an opponent. Strictly speaking, he needed my permission, but I'd have to be an idiot to raise an objection, let alone show him a yellow card. There is barely a complaint about a decision all afternoon, bar one or two courteous questions. The captain of one team, a central defender, wins every single challenge — both aerial and on the ground—without committing a single foul. There are around 150 spectators, but there's no caterwauling and cat-calling about offside decisions. After the game, the teams drink beer together around a barbeque.

I'm not a fan of mawkish homilies about football bringing people together, because I've seen way too much belligerence in this city over the past seven years to believe there's much truth to such a trite simplification. But I tell the Serbian journalist after the final whistle that it was an absolute pleasure to ref this one, from start to finish. If I had a good game, it was because the players made it easy for me to have a good game. There's not a single incident where I even think about pulling out a yellow card. It's as though the weight of a traumatic, violent history is leaning on the players to practice good behaviour. An optimist might venture that the feud is so exhausted that it has no energy left for even the slightest confrontation.

At half-time, one of my club-appointed linesmen comes over for a chat. "I was a ref for 35 years," he says. "It's a shit job. You're running a good game." But when the teams are disciplined and just here to play sport, this shit job is a breeze.

Final score: 4-0 (no cards)

The referee's a preacher

Sometimes the Gods deliver their own kind of verdict on the games that I referee. With around 15 minutes left to play on this sultry Sunday afternoon, the clouds burst and unload, there's an impressive drum-roll of judgmental thunder right above our heads, and then the conclusive blast of my whistle as I direct both teams to run for the changing rooms. Part of me's hoping that the rest of the day's a washout.

The first half passed without too much incident. There was one yellow card against the home team for a reckless foul, and three very well-taken goals by the visiting number 9. A 'crystal-pure' (*lupenrein*) hat-trick, as the Germans call it — three consecutive goals by one player, all scored in the same half. There's been nothing crystal pure about the second half, though. Fouls have turned niggly and deliberate, players have thrown themselves to the floor with the stricken cries of part-time pantomime thespians, and there have been three major arguments. These result in a flurry of cautions for poor conduct and a series of short lectures about keeping a lid on it.

The away team's number 5 is involved in the histrionics time and again, claiming that he's been insulted by his opponents in his native language. I don't doubt for one second that he's telling the truth, but I have no knowledge of his native language, and the claimed insults are being whispered in his ear rather than shouted across the field. He already has a yellow card for his role in one incident of tempestuous shoving, and when his coach decides — sensibly — to sub him out, he freaks out as he leaves the pitch, throwing his shirt on the ground and claiming that he's being insulted yet again. Once off the field, he has to be restrained by his coach and the substitutes from coming back on. I walk over for another chat, and the away bench assures me that they have the situation under control.

The storm only lasts a few minutes. Suddenly, the sun's shining, but the air has cooled. A player knocks on my door and cheerfully informs me that everyone's ready to continue. Before we resume, I gather both teams around me in a circle like it's assembly time at kindergarten. "This game just got the weather that it deserved," I tell them. "Since half-time it's had nothing to do with football, and the behaviour of both teams has been an absolute disgrace. You should count yourselves lucky that we're able to play at all with the pandemic still out there. Maybe all sport will be cancelled again soon, so I suggest you try and enjoy the last 15 minutes, actually play the game, and treat each other like human beings."

The effect is unexpected. Both teams applaud, and the last 15 minutes pass without deliberate fouls, without the exaggerated tumbles, and without any indignant squaring-up. At the final whistle, everyone's calm and conciliatory. The home team's coach asks politely why I didn't red-card the away team's number 5. "Under the Laws of the Game," I say, "he should have been sent off. But sometimes it's more important to try and preserve the peace than deliver punishment by the book."

The number 5 comes to my changing room to apologise, and to reiterate that he was being severely provoked. I appreciate that, I say, but you should also know that next week a different referee will send you off. I can't understand every language being spoken on the field, and I can't hear everything said between 22 players, so you have to keep yourself in check while you're out there and concentrate on the game. It occurs to me later that I should have offered him the chance to lodge an official complaint, but in the past that option's never been taken up. More often than not, these matters are taken care of during post-match handshakes and — for better or worse — I'm spared the bureaucracy.

I've experienced few games where so many players have thanked me after the final whistle. Some days, this job feels like another vocation practiced on a Sunday — I'm part righteous preacher delivering the loud moral sermon, part counsellor dispensing guidance along amateur football's narrow, rocky path. If I wasn't an atheist, I might have been better suited to a life behind the pulpit, showing yellow cards to the congregation:

"Thou shalt not venture into the dark realm of the offside, and thou shalt abjure foul play against thy neighbouring player, whom thou shalt love as thyself!"

The mighty storm flushed away the sins of this ungodly game, prompting a brief half hour of enlightenment and redemption. Will next Sunday be any less foul?

Final score: 0-3 (7 x yellow cards)

Ignorance of the laws

Twenty minutes into a boys' U19 game, and I blow for offside against the home team's number 15. His reaction is to kick the ball far out of play, and so — predictably enough — I show him a yellow card. He looks at me all hurt and confused, like a rabbit whose previously loving owner has just shown him a pot of simmering stock and invited him to take a seat on the chopping board. "What was that for?"

Every week, players demonstrate how clueless they are about the Laws of the Game. Rather than sitting down to read them (you may be unsurprised to know that they are available for free on a global information network), they prefer to learn by a slow process of accumulating cautions. 'Delaying a restart' is a particularly common bone of contention, because for some reason players think that prodding the ball away from an opponent before they have the chance to take a throw-in or free-kick is absolutely normal practice and totally permissible. Perhaps they've seen it go unpunished on TV a few thousand times (thanks again to our wonderful pro refs for setting a great example to the amateur game. See also: Dissent).

Here are some other aghast reactions for yellow cards, from this one weekend alone:

Example 2: *Unsporting conduct.* Two teenagers square up and exchange loud and rowdy words with each other, a sight as common in this city as pigeons shitting on a window ledge. I take them to one side, invite them to calm down and focus on the game, and show them both the yellow card. "What did I do?" exclaims one. Well, young man, what do you think the lecture was just about? (If you deliver the lecture without the cards, you can be certain they'll be at it again within a few minutes, sometimes a few seconds.)

Example 3: *Dissent*. Before Sunday's game (men's Level 10), I gather both teams in the centre circle to make sure they're on board with the new trial punishment scale in our state — yellow card, followed by a 10-minute time-penalty for a second yellow-card offence, followed by a red card for a third yellow-card offence. "For example," I say, "if you speak disrespectfully to the referee, you will immediately receive a yellow card ..." And so on, always using the example of dissent. Everybody nods. Ten minutes in, the away team's defender is the first to yell at me about an offside call (or something), and he just cannot believe it when I show him the yellow card. "What did I just tell you before the game?" I ask. Oh, yes. And that's it with dissent until the game's dying minutes, when one of his team-mates concludes that I have "no clue" how to ref following a free-kick given for handball. Instead of saying, "And you have no clue how to defend against 10 men" (his team conceded two goals while a man up — see Example 4), I speak the referee's silent language of a yellow card thrust into the damp afternoon air.

Example 4: *Time-wasting*. The home team is 2-1 up with 15 minutes left. Their big forward is called for offside just inside his opponent's half, but he continues running with the ball all the way to the goal. He's already seen yellow for flattening a defender, so he gets sin-binned for 10 minutes for time-wasting. Whaaaaaat? He's so outraged that after leaving the field he kicks the ad hoarding. I let him off the theoretical red card, generously interpreting his rage as anger at his own stupidity.

Two games, with a total of 17 cautionable offences (15 yellows and two time-penalties), and that was an absolutely normal weekend. These games were by no means off the radar — there was the average amount of fouling, moaning and squaring up. I haven't even mentioned the away team's captain in Sunday's game, who insists that he's allowed to question every decision against his team by dint of his armband. He never gets loud, it's more of a constant nagging commentary, so after telling him the captain has no special rights, I just ignore him for the entire game.

Here's a new idea that will never be implemented: before a player is issued with a pass from their state FA, they have to pass a really simple test on the Laws of the Game, with a focus on what constitutes a yellow- or a red-card offence.

Saturday: 1-3 (8 x yellow, 1 x time-penalty)

Sunday: 5-1 (7 x yellow, 1 x time-penalty)

Missing a clear penalty

When the coach is screaming at you, there are usually two options. Either ignore him (it's almost always a him), or card him. Sometimes there is a third option, though it's not the ideal path. You try and talk to him and justify your decision. Because perhaps you already know that you fucked up.

It's the second half of a boys' U13 game, and so far everything's been quiet. The away team is leading 1-0, and is clearly the better side. On a rare home team attack, a forward is through on goal on the right side of the penalty area and tries to lift the ball over the keeper. His lob is so hopelessly wide that the ball remains in play out on the left side. I keep my eye on the arc of the ball (an error), and only see out of the corner of my vision that the goalkeeper has crashed into the forward. The home coach screams for a penalty, but I'm already following the play. When the forward doesn't stand up, I stop play and wave the coach on to treat him.

As he's tending to his forward, he has some strong words about the challenge. My main concern is the player's health, and so I ignore the penalty issue. The player's okay to continue, though he's a little shaken, and I restart the game with a drop ball.

The home team loses 2-0, and after the game the home coach comes over to say thanks and bump fists. It's me that brings the penalty incident up. "I didn't give a penalty because I saw it as a collision between the two players ..." I start, but he interrupts me, suddenly incensed again, and says, "The keeper laid my player out flat. It was a clear penalty." And he leaves it at that. As I walk back to the clubhouse, I start to admit to myself that he's right. I've given decisions like that before against goalkeepers, and I can't explain why I didn't give it today.

A few minutes later the coach comes into my changing room to pay me. "Look," I say. "About the penalty call. I think you were right. I'm sorry, I screwed up, it should have been a spot-kick." Immediately he relaxes and sits down, and we talk about the game. His team's just been promoted to a higher level and are still getting used to playing stronger teams, he says. He knows that the end result was a fair reflection of play, but still, it would have been nice to have had the chance to gain a point — if the referee hadn't inexplicably failed to award them a penalty. He doesn't say this last part out loud, and we part on amicable terms. I know he's doing a demanding job in his free time on a volunteer's salary of nil, and for once I feel no resentment at a coach for having lost his rag.

I've also argued before that a foul in the penalty area is a penalty, no matter how 'soft'. At the same time it's true that most referees, even subconsciously, set a higher bar for fouls in the box. It's often a game-changing decision, after all. And it's much easier to wave away a penalty appeal because the protests dissipate much quicker and the game moves on. Call a penalty on a borderline decision and you might find yourself surrounded by angry players (though not, hopefully, at U13 level), and the reproaches can continue long after the final whistle. In this case, I bottled the decision because a foul by the goalkeeper coming out to challenge a forward can so easily be dismissed as a collision.

Every game, we learn and move on, even at my age. I'm still unhappy with my own error, but at least my apology was accepted.

There had already been one apology during the game after an away player absolutely wiped out an opponent with a very late challenge. There are no yellow or red cards at this level, but you can give a five-minute time penalty. When the lad returned to the field after his punishment, he came up to me and sincerely said sorry for the challenge, which I knew had been ill-judged rather than malicious. We all make mistakes, lad. And we'll all continue to make them.

Final score: 0-2 (1 x time-penalty)

All the crap and chaos

Saturday 4pm. Boys' U19 match in the city's east park. It's a beautiful autumn day, there are multiple pick-up games, families grilling food, dog-walkers and drinkers hanging out at the kiosk. The home club is friendly, the away team remembers me too. I've not given a penalty all season, but towards the end of the first half the home team gets two in three minutes, both of them unnecessary fouls, and both greeted without a single complaint. The only other incident of note is when a home player yells at me after he's been fouled and I've already whistled for the free-kick. His coach tells him to calm down, while I give him a yellow and a ticking-off. A mostly fair and stress-free game. Pay: €14.

6.48pm. Tomorrow I'm due to ref a Level 8 men's game in Wiesbaden at 3pm. I receive an email from one of my assignors saying that "unfortunately, we're losing refs in droves, so I'm asking you to take on a youth game tomorrow morning at 11am, otherwise this game won't be covered. Lots of other refs are doing two games tomorrow." I write back pointing out the physical impossibility of me finishing that game at 1pm in the east end of Frankfurt and then making it to Wiesbaden in time for kick-off at 3pm. I don't hear back from him, but am left somehow feeling guilty that I've turned him down.

[A couple of things here — when we turn back a game at short notice, we're told to always phone the assignor rather than email if there are less than three days to kick-off. That's a fair rule. But when we receive a game at less than 24 hours notice on a Saturday evening, sandwiched between two other 90-minute games, we're only told by email, and an imperatively phrased email at that, implying we're letting the side down if we don't take the game. Second, I know my own body pretty well because we've been together for 56 years, and so I have to ration my daily exercise.

272

Finally, it's no bad thing to let the clubs ref some games for themselves to find out what that entails, and so they also know that we're facing a shortage of match officials largely due to shite pay, choleric coaches and insane player behaviour.]

Sunday 11.40am. I take my bike on the train for half an hour, then have another half hour's cycle ride to reach my game — I leave early because any number of things could go wrong (cancelled trains, punctured tyres), and because I want to see some of the preceding game between the two clubs' reserve sides. Just as I'm setting off on the second half of the journey on a path through country fields, the clouds rumble and then dump their wet and heavy load to give me a thorough soaking. When I reach the club, I have to wring the water out of my tracksuit bottoms into the changing room shower. At least my side-saddles are water-proof, so my reffing gear's still dry. I watch the second half of the reserves' game from the clubhouse entrance (it's still tipping down). There's the usual level of moaning at offside calls, but the ref deals with it well — good communication, and a yellow card for the loudest mouth.

2.50pm. On my way out to the field, I pass a reserve team player with a cigarette in his mouth and a can of Jack Daniels with Coke in his hand. "What if you get called up to the first team now?" I ask him. "No problem," he says. "I play much better when I'm pissed."

3pm. Kick-off, with around 100 spectators in the ground. The home team is top of the table and unbeaten, but the game's balanced and of a decent standard. There are three cautions in the first half, and one of those is for an early bout of dissent from a home team player. Right after I blow for half-time (the visitors are 1-0 up), there's a sudden flare-up out by the touchline between two opposing players (both number 14s) and the away team's coach, then suddenly everyone's over there shoving and shouting. I break up the melee, then yellow card both number 14s and the coach.

3.47pm. The two changing rooms are door by door, and the hallway is tiny. Both teams are crowding in there (I'm still outside) because the doors are still locked. There's yet more outraged shouting and disorder from within. The away team coach summons his team back outside. They claim the home team's captain shoved one of them over. I gather both coaches and tell them we've a choice — I call the game off, go home, and they can explain themselves to a Disciplinary Hearing. Or, they can go and talk to their teams and tell them to calm the fuck down. Also, they should both sub out their number 14s (I can only recommend this, but I make it sound like an order). Also, if there's any more of this shit in the second half, we're done. They nod and disappear. I take an extra long break (still wringing out my tracksuit trousers) to give both teams more time to cool off and think about it.

4.05pm. Second half kicks off, without the two number 14s. The home team equalises. They all go nuts. The home team then takes the lead, but I cancel it out for offside. They all (including the crowd) go nuts, but not in a good way. I give a free-kick to the away team just outside the penalty area, they score to take a 2-1 lead. It's now the away team's turn to go nuts, while the home team continues its policy of going nuts at me — within the space of nine minutes, I dish out three yellow cards for dissent. But at least the teams are no longer going nuts at each other.

4.45pm. With 10 minutes left, the away team keeper comes off his line and takes out an on-rushing attacker. Cheers, mate — it's a clear penalty kick no one argues about, and in the eyes of the home team and fans I'm partly redeemed. The kick's well-placed, it's now 2-2. There follows a mad end-to-end game as both teams pursue the winner. In the fourth minute of injury time, another free-kick just outside the box, this time for the home team. It's not that well placed, but it's well struck and it swerves and the keeper misjudges it. 3-2, and this time everyone in the stadium bar me and the bedraggled away team goes absolutely screaming nuts. Best of all, everyone's forgotten that absolute shit-head of a referee who had the audacity to cancel out a goal for offside.

5pm. After eight minutes of injury time, I blow the final whistle. I hang around to check there's no more twat-like behaviour, but the home team (too elated) and the away team (too exhausted) aren't up for any more conflict. The home team who yelled at me for most of the second half are now shaking my hand and thanking me. As I walk off, a stern-looking, tall man among the spectators says, "Well reffed." I nod and thank him — I definitely feel like I need some kind of affirmation, however fleeting.

7pm. I'm home — a seven-and-a-half hour endeavour for €25 plus train fare. In some ways, the game was a nightmare. In many ways, though, it was just a typical afternoon of sport. Intense, idiotic, thrilling, loud, belligerent, strange, funny, perplexing, and for the bloke who scored the 94th-minute winner direct from a free-kick — unforgettable. "Good goal," I'd said to him at the final whistle. "Thank you," he smiled, then added, "Sorry about all the crap and chaos."

Saturday: 2-5 (3 x yellow)

Sunday: 3-2 (13 x yellow)

Quick cards for dissent

Three very quiet matches in a row, perhaps due to them all being one-sided, but also helped in two games by me being able to set the tone for the 90 minutes. That is, the players give me the perfect opportunity to show an early yellow.

Both are boys' U19 games, the first one a City Cup quarter-final. A home defender strongly disagrees with my throw-in call just five minutes into the game, cursing and throwing the ball down hard against the ground. Young man, that's not the kind of behaviour we want to see here tonight, I say loudly (and much less diplomatically), so that players and spectators alike get the message. In the book he goes, and he's the only one of the night until a team-mate joins him five minutes before the end, for the same offence. Having made the decision to be ruthless on dissent this season, the yellow card now comes out of the pocket without me stopping to think about its necessity. It's the Law, lad.

The following Saturday, it's a hard, late challenge from an away team defender in the third minute, but initially I play advantage because the ball has run on to an attacker in space. That move fizzles out, but the ball stays in play for a good two minutes. I'd planned to show the defender the yellow card at the next stoppage, but then I start to doubt the decision. Will anyone even remember the offence by then? The more time you have to think about a decision, the harder it can be to decide if it's the right one. Ask any VAR.

When the ball finally runs out for a throw-in, I whistle and show the defender the yellow card after all, pointing approximately to the spot where the foul happened. It turns out to be a good call — there are no more such illegal challenges, and just one more caution during the game, for a tactical foul. I don't know whether the players consciously think, "This ref won't stand for any bollocks," and then it has a positive effect on the game, or if it's just dumb luck. Some games are destined for dirt no matter how keenly you try to set a precedent.

One-sided games are not all necessarily low-key and easy to manage. Sometimes a team will take out its frustration on the legs of its opponents. In Sunday's game, the home team's record this season is: scored two, conceded 67. They're playing a mid-table team with a respectable record, so I already have a feeling that it's not going to be close. But the home side also has the division's cleanest disciplinary record. They make me very welcome, while telling me they lost a lot of players during the pandemic and that they had to scrap their reserve team. Left over is a combination of very young and very 'experienced' players (one player on the bench is almost as old as me). They're overwhelmed from the start, but never try to deliberately kick their opponents.

And they almost get that elusive third goal of the season. With the score at 0-8, I award them a penalty when their number 18 is shoved over in the box. The away team, despite the scoreline heavily in their favour, dispute the call with vehemence. The afternoon's two cautions have already gone their way, and I can tell they'd be a handful in tighter games. The keeper, though, saves the spot-kick ("Justice is done!" cries one of his team-mates, as though we've just come down the courtroom steps after a 10-month trial), and by the end of the afternoon the home team's goal difference for the season is at minus 75. We're barely into October.

"Glad I gave you something to do," I say to the away keeper at the final whistle. He laughs and says, "Good game. And, by the way, it was a penalty." Dude, of course it was.

Tuesday: 0-3 (2 x yellow)
Saturday: 8-1 (2 x yellow)
Sunday: 0-10 (2 x yellow)

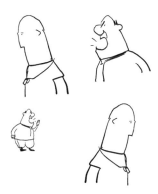

The designated heckler

It was a clear and chill autumn weekend, and I really enjoyed both games that I refereed, but there was one disturbing factor in the boys' U19 game on Saturday — the away team's assistant coach. As I wrote in the inevitable disciplinary report, I wasn't quite sure what his role with the team was supposed to be, besides 'designated referee heckler'. His entire performance felt like something out of a comedy sketch show, where the repetitive absurdity of a personality disorder is played for laughs.

It starts with a yellow card for the away team's number 12 for a tactical foul on the quarter-hour mark, a clear and uncontested call. Except for the above-mentioned assistant coach, who starts yelling about this or that foul I supposedly haven't called for his team. I ignore his protests, but when I notice that the number 12 was listed as starting on the bench, I go over to ask whom he replaced in the starting XI. "I don't know," says the assistant coach dismissively, and continues instead to rant on about the injustice of the caution. I ask him to stop, but he doesn't, so I show him the yellow card.

This causes him to have an almighty row with the team's head coach. The now steaming and indignant assistant pulls on his jacket and strides for the exit, which would have been the best possible solution at this point. But then he comes back and stands on the touchline again, only now far away from his own bench. From there, he continues to moan about every decision given against his team, even though they've turned around an early 2-0 deficit and are leading 5-2.

Just before half-time, one of the away team players is fouled directly in front of the choleric assistant coach. He screams in outrage, but the ball's run to his own number 10, who sprints through on goal and narrowly shoots wide. The assistant coach is still remonstrating about the foul.

I turn around and say to him, "Did you not see that I played advantage there?" He doesn't care, he's still gesticulating and shouting at me for not giving a free-kick. Then he invites me to show him the red card, and I'm more than happy to oblige. Triumphant, he jumps behind the spectator barrier and says he'll continue to 'coach' from there. After another two minutes of shouting at me, I pause the game and order him from the ground under threat of abandoning the match.

He leaves, but points to a schoolyard that overlooks the ground and crows that he'll now watch from there instead. At half-time, he accompanies my walk to the changing room with slow, sarcastic applause (his team is 6-2 ahead by this point). When I come back out, he yells, "Ref! Ref!" I don't even look in his direction, and in the second half his vantage point is too far away for me to hear him, let alone have to pay him the attention that he's craving. His near future as a coach is now a matter for the disciplinary panel.

Sunday's game is a seven-goal cracker at the men's 10th level — all fire and intensity, a couple of obligatory flare-ups, just a handful of heinous fouls, plus myriad mistakes and missed chances. I keep a lid on it, and dissent is confined to the away team's number 8. Just before half-time, I show him yellow for screaming about me not having given offside in the run-up to the home team's first goal (the reason being — I didn't think it was offside. Though, who knows, maybe it was). In the second half, during a brief break in play, he somewhat belatedly apologises. Then, with the game almost over and his team hanging on to a one-goal lead, he screams at me again, I can't even remember why. He seems surprised when I send him out for a 10-minute time penalty, meaning his game's over. Perhaps he thought the apology meant that the earlier yellow card was annulled, but there's not yet a 'Law 18: Remorse.'

Afterwards, there's an excellent home-made cheesecake from the food hut. The home coach is not unhappy, despite the defeat, which is always a good sign. And I'd got to pick the ball off a Champions League-style podium while running out with the teams. It was a little bit of lower-league gimmickry, of course, but it was a nice touch too — what player, coach or referee doesn't fantasise about gracing a grander stage?

Saturday: 3-9 (4 x yellow, 1 x time-penalty, 1 yellow-red)

Sunday: 3-4 (5 x yellow, 2 x time-penalty)

Why the fuck do I bother?

Imagine you're reading a book, sitting peacefully on a bench by a quiet river on a still afternoon, when someone stops in front of you and starts to yell in your face, "Ian McEwan? IAN FUCKING MCEWAN? What are you reading that shit for, you idiot — you should be reading David Keenan's *This Is Memorial Device*!" Or you're hiking the Pennine Way from Steel Rig to Bellingham when another walker stops you and screams, "You didn't take the detour for the view from Cuddy Crags, and to look at the excavated Roman fort at Housesteads? WHAT THE FUCK IS THE MATTER WITH YOU?"

I'm just trying to think of another hobby apart from refereeing where you'd have to put up with a similar level of loud verbal abuse. Just recently I'd had a run of games which — while they were not exactly peaceful — were definitely under control, and I was really starting to enjoy football again. Then came a match last Thursday night that set me back and left me feeling crushed. As I wrote in a somewhat tired and frustrated state after the game on Twitter: "An absolutely miserable men's game tonight — fouling, moaning about every decision, diving, players squaring up, spurious offside appeals. Back to the basic question: why the fuck do I bother?"

The tweet has had an unprecedented 57 'likes' (roughly 10 times my average), which suggests that it resonated among fellow refs. I'd just come off filing the statutory match report (goalscorers, substitutions, cautions etc.), but had opted against a disciplinary report because I was mentally exhausted. But there's also a section in the report for 'Particular Incidents'. I was in the mood to vent, so I wrote the following:

"Massive bundle in the 75th minute. Spoke with both captains and threatened to abandon the game [I also had them gather in a huddle with their teams to appeal for calm]. After a second fight in injury time, I blew the final whistle. I'd had enough. I've had enough of the Level 10 League in Frankfurt, where the players constantly moan and whine like they're in kindergarten. I didn't want any money from these two teams — please donate my match expenses to a good cause. Unfortunately, I don't have two hours to write up a disciplinary report (it's 11pm, and tomorrow I have to work) — and anyway, they don't change anything, you never hear back from the FA as to whether or not they got the report, if there were any measures taken, not even, 'Thanks for the trouble'. No surprise that referees are quitting in hordes, we've all had it up to here. 'Respect' and 'Fair Play' are just slogans, out on the field there's all too often no sign of them at all. Thank you and good night."

Two refereeing friends talked me down from quitting on WhatsApp the next morning, and a weekend away helped me stop dwelling on what was certainly not my best game. There's a penalty for handball just inside the area, for example. At least, that's how I see it. The home team sees it differently — for them, the handball was outside the box. What should I do? Pretend that I think it was outside the box after all and change the decision? Of course not, so instead I have to put up with them screaming in my face that I've made the wrong call. Maybe I did, but without a TV camera at the pertinent angle, we will sadly never know.

The converted penalty, the third of the night, lets the away team back into the game at 3-2. The home team are down to 10 men because their central midfielder, the number 13, is off the field serving a 10-minute time penalty. This filthy player is the main foul cause behind the game having turned from normal (a bit of moaning, a bit of fouling) to intemperate (non-stop moaning, non-stop fouling). While he's still off, the away team make it 3-3, which is at least good publicity for the time penalty (currently under trial for two seasons). The goal apparently includes a foul on the home team's defender, but being a myopic, useless twat I don't see that either ("WHAT IS WRONG WITH YOU?"). By the final whistle, I'm swearing under my breath in a manic fashion and telling players to keep away from me, I'm no longer interested in what they have to say.

The home team's coach comes into my dressing room with a half-apology. One of those, "Hey, it's just football, right?" apologies. On many days I'll take that and say it's fine, I appreciate you coming by. But not on this night. I know full well he sent his number 13 out there to foul the fuck out of the opposition's best players. That not only lost him the game, but it shitted up the whole evening, leading to the mass confrontations, the alleged insults, the uptick in fouling, several dives, all the shouting and shoving, all the reproaches and the bellicose confrontation. All the things you don't want to see and hear while you're engaged with the hobby you took on because you want to keep fit and you love the game.

So I said, "It's not just part of the game, though, is it? It's about an overall lack of discipline. How am I supposed to focus on refereeing 22 players, on every last foul and offence, when I'm constantly being de-motivated and distracted by players moaning at every single decision and telling me that I'm doing a shit job?" This puts him on the defensive. "Yeah, well, that was never a penalty … " he starts, but I'm on my way out, storming off to my bike and into the dark, autumnal night, thinking about possible new pastimes like crochet, meditation, or painting water-colours of a very quiet and still life.

The night before had been another fraught but invigorating game, with eight yellow cards, though just one for dissent — the home team's goalkeeper. He knocked on the dressing room door afterwards and, with a shit-eating grin, apologised for his behaviour. Yeah, sure, it's okay, I reply. Until the next time, and the time after that. Until there's no next time because the referee couldn't be bothered to show up. He stopped by the river on his way and started to read a book instead.

Wednesday: 2-2 (8 x yellow)

Thursday: 3-5 (4 x yellow, 1 x time-penalty)

Phantom goal

Thursday evening: Boys' U11 Cup. At half-time the home team's coach tries to pull rank on me. "I referee at [such and such] level, and that was a clear penalty we should have had." For the record, it wasn't a penalty, I was two yards away from it. Much more importantly, don't pull that 'I'm a referee too' shit when you're coaching, except to offer support. Tonight you're the coach, I'm the ref.

He could do with paying more attention to his coaching. Twice I have 10-year-olds from his team disputing decisions, and his goalkeeper kicks the ball away to waste time. The disease of dissent is seeping down the age groups, but there are no cards at this level so I'm left with three short lectures. But those lectures need to be coming from the coach, not me. From the opponents, though, a kid comes up to me and says very humbly, "I think you may have made a mistake on that corner kick." And, very politely, I explain back that due to the nature of the deflection, I did not. Cute.

Final score: 2-2 (5-6 after penalties — the time-wasting by the keeper didn't work, his team conceded a late equaliser. Football crime doesn't pay, kids!)

Saturday afternoon: Boys' U19 on a notoriously filthy field that's already hosted a game today, so it's bumpy, muddy and slippery. Best just to cut straight to the disciplinary report:

"Everyone's known for years that this pitch is catastrophic and that after even the lightest of rains, decent football is very difficult. Today it was barely playable and from the start the players had problems with the uneven, muddy surface. This was a contributing factor to the high number of fouls and yellow cards in the first half, but the playing surface wasn't the only reason the atmosphere was miserable. There were also three yellow cards for unsporting conduct — twice when quickly-taken free kicks were blocked, and once when a player needlessly whacked the ball far away after missing a chance. All avoidable cautions reflecting the lack of discipline on both teams. After certain fouls there were also a few incidents of minor friction between individual players.

"Also, after 30 minutes (score: 0-2) there was a 'phantom goal', for which I take full responsibility. I'd checked the goal nets — which are in a desolate state and repaired in a thousand places — while the previous U15 game was still on, but I overlooked a hole in the bottom right hand corner of the home team's goal. A shot on goal from the away team went exactly towards this corner, but — in the intervening second I had my view blocked by a defender — the next thing I saw, the ball was rolling past the goal towards the clubhouse, so I presumed it had missed. The away team players strongly claimed the ball had gone in. I appealed to the defenders to confirm to me that it had been a goal, but no one would answer, while their coaches claimed, "We didn't see it." What a shame, because at half-time two spectators attached to the home team confirmed to me that it had indeed been a goal. Fortunately, it had no effect on the game's outcome, but of course it would have been great if just one player or coach had used this opportunity to act in a fair, sporting and honest manner. [I typed in here the German equivalent of 'Fat fucking chance', but then deleted it.]

"At half-time I spoke with all four coaches of both clubs and asked them to talk to their teams about their shockingly poor conduct during the first half. Because what we'd seen so far had nothing to do with sport — it was instead a mixture of fouling, unsportsmanlike conduct, macho behaviour, and shite attitude. They agreed to my request, and after the break the game was somewhat better. Until the 85th minute..."

I then described in detail how — after a brief but futile wrangle over a throw-in, then a fair challenge between the same two players, following which the ball had been passed forward to a team-mate — one player physically assaulted his opponent with a kick of excessive force to the legs that mercifully didn't lead to a serious injury, but which sent the player flying. There was immediately a mass ruckus, but I kept the offending player away from his opponent (who was understandably furious and ready to address the matter illegally) before showing him the red card. He seemed surprised, somehow, but after the game couldn't explain to me why he'd lashed out. Rather than apologising to his opponent, he wanted to know how long he'd be suspended for. I said I'd no idea, it's not up to me. "What are you going to write in your report?" I'm going to write exactly what happened, I told him. He walked away, head down.

Final score: 1-4 (7 x yellow, 1 x time penalty, 1 x red)

Sunday afternoon: Men's level 8, out way east of the city. A stadium of sorts, with terracing, and a huge grass field, softened by rain. Lots of negative noise in the first half — from the players, from the benches, from the spectators. Some of it's aimed at me, and there are three yellow cards for dissent before the break. Mainly, though, the home team's players especially are screaming at each other. At half-time, they're 0-1 down due to a penalty for a goalkeeper foul. ("I played the ball" he screams five times, louder and louder until he gets the caution. He also played the man — I repeat for the thousandth time, there's no special law for the goalkeepers, you already have the advantage of your hands). My changing room is only accessible through the home team's, so I'm expecting to hear more bawling in the break, but it's actually pretty quiet. As we walk back out, the captain apologises for the noise from the bench. In truth, I'd tuned it out over all the other cacophony.

They start playing football, even though they're now kicking into a quite stiff wind. They score twice, the winner coming just before the end. There have been some shockingly late fouls, meaning even more yellows, plus two players kicking the ball away to prevent quick free-kicks (and, as always, astonished and indignant that this means a caution). But I seem to have a full handle on the game, there's no squaring-up, and no one's getting on my case any more — not even the crowd, including several away fans who had vociferously booed some calls in the first half. And of course the home team, after their comeback, are generous with their post-match praise and handshakes. The losers ignore me completely — as predictable as cows farting in a field.

The club president gives me a lift back to the train station. On the way, I tell him that the change in attitude had paved the way for the victory — concentrating on football and not undermining their own confidence by screaming at each other (and at me). I sense that he doesn't really agree. He even brings up a first-half penalty "that we maybe should have had". Maybe, I reply, if it hadn't been your player that actually committed the foul. He goes quiet at that. We're at the station. I thank him for the lift — I'm just in time for the next train and it's saved me an hour's wait on a cold, dark, windy and deserted platform. Despite the foul mouths, the foul play and the foul weather, it rounds off a great afternoon.

Final score: 2-1 (11 x yellow)

The Moroccan derby

Some weekends, I feel like I'm living in a referee's version of The Truman Show, and that the games I'm assigned are merely staged to provoke drama for the sake of my viewing figures and the delight of a sofa-based audience high on popcorn and catastrophe. I already knew before Sunday's game — a Level-8 local diaspora derby between two clubs not known for taking a placid approach to sport — that it would be a tough afternoon. Even with all my experience of football in this city, though, I wasn't expecting enough material for a five-act play. And what I only found out later — the last time these two teams met the game was abandoned, and some players on the away team physically assaulted the 17-year-old referee. And yet here they still are. On to the issues:

1. *The Suspended Player*. The away team's side includes a player (the number 3) I red-carded back in August (see 'Amateurs on Steroids?'). One of the team officials recognises me, and while we chat I ask him how long the player was suspended for. Six weeks, he replies, and the club only let him return after that because he'd pleaded for mercy — this red card hadn't been his first. "He's a good player, but has absolutely no mental control," is the club official's assessment. Curiously, just before kick-off, another of the away team's officials asks me if I can make the player's name 'non-public' in the match report. Why? "He just doesn't want his name out there." Hmmm, okay.

2. *The Brothers*. There's a brother on each team, and this is the first time they've ever played against each other. "I promised our mum I would take him out with a wild tackle — just once," the older one says. "He needs taking down a peg or two." All in jest, of course. But just to be on the safe side I say, "Of course you can, as long as you don't mind taking the

yellow card that comes with it." A very 'ref' thing to say — I'm great fun at parties, honest.

3. *The Crowd.* There are over 300 spectators in the small ground. It's the same place where I reffed 'the Game From Hell'. It's also the place where I oversaw the expulsion of several spectators a few years back during a reserve team game, for anti-Semitic abuse aimed at the city's only Jewish team (see 'Hatred on the Touchline'). It's compulsory for clubs to designate two stewards in yellow jackets to keep order. Today there are five.

4. *The Opening Minute.* The home team's number 7 scores within seconds of the start, but he's offside. There's no disputing the decision, but he immediately gets into a verbal and physical confrontation with his direct opponent, who is ... the number 3 (see above). "Is there a problem here already?" I ask. Instead of shaking hands and assuring me there's not, they keep arguing. I show them both yellow cards. The game is 40 seconds old.

5. *The Drama Queen.* I'd watched the home team's number 10 playing for the reserves earlier. Every time he's fouled, he falls down and lets out a cry of pain and despair. The first time this happens in my game, I have a quick chat. "When you go down you always scream like you've been shot. How am I going to know it's serious if you're genuinely injured?" It's the last time he carries on.

6. *Some spectacular football.* The two cautions in the first minute, and an early yellow for the away team's number 6 for his second bad foul of the game in just the eighth minute, keep the disciplinary lid on a thrilling first half when both sides actually concentrate on playing football. In fact there's a spectator or team official who keeps screaming, "Play football!" every time the home team looks like committing a foul. The scoreboard oscillates: 0-1. Then 1-1, then 1-2, then 2-2, then almost immediately 2-3. Both home goals are scored by the number 7 (and both very well taken), who has his own fan club of about 20 young boys behind the goal he's attacking. After each goal, he runs over to celebrate with them, a star in this corner of the city. Eventually, the goalkeeper complains that the rowdy urchins are distracting him, and the stewards move them to the sides.

7. *The Turning Point.* Almost an hour in, with the score still 2-3, the home team's number 14 goes on a weaving run through the midfield, then plays the ball too close to a defender, who clears. Number 14 follows up with a studs-up tackle, and even a short after-kick to his opponent when he's on the floor. He's incredulous at the yellow card and offers up some sarcasm, which upgrades his sanction to a 10-minute time-penalty. In this time, the away team scores to make it 2-4, but then immediately concedes to a cracking long shot: 3-4. The home team's coach goes nuts at me for another caution — for his consistently dirty number 9. "It was a completely normal challenge!" he yells. Maybe for this team it is. It's raining fouls and cautions

now, and when the coach yells at me again for something or other, he sees yellow too.

8. *The second time-penalty.* On 73 minutes, it's the away team's number 10 who's sent out — a useful but physical player who'd already seen yellow for blocking a quick free-kick. This time it's for a very hard foul. He doesn't complain, just wants to know how long is left in the game. While he's out, the home team's number 7 completes his hat-trick with a beautifully taken header. The defence screams for offside, but he wasn't — I was directly in line, having lingered there following a previous free-kick, and one defender was too late coming out. Three away players stalk up to me and I wave them away — they see where I was standing and decide to give up. The pre-teen fan club again goes nuts for its hero: 4-4.

9. *The late penalty kick.* The home team is pushing for victory, the away team's wasting time and holding out for the draw. In the 89th minute, number 7 is up-ended just inside the penalty area when a defender goes through the back of him. "He played the ball!" scream the away team. He maybe did, but he also laid out the man. Penalty. They surround me, seven or eight of them, yelling for 30 seconds until I clear them out of the area. Number 7 converts the kick: 5-4, and the home crowd is duly ecstatic. The away captain talks himself into the book but declares he doesn't care. Me neither, mate.

10. *Injury time.* For all the stoppages — injuries, cautions, substitutions, time-wasting — I add five minutes. The crowd is now somewhat persistent in calling for the final whistle, the home coach is dancing around like he has hot coals strapped to his soles. When I finally blow up, the away team, almost as one, starts to run towards me. I take several steps back. I hear someone yell, "He has to be told!" But then the five stewards, bless them, sprint on to the field and hold them back. There's the usual load of shouting and shoving. Someone escorts me to my changing room and suggests I lock the door from the inside. I fill in the online game report (cards, goals, subs etc.) while outside the tumult gradually subsides. I don't get to see if the opposing brothers are still talking to each other, or if the older one's now on the phone to Mum complaining about the ref.

11. *The Number 3?* Just after I've pressed the button to send the game report off, the away team official who'd asked for number 3's identity to be concealed from the public knocks on the door. He's very friendly, wants to know if everything's okay. I know what he means by that — "Are you going to be writing up a report about our players' threatening behaviour?" I tell him everything's fine, that I can understand the players' frustration, but that they should aim their questions at the defender who committed the foul, not at me. Once he's gone, something belatedly occurs to me. I look again at the photo on the number 3's player pass. He doesn't look anything

like the number 3 who was out on the field. It's too late to check now, he'll be long gone. So — they tried to cheat and lost. Another good plot line for The Referee's Reality Show.

12. *The Happy, Smiling Home Coach.* I honestly don't recognise him, standing in the doorway all cheerful and thanking me for having officiated today's game of association football. The number 7, full of himself after his four-goal haul, chirps up in the background, "Don't forget to input his yellow card!" Wait, you were the guy yelling at me from the touchline all through the second half. Yes, he admits, but after the game everything's fine, right? Not really — you were utterly disrespectful to me and the game of football, and your behaviour was a disgrace. But he doesn't give a solitary turd about that. He won. He's still smiling as he turns and leaves.

13. *Really*? When I leave the clubhouse, the away team's captain is waiting. He still wants to discuss the penalty call. "I'm done here, have a great evening," I say as I stride past him towards my bike. Cycling across the car park, I'm semi-expecting the sound of a revving engine followed by the screech of tires and rapid acceleration. But of course there's no such thing. It's not that kind of reality show. Yet.

14. *The Night Before.* A boys' U19 game, regional league. At the first sign of dissent (fourth minute), I show the away team's number 20 a yellow. That's it for the evening. I'm not kidding. For the remainder of the 90 minutes, not one player on either side disputes a single call (there's just one more yellow card for a bad foul), although it's also a fast and physical clash. This quiet and (for me) superbly enjoyable game feels like the conspicuous exception. But why can't it always be like that? "Ah, you know, ref — emotions!" But it's all okay after the game, right? Yeah, right.

Saturday: 0-5 (2 x yellow)

Sunday 5-4 (10 x yellow, 2 x time-penalty)

VAR marks in the grass

Although I despise the Video-Assistant Referee (VAR) when it cancels out goals for fractional offsides not visible to the human eye, I'm a big fan of it in certain situations of clear injustice. This is especially applicable to penalties, which are in any case inherently unjust — an innocuous foul close to the edge of the penalty area doesn't deserve the same punishment as a deliberate handball on the goal-line (but that's an argument for another day). When a game-changing decision is reversed thanks to close-up proof of an ankle-tap or a dive, then it's certainly to the benefit of football, and serves to smother at least some of the toxic anger aimed at referees for controversial calls.

Of course, amateur referees have no VAR, as we'll often point out to players in the thralls of protest and gesticulation. Sometimes, though, we have other clues and pointers when we're uncertain. On throw-ins and corner-kicks, for example, when two players have challenged for the ball and you're unsure who touched it last, you can often tell from the players' body language which way to point. If the attacker runs off to retrieve the ball and the defender runs back to the six-yard box to defend the corner-kick, then you know for sure they were the last player to touch the ball. (But if they both yell, "Corner!/Goal kick!" at the same time, then you just have to make a wild guess, while looking bold and full of conviction.)

Anyway, in the second half of a Level 8 men's game, with the hosts leading 2-0, I'm caught out of position by a long punt that launches a swift counter-attack by the home team. As two players challenge for an aerial ball on the edge of the away team's penalty area (I'm probably just over the halfway line by now), the defender climbs all over the forward's back and flattens him. It's such a clear foul that the defender and forward are both laughing as they help each other back up. The question, though — was it in the area or out? Quite simply, I'm too far off the play to see for sure, but my initial reaction is to whistle and point to the penalty spot.

One of the home team players, though, hasn't seen that I signalled for the spot-kick and has now placed the ball just outside the area for a free-kick. The away team points to him amid a choral protest — look, even the home team thinks it was outside the box! They also present as further evidence for the defence a skid mark on the damp pitch just outside the box. By now, though, the home team has placed the ball on the penalty spot and the home crowd is awaiting its third goal of the afternoon.

I change the call to a free-kick. I still can't decide if this was a courageous call (it provokes the wrath of the home players and crowd — not that it's massive, maybe around 100 spectators), or a cowardly one (caving in to the loud and carping demands of the away team). But using the evidence available (home player's body language, and the mark on the grass) is a kind of real-time VAR experience. Either way, one of the teams is going to be pissed off, but I feel that I've corrected an erroneous decision. Which doesn't stop a home player grumbling, "Everyone in the ground saw that was a penalty."

The home team almost score from the free-kick, which would have bailed me out, but they go on to win 4-0 anyway. A short while after the game, just as I'm coming out of my changing-room, I hear a club official at the entrance to the building (and who has his back to me) say to one of the players amid a group of spectators, "I suppose the referee thought that foul was five millimetres outside the box." I pop up just behind him and say, "Yep, that's exactly where it was." Everyone laughs, and the surprised club official tries to apologise, but I'm just grateful no one's pissed off about it. "To be honest, I got caught out of position," I tell them. "It wasn't my proudest moment as a referee." And I've been wondering ever since if the foul was in or out, and how nice it would have been to see a quick replay on a screen so that I'd have known for sure.

* Misconduct update: I could easily have made this week's blog another lament about lack of respect and verbal violence (boys' U17 game — extensively yelled at and insulted by two players right after the final whistle, pissed off that they've lost 3-1 to a team they beat 8-4 just three weeks before), as well as a red card for a barely prevented physical attack by a player who ran off the field to go for one of his team-mates (from the above men's game). But, dear readers, you deserve a break from all that shit once in a while. I wish I could have a break from it too, if only to avoid sitting up late to type detailed disciplinary reports.

Saturday afternoon: 0-13 (3 x yellow, 1 x time-penalty)

Saturday evening: 3-1 (6 x yellow, 1 x time-penalty, plus post-game disciplinary report on two players for disgraceful conduct)

Sunday: 4-0 (5 x yellow, 1 x red)

The naughty step

An elderly spectator comes up to me at half-time as I'm on my way to the dressing room. That's not always a good thing, and after today's testy first 45 minutes I'm expecting a Strong Opinion — there have been two penalties for handball offences, four yellow cards, and a time-penalty for a player on the home team, during which the away team took advantage of its extra man to equalise. Score: 2-2. But the gentleman only has encouraging words: "When you took the two players off to one side there for a talk, that was great — well done."

He's referring to a typical scene that seems to play out now in every game, regardless of level or age group (with the exception of the U11/U12 games I recently reffed). Two players go for the ball, one of them commits a foul, the other has something to say about it, the fouler makes a comment back, and then they're both squaring up and pushing each other in the chest. WHO FACKIN' WANTS SOME???? And then comes the bandy-legged old ref with his whistle, ordering them both off to one side and on to the naughty step. I want them to feel like this is a visit to the headmaster's office. The good thing is that my speech is so well honed by now that I don't even need to think about it.

The first task, though, is to get one or both of them to shut up. Just like in the school yard, they want to let you know that it's the other guy's fault. "Ref, he said, he did blah blah blah." I interrupt this infantile babble with, "Quiet, I'm the only one talking here!" Then off I go: "Are you both off your heads?" (I like to act a little outraged, like this is the first — rather than the 500th — time I've seen such a scene on a football field.) "You realise this is a football match, right? So make a decision, do you want to stay on here and play football, or do you want to act like idiots? If it's the latter, you can get on with your moronic macho posturing in the clubhouse for all I care.

On here, we're playing football." By now, both players should be nodding. I stop talking, whip the yellow card out of my left pocket, and raise it twice as the concluding choreography to my short one-act play.

In Sunday's game, the speech comes after just 13 minutes. I make it twice more during the course of the afternoon, once even for two players on the same team. Generally, I leave team-mates to it when they vent at each other because it's done and dusted in a second or two, but in this case the away team's number 8, playing at centre forward, enters into a long and loud verbal exchange with his captain on the right wing, the number 7, who's just shot from an unlikely angle rather than passing to his better-placed striker. It's threatening to escalate, as it did in last week's game, so I take them to one side for another short word. "You're meant to be team-mates, right?" I ask, again laying it on thick with the disbelief.

A few minutes later, number 7 sets up number 8 for the equaliser referred to in the opening paragraph. They pointedly ignore each other during the celebrations, but I say to the number 7, "Nice pass to your team-mate", and he smiles. In the second half he sets the number 8 up for two more goals. "Nice pass from your captain there," I say to the scorer, and he also smiles. Everyone's happy after a goal. At the game's end, with three points secured, they are friends again. Awwww, and just in time for the season of goodwill to all our fellow men. You're welcome!

Once when I reffed at this club it ended badly when a player threw his shirt in my face after a red card (see 'Coward!'). He's playing again today, in the centre of defence for the home team, and he's the model amateur — not very good, but he commits no fouls and doesn't moan about a single call. When I'm lecturing the other team's numbers 7 and 8, who have both been giving him the run-around, he even quips, "Just send them both off." This State of Zen has not yet affected his coach, who was also barking hysterics on that same sunny day. When I give an early penalty to the away team for a clear handball, he rants and raves on the touchline. Today I stand with my back to him and just ignore the tantrum, and eventually his defenders tell him to shut up, because they're not disputing it. Sometimes it's best to just leave the coach standing there, boiling like a rancid cabbage stew that no one wants to taste or even smell.

It doesn't always work, but the first-half lectures seem to have a positive effect on the atmosphere, and the second half is peaceful. Both teams are in a conciliatory mood at the final whistle, there are handshakes all round, and no belated settling of scores. After weeks of murky, wet and depressing weather, the sun even comes out for an hour or so. Two more boys' U19 games until the Christmas break, then I'll be huddled over my conflict management portfolio. Or, more likely, downing a barrel of Glühwein and thinking about something other than football.

Final score: 3-5 (7 x yellow, 1 x time-penalty)

Try saying something positive

In 'Phantom goal', I wrote about a toxic boys' U19 game where the home team passed up the chance to be good sports by admitting that a goal scored by their opponents had actually gone in (but back out through a hole in the net). Later, one of their players received a straight red card for violent conduct. It was the team's last game. They withdrew from that league a week later and all their results were annulled.

It was no surprise. The coaches seemed indifferent, and that was reflected in the players' attitude. Numerous U19 teams drop out in the course of any given season because there's not much more to play for — no more promotions to a higher level, for example. Even the most deluded players have realised by now that they're not going to play at a professional or even semi-pro level, while the distractions of exams, relationships and the imminent prospect of possibly leaving home and starting a new life all mean that football is pushed down their priority list. Why bother showing up for another six months in a losing team with no sense of spirit or togetherness when you can quit now and enjoy a few extra free Saturdays?

This age group is not helped by its games being mostly scheduled for 4pm or 6pm on a Saturday. Saturday afternoons often clash with home games for Eintracht Frankfurt, while on Saturday evening the world's an open book when you're 18 years old. Meanwhile, the coaches are often waiting to be released from the burden of their voluntary jobs, especially if they're only doing it out of a sense of duty towards their children, rather than out of a love for the game. Which brings me to the coach of the home team on Saturday afternoon.

He's all smiles and super-friendly before the game. He's the same afterwards. He and his coaching assistant insist that both myself and my friend Helmut — who's come along to watch — should share a beer with them. That's very much appreciated, and it doesn't happen often enough. But because Helmut has been running the line for them right in front of the bench, he hears everything they say during the course of the afternoon. That includes not just a negative running commentary on my decisions, but a shouting match on the bench with the team's captain after he's subbed himself out. "Catastrophic," is his verdict. "They have no clue about football, or how to coach a team and interact with their players."

Admittedly, the captain's a bit of a head-case. The last time I reffed this team, he took a caution for excessive moaning, and nothing has changed. He's very keen to call offsides that he's 50 yards away from, and then to emit a whelp of outrage when I don't give them. I ignore it for a while, then I show him yellow in a game that's otherwise lacking nastiness or controversy. At this point, with the score at 1-5, he walks off the field and straight into the verbally violent shouting match with his coach. The only other sub is already injured, so his team is now down to 10 men. Just what you need from your captain, who in the course of a lively exchange informs the coach that he's quitting the team.

At the end of the game, the coach loudly and publicly upbraids another player, and orders him to the shower. "Then," he barks, "we'll sit down and talk." This second player also looks like he's ready to quit. If you could write the book on how not to train and motivate a team of adolescents, this coach would be your prime exhibit.

Not a single player on either team offers me a fist-bump or a thank-you at the end of the 90 minutes. This inherent lack of basic courtesy and sportsmanship is no more front page news than the away team's coach yelling at me for something or other completely inconsequential connected with a drop-ball (like Cristiano Ronaldo, many players and coaches still haven't cottoned on to the new drop-ball law two and a half years after it changed). I just ignore the vociferous twat, whose faecal gob is completely out of sync with the tenor of the game.

After the half-time break, though, one of his players also has something to say. He points to Helmut and says with righteous conviction, "The linesman keeps pointing in the direction of the throw-in. He's not allowed to do that, he should only signal if the ball's in or out." I point out that the linesman can do whatever I ask of him, and that's exactly what I'd asked him to do because I know that he's neutral.

"But," I add, "it's nice that you found something to complain about, however trivial." Then, as we're still not ready to re-start, I take it a little bit further. "On the other hand, you could say something positive too.

Like, 'Hey, isn't it cool that on a wet and very cold winter's afternoon, someone's prepared to volunteer to stand on the sideline for 90 minutes, holding a flag to help make my football game run a little more smoothly.' Am I right?"

The player doesn't concede that I may have a point. It's also possible that he doesn't have a fucking clue what I'm talking about. Say something positive? Who the hell does this wanker with the whistle think he is?

Saturday: 1-5 (3 x yellow)

Sunday: 3-2 (2 x yellow)

The Manifesto

This book documents five and a half seasons of often abusive, insulting and disrespectful behaviour towards referees in and around the amateur and youth football scene in Frankfurt. At some point, though, merely describing what's going on — and it's not just in my games, it's universal — is insufficient. The time has conclusively come to take a stance.

Myself and a small group of local referees are working on a list of demands and proposed actions to try and tackle the endemic problems in amateur football that have escalated to the point where every weekend brings some form of trouble, even in the quietest games. What can be done to curb the dissent, the tantrums, the threats and the all-round prevalence of unpleasant attitudes and total lack of sporting enjoyment? One thing is clear — posters saying 'Respect!' and 'Thanks, ref!' are not doing the job, whatever their grandiose, committee-endorsed intentions.

After dozens of negative and hair-raising experiences, my personal tipping point came a week ago. A month back, I'd refereed a boys' U17 match which ended with a number of players on the losing team insulting me and screaming at me after the final whistle (see footnote to 'VAR marks in the grass'). I walked through the cacophony without reacting, but noted the numbers of the players and duly wrote up a disciplinary report that same Saturday evening when I would rather have been doing something more relaxing (they have to be submitted "within 24 hours" of the final whistle). As usual, I heard nothing back. The team in question didn't play for another three weeks. But when they did play, all three players that I'd named in the disciplinary report were in the starting line-up. There had been no punishments at all for 16-year-olds screaming indiscriminately at a referee, frustrated at their loss in a game they'd expected to win (with no intervention from their coach — a fellow referee, by the way).

So a week ago, I fired off an email to my refereeing association, the league administrator and the state FA demanding to know why there had been no sanctions against the three players. What was the point in referees making the effort to urgently write up these reports (remember — "within 24 hours") if no one was acting upon them? Were they even being read? Due to this disgraceful inaction and ineptitude, I went on, I was withdrawing from all U17 and U19 games until further notice.

My refereeing boss followed up with a fully supportive email pointing out to those concerned that "we're in danger of losing yet another referee for youth games". Besides that, there has — predictably enough — been no acknowledgment or response at all. On Saturday, I was supposed to take a boys' U19 game, but I pulled out. In exchange — you can view it as a punishment or a reward — I refereed a U11 game instead. Forty minutes shorter, but only €2 less pay, and no aggro whatsoever.

Of course I missed the challenge of a full-on, 90-minute game, and my body won't benefit from having run about one-fifth of the distance that I would have covered on a full-sized pitch with almost fully developed teenagers rather than 10-year-olds. But I didn't miss that nagging pre-match fear about what could be waiting for me this time around. Which trifling decision might push a coach or a player over the edge? Which throw-in call will render a grown man ballistic? Will I make it back to my bicycle without being told I'm the shittiest ref in the history of the game?

Our nascent manifesto will outline what we think needs to be done to shift the current football culture in our city. Although the last thing I feel like doing right now is refereeing, I'm still not yet willing to give up, no matter how tempting the prospect of stress-free weekends for the rest of my life. We will be positive and constructive, but firm in tone, demanding justice, transparency and a concrete support network. We will summarise what needs to be done at all levels of the game to support football's sporting values from the bottom up. If we don't raise our collective voices now, the clubs will not pay any attention until, one day, they're forced to referee all their games with a parent plucked from the touchline, or a passer-by out walking their dog. Or even the dog itself ("Bloody hell, Rex, what's the matter — you fucking colour blind or something?")

I'll keep you posted.

Final score: 2-8 (no cards)

ADDENDUM

THE MANIFESTO'S MAIN POINTS

Manifesto

* An intensive campaign to protect all young and newly qualified referees from abuse, inspired by the Worcestershire FA's #seemysocks initiative. Goal: to improve awareness among clubs, and to improve long-term coaching and mentoring of young refs.

* Transparency throughout the disciplinary process so that referees know poor and disgraceful conduct has been duly punished. Disciplinary hearings to be made accessible to all referees.

* A statutory FA D-licence for all coaches and team managers from U11 upwards. Qualification upon completion of a two-day course, with exam. Focus on handling young players, the Laws of the Game, and how to interact with and treat referees. Re-qualification every 12 months. Only licensed coaches/managers allowed in the technical area.

* A digital ID card for all coaches/managers, to be presented to referees before every game. Card to be suspended or annulled for failure to pass the D-licence exam, or for punishable behaviour.

* Youth teams to be docked points when their coaches are carded — one point for a yellow card, three points for a red. Coaches to be suspended for one game for a yellow card, four games for a red.

* The appointment at all clubs of a designated official, or officials, responsible for the welfare of referees on game days, and for monitoring coach behaviour (youth and adult teams). A dedicated 'referee officer' at all clubs to oversee all issues involving referees.

* Harsh and consistent penalties for discriminatory behaviour of any kind from coaches, players and spectators.

INDEX